Social Theories of the Press

Critical Media Studies: Institutions, Politics, and Culture

Series Editor
Andrew Calabrese, University of Colorado

Titles in the Series

Interactions: Critical Studies in Communication, Media, and Journalism, Hanno Hardt
Communication, Citizenship, and Social Policy: Rethinking the Limits of the Welfare State, edited by Andrew Calabrese and Jean-Claude Burgelman
Public Opinion: Developments and Controversies in the Twentieth Century, Slavko Splichal
Redeveloping Communication for Social Change: Theory, Practice, and Power, edited by Karin Gwinn Wilkins
The Information Society in Europe: Work and Life in an Age of Globalization, edited by Ken Ducatel, Juliet Webster, and Werner Herrmann
Tabloid Tales: Global Debates over Media Standards, edited by Colin Sparks and John Tulloch
Ferdinand Tönnies on Public Opinion: Selections and Analyses, edited, introduced, and translated by Hanno Hardt and Slavko Splichal
Deliberation, Democracy, and the Media, edited by Simone Chambers and Anne Costain
Deregulating Telecommunications: U.S. and Canadian Telecommunications, 1840–1997, Kevin G. Wilson
Social Theories of the Press: Constituents of Communication Research, 1840s to 1920s, second edition, Hanno Hardt
Floating Lives: The Media and Asian Diasporas, edited by Stuart Cunningham and John Sinclair

Forthcoming in the Series

Continental Order? Integrating North America for Cybercapitalism, edited by Vincent Mosco and Dan Schiller
Global Media Governance: A Beginner's Guide, Seán Ó Siochrú and W. Bruce Girard
The Global and the National: Media and Communications in Post-Communist Russia, Terhi Rantanen
From Newspaper Guild to Multimedia Union: A Study in Labor Convergence, Catherine McKercher
The Eclipse of Freedom: From the Principle of Publicity to the Freedom of the Press, Slavko Splichal
Elusive Autonomy: Brazilian Communications Policy in an Age of Globalization and Technical Change, Sergio Euclides de Souza

Social Theories of the Press

Constituents of Communication Research, 1840s to 1920s

SECOND EDITION

Hanno Hardt

ROWMAN & LITTLEFIELD PUBLISHERS, INC.
Lanham • Boulder • New York • Oxford

ROWMAN & LITTLEFIELD PUBLISHERS, INC.

Published in the United States of America
by Rowman & Littlefield Publishers, Inc.
4720 Boston Way, Lanham, Maryland 20706
www.rowmanlittlefield.com

12 Hid's Copse Road, Cumnor Hill, Oxford OX2 9JJ, England

British Library Cataloguing in Publication Information Available

Library of Congress Cataloging-in-Publication Data

Hardt, Hanno.
Social theories of the press : constituents of communication research, 1840s to 1920s / Hanno Hardt.—2nd ed.
p. cm.—(Critical media studies)
Includes bibliographical references and index.
ISBN 0-7425-1133-2 (alk. paper)—ISBN 0-7425-1134-0 (pbk. : alk. paper)
1. Communication—Social aspects. 2. Mass media—Social aspects. 3. Sociology—Germany—History. 4. Sociology—United States—History. I. Title. II. Series.

HM561 .H37 2001
302.2—dc21 2001019018

Printed in the United States of America

∞ ™ The paper used in this publication meets the minimum requirements of American National Standard for Information Sciences—Permanence of Paper for Printed Library Materials, ANSI/NISO Z39.48-1992.

To Allie, Liam, and Isabel,
grand children, indeed.

Contents

Foreword

The first edition of Hanno Hardt's *Social Theories of the Press: Early German and American Perspectives* (1979) brought to light for English-speaking readers a buried tradition of German thought concerning communication, the press, and the mass media. Of the theorists Hardt elucidated—Karl Knies, Albert Schäffle, Karl Bücher, Max Weber, Ferdinand Tönnies—only Weber was well-known, though his work on the press was the least visible of his writings. So little of Tönnies had been translated that he was understood only in caricature; he was simplistically identified with, even embalmed by, his contrast between *Gemeinschaft* and *Gesellschaft* types of social organization. This new edition adds Karl Marx's writings in and about journalism to the analysis. When paired with *Ferdinand Tönnies on Public Opinion*, the recently published translation by Hardt and Slavko Splichal (2000), this volume, particularly with its spirited conclusion, lays down a major challenge to our understanding of the history of communication research.

The standard history of communication research is largely an outgrowth of the liberal tradition and is distinguished by the adoption of an essentially economistic point of view. This view of communication emphasizes the choices and consequences individuals face when selecting from the marketplace of things to read, listen to, and watch. Choice is governed by utility or individual satisfaction, and the only theoretically compelling question in this equation concerns the conditions of freedom that support the process of individual decision making. About the objects of choice, the liberal tradition is silent; it is always and only a matter of individual taste and the freedom to choose for oneself.

But if communication is simply a matter of individuals pursuing their own taste—I like poetry, you like pornography—and of the structural guarantees for our self-indulgence such as the First Amendment, two very large questions remain. First, how do disconnected individuals jealously in pursuit of their own happiness, using others as means to their own ends, ever manage to form a functioning (let alone an equitable) society? Second, once you release the assumptions concerning the origins of the tastes of individuals, how are preferences to be explained? Why it is that I like one thing and you like another? To the first question, the liberal tradition has but a metaphysical answer: societies of selfish individuals are held together by the "invisible hand of Providence." More concretely, they are held together by the market, which coordinates their actions and ensures that, by guaranteeing the freedom of one person to pursue his own selfish ends, the freedom and happiness of all will be maximized in a manner never quite revealed. To the second question, the liberal tradition has but a couple of answers: tastes and preferences of individuals are governed by heredity or environment—the real invisible hand of genetics or conditioning—or by the functional demands of the social system: we want what we want because society invisibly demands that we want it, though we are never told how this demand is exercised.

The liberal answers to these questions never satisfied thinkers who stood with a foot outside of the liberal tradition or, to put it geographically, lived on the "other" side of the Rhine. Contrary thinkers wanted a more theoretically specific, empirically apprehensible understanding of how it is that "individualistic" *Gesellschaft* societies held together and how it was that individuals wanted what they wanted. Just as importantly, such thinkers wanted a critical answer, one that did not doom us to be silent servants of the market, our genes, or our society.

Hanno Hardt in this book excavates this contrary tradition as it concerns communication in the work of frequently obscure German scholars and, at the same time, elucidates an important chapter in American social thought. These German thinkers attempted to go beyond views of communication as exclusively a matter of freedom of choice and choice as a matter solely of individual will. In one way or another, they asked this question: what are the other sources of social order that are transcendent to and that guarantee the functioning of markets. In the nineteenth century the greatest of these social theorists looked at premarket factors as sources of the problem of social integration. Religion, which existed before but continued into the industrial age even if in secularized form, was the most important source of social cohesion they examined. But gradually religion became reidentified on a wider scale as culture and often ideology, and both were increasingly seen as the bedrock of social communication.

In addition, they saw that individual desire was not just a product of an abstract society but resulted from the practices of daily life as such practices were embedded in structures of class, status, and power. Men and women did make history, so there was room for human agency; but they did not make history in conditions of their own choosing. Within modern societies there had to be room for both human agency and social determination. A common culture and common values still mattered but did so within the constraints of societies riddled by inequalities, conflicts, and political struggle.

From multiple sources Hardt elucidates this alternative tradition of social thought that emerged to challenge the consensus of the liberal agreement, that brought to bear a different understanding of social life. It was a tradition that continued to emphasize conditions of freedom but was more sensitive to the constraints and contradictions of actually existing societies. It was a tradition that continued to emphasize human rationality but the rationality of ends, not just means. And it was a tradition that paid greater and more circumspect attention to the nonmarket elements present in market societies: the cohesion (or domination) that stemmed from shared cultural orientations, rooted in religion and other primordial factors, even if these factors, as in ideology, were often exploited and rationalized by the market.

The significance of Hanno Hardt's research, particularly for American readers, lies in the questions he raises, often implicitly, about the relation of European and American scholarship. This relationship is particularly problematic at the moment because for many years American scholars were out of touch with European work. Now they are threatened with being overrun by it or, better, by a small and often unrepresentative, contemporary portion of Continental writing and, in the process, abandoning a vital German-American tradition.

In the years after World War II American scholarship, like American politics and power, culture, and economy, exerted a widespread dominance. This was a temporary artifact of the war itself. From our comfortable distance we failed to grasp the ruinous effect of the war on European scholarship: a major part of a generation lost, universities in disarray, publishing houses disbanded, research traditions fractured. In the 1940s and 1950s a kind of intellectual Marshall Plan grew up that led to the widespread exportation of American scholarship and an unprecedented, though temporary, influence for American ideas. The situation is rather different now, and it is necessary for American scholars to regain intimate contact and familiarity with European work but in fullness and not in stereotype.

American scholars need to be in touch with something more than a thin stream of contemporary writing. Many of the originating impulses behind research on mass communication were German, and Hanno Hardt's work succeeds in making this scholarship accessible to us by negotiating the discrepant frames of meaning of German and American traditions. It was not until the twentieth century that journalism and the mass media became subjects of scholarship in the United States in any significant way. Up to that time the nature of the media, their relation to society, and their consequences were taken to be relatively unproblematic. Anglo-American scholarship was devoted almost exclusively to the problem of the nature of freedom of expression. It was generally agreed, however, that if the conditions of freedom were maintained, then the consequences of mass communication were relatively automatic—an invisible hand leading the will of individuals to the maximization of the social good.

Operating within a different national tradition of scholarship, a tradition with much more skepticism concerning the doctrines and consequences of the Enlightenment, German scholars found the press a problematic institution—its consequences unclear, as well as its contribution to the state, to the capitalist economy, and to the social order generally—that could be troubling, sometimes menacing. For these reasons the press became an object of scholarly concern earlier in Germany than in the United States. We are familiar with the work of the towering and dominating figures of late eighteenth- and nineteenth-century German scholarship—Herder, Kant, Hegel, Marx, Dilthey—though we are not necessarily always aware of the implications of their views for the study of communications and the mass media. We are also familiar with those figures who migrated to the United States and published in English—Cassirer, Adorno, Horkheimer, Marcuse, Löwenthal—for they sometimes made an attempt to translate their ideas into terms congenial to American understanding. But of other German scholars who were concerned with the press and mass media over the past hundred years or so, we know little. Professor Hardt corrected a major part of this deficiency in the first edition of this book and here he extends and consolidates those gains by bringing out the contrasts in sensibility and intellectual position between German scholarship and our own.

The story he tells is part of a curious chapter in the transatlantic migration of ideas on mass communication. Many of the greatest American scholars of the late nineteenth century were trained in Germany, since there was not at that time an adequate system of graduate education in the United States. On their return they brought with them the model of what a graduate school should be and many of the ideas of the German classical tradition: ideas loosely grasped by notions such as the materialist theory of history, the distinction between *Naturwissenschaft* and *Geisteswissenschaft*, of hermeneutic understanding, of the necessity of reconstructive imagination, or *Verstehen*, in understanding human action. But they returned with more than a few foreign concepts. Because the German tradition of scholarship is grounded in philosophy, they also learned to examine society and its institutions in a more synoptic frame than was possible given the narrow and disciplinary forms typical of American understandings of the social world. They saw, in other words, the mass media not in the narrowed context of psychology and the small group but in the larger framework of politics, economics, and culture.

Three of these figures—Albion Small, E. A. Ross, and William Graham Sumner—are the subject of a later chapter. Nearly all of the major figures in early American scholarship on mass communication—John Dewey, Robert Park, George Herbert Mead, W. I. Thomas, Franklin Giddings—were either educated in Germany or struggled all their life with the German intellectual tradition (Dewey is a good case). In making certain German ideas accessible to domestic audiences, these men had to convert this scholarship into an American idiom. Inevitably distortions crept into the exposition if only because German ideas had to be adapted to a quite different landscape—geographic and social. However, it is impossible to understand these men, to understand the problems they were setting before us, the tacit meanings of their arguments, and the significance of the concerns they announced, without recognizing the German background—the absent presence in their work like the sky trail of a vanished aircraft.

To complicate all this coming and going, the scholarship of these Americans has recrossed the Atlantic in recent years, and important aspects of the American pragmatic tradition are found in recent German and British work on communication. For example, the critical theory of Jürgen Habermas begins in a traditional German strategy of contrasting philosophical positions among German scholars: Kant versus Heidegger, Marx versus Hegel, and so on. He then, in the theory of the public sphere, turns to Peirce, Dewey, and Mead along with the speech-act theory of John Searle and J. L. Austin. As a result, Habermas's analysis of the public sphere bears a close resemblance to Robert Park's. Similarly, when work at Birmingham on Cultural Studies reached out to continental sources of inspiration in the 1960s, it also imported significant portions of the Chicago School theory of symbolic interactionism to ground their outlook on the empirical regularities and inequalities of daily life.

Professor Hardt's chapters on nineteenth-century German scholars resound with arguments announced later by Robert Park, John Dewey, and even the Canadian economist who studied in Chicago, Harold Innis. But they also resound with elements that American scholarship in mass communication lost: a thoroughly critical attitude toward its subject, a sense of the larger framework of social theory within which studies must proceed. More than merely a history of pertinent German thought on mass communication, this book reminds us of valuable ideas shared by German and American scholarship that form a vital tradition that can vivify work today.

James W. Carey
Columbia University

Preface

This book is an enlarged and revised edition of *Social Theories of the Press: Early German and American Perspectives*, originally published by Sage in 1979. It has been closely edited, revised, and expanded to accommodate two additional chapters (2, 9), which address the contributions of Karl Marx as an active participant in the nineteenth-century struggle for press freedom and the rise of an alternative theoretical perspective on communication and society since the 1970s, respectively.

More specifically, chapter 2 focuses on a neglected contribution of the early Marx to the struggle over press freedom in Prussia. It addresses his initial political engagement as a journalist and provides an example of the merger of theory and practice as editor and political activist. His interests in the relations of press and society, the importance of a free flow of information and opinion, and the role of communication in the making of society provide insights into the journalism of Karl Marx and help enrich our understanding of the intellectual atmosphere surrounding nineteenth-century social theory in Germany.

Chapter 9 summarizes the theoretical contributions of German and American social scientists; it also reflects on the decentering of traditional theories and practices at the end of the twentieth century and the emergence of an alternative discourse about the relations of communication, media, and society beyond the rise of the social sciences in the United States—an outgrowth of these early considerations in German and American scholarship. The chapter addresses the consequences of a paradigm shift in "mass communication research" based on the neo-Marxist response to issues of culture, communication, and media through the contributions of Critical Theory and British cultural studies, in particular.

The need for such an alternative discourse, which I addressed in the original preface to this book, still exists, while solutions to the problems of media and communication become more urgent with the failure of traditional models of democracy in a world that is dominated by centralized production of news and information and threatened by decreasing communicative competencies vis-à-vis the complexities of modern existence.

This book reflects my belief in the importance of historical consciousness as a considerable force in the intellectual life of the field; it also promotes an understanding of the concrete theoretical discourse regarding communication, media, and society that emerges from the political economy and sociology of the nineteenth century to inform the social scientific analyses of communication and produce an ideology of "mass communication research"; the latter controlled the field throughout most of the last century. At the same time, the book confirms the centrality of communication and media in a theory of society—as expressed by German and American social thought—and suggests that a critique of society must begin with a critique of its process of communication.

I am indebted to Andrew Calabrese, the series editor, and his interest in publishing a second edition of this book, and to a number of anonymous students in the School of Journalism and Mass Communication at the University of Colorado in Boulder who meticulously reproduced the original, out-of-print edition on disk to provide a workable copy, including Zhang Weidong, my graduate research assistant at the University of Iowa, who labored on the last phase of the project. Thanks also to Brenda Hadenfeldt at Rowman & Littlefield for taking on this project, Jehanne Schweitzer for an efficient production schedule, and Chrisona Schmidt for a judicious copyediting effort.

Parts of chapter 9 have been reprinted from *Mass Communication and Society*, whose progressive editorial policy under the leadership of David Demers protects the right of authors to use their own material without special permission from the publisher.

I am also grateful to my respective home departments at the Universities of Iowa and Ljubljana and their continued encouragement and material support of intellectual labor.

Social Theories of the Press

The first freedom of the press is not to be a business. However, when the press exists as a business, it is not an interest of writers, but of printers and booksellers.

Karl Marx, 1842

Not everybody realizes that a really good journalistic achievement requires at least as much genius as any scholarly accomplishment.

Max Weber, 1918

The press is the real instrument . . . of public opinion, weapon and tool in the hands of those who know how to use it.

Ferdinand Tönnies, 1887

The newspaper-owner manufactures the impressions that breed opinion and, if he controls a chain of important newspapers, he may virtually make public opinion without the public knowing it.

Edward A. Ross, 1918

It is idle to deny that the worst papers are the most popular and make the most money.

William Graham Sumner, 1934

1

Mass Communication Research and Society: An Introduction

COMMUNICATION IN SOCIETY

The development of communication and mass communication theories in the United States constitutes a small but significant chapter in the twentieth-century history of social, philosophical, and political thought in Europe and North America. It dominates the earlier part of the twentieth century with the rise of pragmatism and the success of the social sciences, which helped legitimate the field of communication and media studies, reinforced its identity, and secured its position among the human and social sciences. Yet considerations of communication as a central social phenomenon began much earlier, during the nineteenth century, with the rise of political economy and sociology amid the specter of industrialization and urbanization in Europe, and Germany in particular.

Although several recent book-length treatments (e.g., Chaffee and Rogers 1997; Rogers 1994; Dennis and Wartella 1996; Hardt 1992; Schiller 1996) have privileged a twentieth-century American perspective on communication studies, celebrating the history of the field, the following account focuses on its prehistory and the scholarly contributions to considerations of communication and the press during the late nineteenth and early twentieth centuries by German social theorists. It also includes (albeit briefly) reflections by first-generation American sociologists, whose own work was influenced by German scholarship and subsequently becomes a reminder of a continuing influence of German social thought on discussions of media and communication. It concludes with the contemporary shift of paradigms in U.S. mass communication research.

The earlier accounts, in particular, advance the rise of academic communication or media studies in Germany (e.g., *Publizistikwissenschaft* or *Kommunikationswissenschaft*) with a sustained theoretical discourse in the scholarly narratives that endured beyond their own times. Consequently, this book traces some of the concrete historical roots of modern communication and mass communication theories and suggests a presence of intellectual kinship, theoretical proximity, and commonality of social-political interests. As such, the book is also a contribution to the history of ideas and their transatlantic migration, signaling the beginning of an intellectual process of acclimatization that culminated most recently in the appropriation of Marxism, British cultural studies, and French poststructuralism (including the encounter with postmodernism) and in a dramatic shift from traditional social scientific paradigms to cultural-historical perspectives in the study of communication and media.

Social thought around the turn of the twentieth century was dominated by the writings of Herbert Spencer, Auguste Comte, and Karl Marx, in particular, which either shaped the contributions to a modern theory of communication or prompted a response to specific theoretical propositions. Observations of social life had led to the Spencerian view of freedom through competing religious or philosophical doctrines, the Comtean realization that religion had to be replaced by a new scientific philosophy to help organize the political and economic conditions, and a utopian Marxian perspective that anticipated the growth of science and technology and the rise of an egalitarian society in reaction to the forces of capitalism. The work of these theorists was supported by others who engaged in closer observations of specific conditions and conducted surveys to report on the failures of society in a more scientific manner (e.g., through observations and descriptions). The latter were not always dispassionate and were often supported by socialist thought or reformist ideas that had also surfaced in the journalism of the day.

At times, social science theory and social criticism, which had been firmly established by the time the nineteenth century came to a close, appeared to flow simultaneously from the work of socially committed intellectuals who published frequently in academic and nonacademic journals and newspapers. But while the social criticism of German scholars dominates mainly as an ideological force, the observations of American social scientists are led by a compulsion for engagement in social reform. In fact, sociology and the study of mass communication as a social phenomenon emerge in Germany as a variation on philosophical and political thought and in the United States as part of an expressed need for the improvement of social conditions. In both instances, these developments had been caused by the rapid transformation of society into a modern industrial state, which had resulted in widespread economic and political inequalities. This expansion is accompanied by the tracing of social consciousness through communication as a definition and an explanation of the rise of modern society. After all, it was Marx who had suggested that social structure must evolve out of the life process of individuals and therefore provide a way for the social sciences to investigate the workings of society.

Accordingly, the production of ideas, conceptions, and consciousness (i.e., the language of real life) is interwoven with the material activity and material intercourse of individuals, while the mental interchange of individuals—conceiving and thinking—emanates at this stage directly from their material behavior. The same applies to mental productions as expressed in the language of politics, law, morality, religion, and metaphysics—real, active individuals conditioned by a definite development of their productive forces and corresponding interactions. Consciousness can never be anything else but conscious existence, and the existence of individuals is their actual life process (Marx and Engels 1970, 47).

This means that considerations of language, public opinion, and media are necessary elements of any explanation of the material or intellectual and spiritual growth of society and provide central themes for discussing those social, economic, and political processes that help shape the human environment.

One of the strongest suggestions that emerges from the work of these early social scientists is that a theory of society—or any attempt to explain more concretely the coming of the modern age—must be based on an understanding of communication as a basic social process. In fact, privileging communication involves paying considerable attention to the socializing or integrating function of language in the construction of everyday realities, ranging from scientific to political worldviews. The production of symbols is crucial for an exchange of ideas, and language as the foundation of knowledge marks the beginning of civilization and functions to preserve and reinforce traditions.

Communication implies the presence of language and the existence of dialogical relationships, which involves the idea of exchange but also suggests the potential of manipulation in efforts to influence personal or public opinions. Therefore, any understanding of human progress, from the tradition of communal relationships to the rise of urban societies, must be predicated on an appreciation of the fundamental role of communication in the life process of society, including the social or political struggle for power.

The communication of ideas for purposes of preserving and transmitting knowledge—or securing the growth and survival of society—calls for the creation of media that are not only accurate and efficient but also fast and durable and, therefore, superior to oral modes of communication. These results were achieved almost instantaneously with the invention of the printing press, the publication of books and pamphlets, and the emergence and circulation of the modern newspaper. The expression of facts and opinions on a large scale with the rise of the print media had the potential, if not the effect, of social and political integration through democratizing access to knowledge and to the means of communication generally. Subsequent inventions of electronic media and contemporary computer-assisted methods of communication successfully build on the nature of a traditional print culture while accentuating immediacy by overcoming time and place with ever increasing speeds.

Thus the press becomes an original, powerful medium for exchanging ideas and advancing the time- and space-binding activities of society in conceptualizations of Western civilization. But newspapers, as technologies of dissemination, are also instruments of political power that play a major role in defining the social and political realities of everyday life; they supply identities, articulate public opinion, and enhance industrial and economic progress as indispensable organizers of public sentiments. While the weekly press (in the United States) reflects the pace of the countryside, the daily press emerges as a child of the city, where the process of public communication is being filtered through economic and political interests; the latter are identified with ideologies of progress that privilege industrialization and embrace urban development. Thus subsequent histories of the modern press typically reflect the rise of liberalism, the establishment of democracy, and the impact of capitalism on the modernization of society.

Throughout this period, the writings of political economists contribute a strong economic bias to the critical treatment of the press. Their views on economic aspects range from interpretations of the press reminiscent of Harold Innis's later work, which produced a unique communication perspective of world history, to assessments of the traditional and unavoidable ties between politics and business that affect the workings of the modern newspaper.

The press becomes central to discussions concerning the production and dissemination of symbols in the form of political facts, opinions, or commercial messages. Thus, when newspapers sell either information or space, they serve the economic interests of other businesses while representing the commercial concerns of the press. The latter helps coordinate production, transportation, and exchange of wealth, aids in the search for ways of disposing surplus and advancing territorial divisions of labor, and also promotes knowledge and education and claims a role in the enlightenment of modern societies.

Press criticism, therefore, focuses on the real or potential conflict between two major functions, which are characteristic of the modern press: public service—as an independent societal institution that produces and disseminates information for public consumption—and private enterprise—as a commercial medium that caters to specific business and political interests. The difficulties of this position are typically described in terms of journalistic work ethics, political as opposed to commercial journalism, or ideological differences regarding the treatment of leadership, newspapers, and public opinion.

More specifically, the German reaction frequently reflects an elitist-aristocratic view that upholds the leader-masses dichotomy in the discussion of social, political, or cultural developments. It extols the intellectual qualities of a minority and delivers a rationale for its place vis-à-vis the necessary presence of the masses. The latter are capable of understanding and reflecting the ideas of their leaders, but they are unfit to assume a creative, innovative role in the rise of modern society. The idea prevails that newspapers serve social and cultural elites in their contact with the masses, and even journalists are often reduced to mere objects, useful for the purpose of transmitting undistorted knowledge and information. Although the press may reflect the opinions of the masses, it is not independent thought or creative insight that is reported by newspapers but more frequently their reactions to the opinions of leaders. In this sense, the press assumes a rather fixed role in the context of describing the forces of history and the distribution of decision-making powers in society when the idea of the individual as participant in the process of social communication is seriously reduced to the notion of a cooperating consumer of information.

The views represented by American scholarship, on the other hand, as it evolves from this study, reveal the tendency to consider the press a forum for the examination of frequently competing ideas. Although the concept of authority may appear to suggest expert knowledge or special interest in the communication process, there is no attempt to preclude others from gaining similar access to society through the press, for instance. The latter offers access to all kinds of commercial or political thought, and, despite its economic interests, it is basically seen in the context of a classless society. This perspective privileges a concept of communication that fits the notion of participatory democracy; in what is really a political process, all information is considered equally important, with the result that anyone may advance propositions that either support or oppose individual or special interests.

Since newspapers do not present windows on the world but rather construct and perpetuate worldviews to direct or affect opinions, the uses of the press by intellectual, political, or commercial elites present a serious problem. Indeed, control over the media of dissemination may suggest control over the mind of society, and especially when press criticism operates with assumptions of an inherently powerful newspaper practice that results in attitude changes and the corruption of minds. Consequently, the notion of effects becomes a focal point of critical observations as a particularly alarming aspect of media practices. Indeed, the workings of cultural and political forces in society are said to become transparent in the process of public communication when purpose and intent of the communicator are revealed to expose an underlying ideology. The suggestive power of the press rests in its position as a public institution *and* in its generation of a specific content; it is met by readers who are said to follow the dictates of the press because newspapers have gained their respect, are considered credible, and deliver facts and opinions convincingly.

Consequently, the effects of the press are typically described at a societal level, where newspapers as institutions of society contribute to the political decision-making process, and at an individual level, where the press changes attitudes and perceptions of reality. How this is accomplished and what are the long-range effects for society are key questions that stimulated the development of empirical mass communication research, particularly in the United States. After all, the preservation of a democratic way of life is closely tied to issues of communication, typically expressed in the late 1920s by John Dewey (in *The Public and Its Problems*).

Differently expressed, the origins of a modern study of the press are bound up in the rise of social criticism. It seems appropriate—especially in the light of contemporary communication and media theory and research—to point to these beginnings and to support and strengthen critical assessments of the role and function of media in society, despite the fact that it could be argued—as Stuart Hughes has suggested (Bottomore 1968, 132)—that social thinkers following Marx "were haunted by a sense of living in an age of merely derivative philosophy and scholarship" and that their major contributions resided in the fact that they "narrowed the range through which such general theorizing might operate and cast doubt on the future usefulness of intellectual operations of this type."

Specifically, the tradition of American mass communication research has been confronted by the crisis of the social sciences and the emergence of a critical approach to issues of communication and culture with a turn to a theory of society that is grounded in neo-Marxist insights and contemplations of neopragmatism. This situation is reflected not only in reactions to specific theoretical and methodological suggestions formulated and discussed under the influence of other disciplines—notably cultural anthropology, ethnography, and literature, or areas such as feminist or cultural studies—but also in self-reflection and reappraisals of communication and media studies after a generation of research activities that had profound effects on contemporary views of media practices as well as on ways in which research itself is defined and executed.

The problems of mass communication research are neither new nor unique; rather, they are the result of an American social scientific enterprise that grew rapidly as a reaction to a number of social problems and attempts to treat specific conditions of society in predominantly political settings. This development suggests the strength and weakness of the field. With its recognized centrality in the life of society, its power of immediacy, and its social, political, and economic impact, the process of communication in everyday life invited academic and commercial research to help solve considerable social and political problems. Consequently, the field of mass communication research grew in prominence and initial success and built a strong rationale for its position among other disciplines and fields of study, particularly after World War II, when its mission spread to Europe, particularly Germany. At the same time, however, there remained a need for moving beyond the concrete, problem-oriented work to a study of the more comprehensive and meaningful contextual relationship among media, communication, and society in the process of an emerging modern civilization.[1]

Questions about the role and function of media in American society are as old as the press itself. However, the felt need for a systematic treatment of communication phenomena is relatively new and coincides with the introduction of broadcasting technologies and the increase of information in commercial and military conflicts. Both situations created specific demands for the social sciences: to summarize the effects of new technologies and provide knowledge about the effectiveness of messages and their impact on the economic and political existence of society. The introduction of new types of media was accompanied by what Paul Lazarsfeld (1972a, 110) once called unanticipated consequences that had to be identified and considered systematically for a complete understanding of real or potential media uses.

Broadcasting not only crossed continents and spanned oceans to collapse time and space, but it was also envisioned as penetrating the minds of people more effectively than earlier media and thus expanding its power as a tool of mass persuasion in the service of commercial or political interests. Subsequent media effects research was legitimized through economic and political support and further strengthened with the outbreak of major conflicts such as World Wars I and II that focused attention on communication as a means of organizing national defenses and conducting psychological warfare.

Lazarsfeld (1972a, 112) had concluded quite correctly some time ago that communication research is a legitimate task of the social sciences, and although new, constitutes "the academic and intellectual shadow of the great changes which have come about in the world." It was a time when the process of industrialization was being replaced by an information revolution, and the notion of transportation expanded beyond railroads and highway systems to embrace the speed of computer technologies and the possibilities of instant access to far corners of the world. When (American) society became the laboratory of mass communication research, much of the initial research concentrated on how to reach large numbers of individuals efficiently and effectively through media practices. This task was quite consistent with one of the prevailing definitions of mass communication—as an activity directed toward a relatively large, heterogeneous, and anonymous audience (Wright 1975, 8). Also, much of the ensuing work treated people as potential or actual consumers of commercial or political messages often at the expense of other critical perspectives on communication as cultural and economic forces with diverse constituencies.

Since modern mass communication research in the United States has it roots primarily in the social scientific traditions represented by individuals such as Harold Lasswell, Paul Lazarsfeld, Kurt Lewin, Carl Hovland, and the work of their colleagues and students, it necessarily focuses on questions of political power, audience effects, and the sociological and psychological analyses of small group communication. Their disciplines provide important points of departure in the 1930s for the rise of mass communication research, although this period of innovative ideas and research designs is relatively short, since their involvement in communication and media phenomena remains peripheral to their major professional interests. Their students and followers (as is often the case) were less successful in generating and advancing new ideas, but they excelled in sustaining interest in particular methodologies and specific disciplinary frames of reference. In fact, mass communication research suffers when theoretical concerns, including theory building, are overshadowed by a preoccupation with the collection of information and the accumulation of unintegrated data.

Most important, however, is the fact that mass communication research continued to operate within the prevailing philosophical mode of social scientific research. Early on, Veikko Pietilä (1977, 34–44) identifies and describes the influence of empiricism, behaviorism, and psychologism on the development of mass communication research. The resulting search for communication causes and effects generated knowledge based on the interpretation of quantitative data, while understanding that the consequences of communication and media activities relied on various schematic models of communication that identified and operationalized their major components (e.g., communicator, message, audience) as pertinent research agendas.

Furthermore, an encounter with functionalism in its sociological and anthropological approaches, which postulate a system of society with stable relationships among its individual elements, means that communication phenomena are treated as sources of information about current states of exchange of information within a social system. Thus a functional analysis of mass communication suggests guidelines for the study of communication as an activity that contributes to the support and maintenance of the social system. Functionalism as it emerges from its psychological roots provided mass communication research with its stimulus-response model and led to a view of the media as deterministic stimuli with direct, cumulative effects on members of society.

These early encounters with empirical mass communication research unveil a dominant way of looking at the world of media practices in a concrete economic or political context. The latter not only provides agendas for media research but proves highly sensitive to expressions of social scientific expertise. For instance, Lazarsfeld (1972b, 124) acknowledges the problems of a commercial partnership and observes as early as the late 1940s that "we academic people always have a certain sense of tight-rope walking: at what point will the commercial partners find some necessary conclusion too hard to take and at what point will they shut us off from the indispensable sources of funds and data?"

Recently there have been some significant changes in conceptualizing communication within a critical (Marxist) or Cultural Studies approach (as suggested in chapter 9), resulting in emancipatory research agendas that threaten traditional mass communication research and signal the consequences of a shifting paradigm.

THE GERMAN TRADITION

The history of mass communication scholarship is considerably older in Germany—where it is known as *Zeitungs-* or *Publizistikwissenschaft*, and more recently as *Kommunikationswissenschaft*—than in the United States. The post–Word War II encounters with an American social science tradition, which include the pervasive influence of mass communication theory and research on *Publizistikwissenschaft*, produced specific reactions against the unreflected adoption of theoretical or methodological premises and helped define a framework for subsequent contemporary criticism.

The discovery of empirical social research for mass communication studies in Germany roughly coincides with the flow of social scientific expertise from the United States through exchanges and study abroad (e.g., Fulbright programs), the return of émigrés (including members of the Frankfurt Institute) from the United States in the early 1950s, and the general reliance of German society on American know-how during a period of physical and intellectual reconstruction within the framework of political renewal. The very notion of democracy, questions of public opinion, and political participation in the new state were based on the tried and tested uses of empirical techniques. Thus Adorno argues in 1952 for abandoning the idea of sociology as *Geisteswissenschaft* and suggests the application of administrative research methods in studying social phenomena (Jay 1973, 346). His comments accompany a widespread use of social science research methods that resulted a few years later in the polarization of empirical and dialectical methodologists. Among the latter are representatives of the Frankfurt Institute and Jürgen Habermas, who exposes the dangers of a strictly empirical study of society. But even Adorno's warning that empirical social research is not "a magic mirror that reflects the future, no science-oriented astrology" did not prevent a *Positivismusstreit* among German sociologists. The clash occurred over the metatheoretical foundation of sociology as science and involved representatives of Critical Theory (Adorno, Habermas) and critical rationalism (Karl Popper, Hans Albert). Although the outcome remained unclear (even to some participants), the problem of the dialectical position is focused on "how to integrate those techniques [of empirical social research] with a truly critical approach stressing the primacy of theory" (Jay 1973, 251).

Habermas and his *Strukturwandel der Öffentlichkeit*, published in 1962, constitute only one, albeit critical, alternative for *Publizistikwissenschaft*. The second one, based on the rise of a postwar generation of social scientists with commitments to developing a contemporary theory of mass communication (and aided by the availability of an American literature on media and communication), was more effective in directing *Publizistikwissenschaft* toward a traditional social scientific discipline.

More specifically, functionalism as an American contribution to postwar media studies in (West) Germany stipulates a particular view of society that is based on the sociological tradition of Talcott Parsons or Robert Merton. Their functional or structural-functional approach describes a tendency of society toward stability, value consensus, and equilibrium, while sudden and profound changes, or conflict and revolution, for instance, are taken into account only in terms of deviations, variances, or dysfunctions. There is no departure from a static view of society. Although critics such as Ralph Dahrendorf (1967, 263–77) suggest a need for studying social change in postwar German society and therefore a need to reject functional models of society, their ideas remain largely ineffective, particularly with respect to work on communication and media projects.

At yet another level, American functionalism may be seen as a conscious alternative to Marxism. Although it is not to be characterized as a political ideology that emerged from the structure of American capitalism, it remains, nevertheless, a product of modern American social thought. For instance, Gouldner (1970, 149) suggests that a group of Harvard scholars—among them George Homans, Talcott Parsons, and L. J. Henderson—engaged sociology in a search for "a theoretical defense against Marxism" at a time in the 1930s when Marxism was brought into sharp focus by the collapse of the American economy and emerged as a new perspective on social practices. Functionalism, on the other hand, projects a politically and ideologically neutral image, while it typically supports order and stability. Thus endorsing change within the context of a status quo does not alter its position vis-à-vis social criticism or efforts of radical social transformation.

In addition, the end of World War II brought along a new style of scientific inquiry—described by C. Wright Mills (1970) as abstract empiricism—which provided social scientists in postwar Western Europe with powerful and compelling descriptions of their function and added to their own definitions of sociology. In a 1948 paper delivered to a group of Swedish social scientists eager to set up research institutions, Lazarsfeld defines the work of sociologists as methodologists of social scientists. He explains, according to Mills, that the first function of the sociologist is to be

> the *pathfinder* of the advancing army of social scientists, when a new sector of human affairs is about to become an object of empirical scientific investigations. It is the sociologist who takes the first steps. He is the bridge between the social philosopher, the individual observer and commentator on the one hand, and the organized team work of the empirical investigators and analysers on the other. . . . Historically speaking we then have to distinguish three major ways of looking at social subject matters: social analysis as practiced by the individual observer; organized full-fledged empirical sciences; and a transitory phase which we call the sociology of any special area of social behavior. (1970, 70)

The promise of empirical methods—as they had been developed in the United States—turned into a stream of mass communication studies in (West) Germany. Method, so it seems, grants status and respectability to the field of mass communication research; it provides a reliable instrument and supplies a scientific context for interpreting communication phenomena in modern society. An identification with contemporary social science methodologies—and the tradition of American journalism and mass communication research in particular—also serves a political purpose at home: regaining the lost credibility of *Zeitungswissenschaft* as a Nazi-dominated field of academic practices by reclaiming respectability among the social sciences under the name of *Publizistikwissenschaft*.

The results were less than encouraging, however, partly because the field was still under the influence of politically suspect professors with traditional visions (Arnulf Kutsch [1984] addresses the problems of a tainted academic field of study after 1945) and partly because a new generation of mass communication researchers missed asking relevant questions regarding the moral or political renewal of (West) Germany's media system. Thus, when young academics like Franz Dröge and Winfried Lerg (1965) observe a lack of theory building in U.S. mass communication research through the 1960s, they fail to comment on an identical trend in the (West) German social sciences, and specifically in mass communication research.

Nevertheless, what Hans Bohrmann and Rolf Sülzer (1973, 101) call the reformed *Publizistikwissenschaft* was now in a position of legitimizing its own role, not only in the university environment but also vis-à-vis professional and industrial interests through an alliance with a respected empirical research tradition.

It is more than a coincidence that the end of World War II marks the beginning of a process of reorientation that led to the exploration of other fields, including sociology, social psychology, philosophy, and political science as related areas that had long recognized the importance of communication and media in their own considerations of social and political processes. The need for a comprehensive view of communication in society activates a search for legitimate intellectual partners in the study of social phenomena to meet the challenges of understanding relations among various social forces in a modern society. In other words, the process of democratization in postwar (West) Germany had resulted in a breakdown of traditional barriers that had separated *Zeitungwissenschaft* from other disciplines through the introduction and acceptance of social scientific frameworks. Finally, since the late 1960s, *Publizistikwissenschaft* entered what could be called a critical or reflective phase in its approach to social research and its own position in society. Controversies in sociology and student and faculty demands for relevant research and teaching helped accelerate internal debates. In addition, there was the realization that a mounting number of empirical studies could neither solve problems of media monopolies and press freedom, for instance, nor satisfy the demands for a comprehensive communication theory that would respond to the need for social or political changes in the communication system. In fact, it was never so much a question of rejecting empirical methods, but rather a problem of interpreting what empirical social research could and should do for a specific theoretical perspective. All the while, the limitations of empirical methods became more obvious: they satisfied demands for reflecting particular conditions of media in society and providing immediate feedback, but they were unable to contribute to a theory of society based on communication and media practices.

The crucial approach to a critical study of media as social phenomena had received support from writers including Hans Magnus Enzensberger, Horst Holzer, Friedrich Knilli, Dieter Prokrop, and Franz Dröge, who seemed to agree that communication research must develop methodologies that will allow drawing conclusions about the interdependence of communication and society.[2] Nevertheless, Adorno cautioned that "the applicability of a science to society depends in an essential way on the state of society itself. There is no general social issue which some scientific method of therapy could treat universally" (Frankfurt Institute 1972, 126).

Into the late 1970s and beyond, the dilemma of communication and media studies was a result of these developments in the social sciences; variations and adjustments to these perspectives continue to exist together with a disregard of the past political condition of the field and its representatives, as well as a general inability to move beyond traditional academic concerns of *Publizistikwissenschaft*. Also, there prevailed a spirit of realism that dominated and controlled the field with an emphasis on facts combined with an intensified search for causes and their consequences for the social system. At the individual level this approach translates into explanations of communication as a process of adaptation to irresistible social forces. It is opposed by what could be called a utopian perspective that views the role of communication and media in terms of creating a desirable social environment and is based on theories or visions of society in which communication performs a major cultural and political task.

The emerging antithesis of utopia and reality, so to speak, reveals itself in a division between critical-intellectual and administrative-bureaucratic views of communication and media. The critical position seeks to make practice conform to theory, is more interested in general principles, and is based on specific human values. Lazarsfeld's description of critical research remains quite useful as a contemporary explanation of this viewpoint. He suggests (1972c, 160) that critical research "develops a theory of the prevailing trends in our times, general trends which yet require consideration in any concrete research problem; and it seems to imply ideas of basic human values according to which all actual or desired effects should be appraised." There is also a tendency for a critical-intellectual position to coincide with politically liberal or radical ideas.

An administrative view, on the other hand, is characterized by its empirical basis and the fact that practice—or action—is more important than theoretical propositions. Also, there are strong ties with existing economic and political powers in society and, generally, with social forces that support the established order. This perspective in particular aims to provide a meticulous account of communication and media phenomena and their role and function in the dominant social and political system; consequently, it tends to lead to conclusions about adaptation rather than conflict and toward a more conservative view concerning communication and media and their role in society.

For the development of Germany's *Publizistikwissenschaft*, however, both positions contain unsatisfactory elements. The critical approach fails to translate theory into practice and, although intellectually convincing in its arguments, it remains relatively ineffective as an alternative to the dominant mode of thinking about mass communication research. Rather, it is an idea that is based on what Lazarsfeld describes as the need "to do and think what we consider true and not to adjust ourselves to the seemingly inescapable" (1972c, 161). This task is quite demanding, however, and it seemed easier to follow an administrative course that supports routinized research activities instead of sharing a fascination with new theories and the flow of ideas. Instead, the introduction of Cultural Studies and its critical interests of media and communication falls outside *Publizistik- or Kommunikationswissenschaft,* from where a critical dimension to media studies emerges to provoke a hitherto neglected and politically provocative discourse about communication and media in society.

While German *Publizistikwissenschaft* struggles with its own history and the mounting challenges to a social scientific perspective on mass communication research, modern American communication (and journalism) studies were initially exposed to a critical perspective on media in a democratic society with the 1947 report by the Commission on Freedom of the Press, whose authors had embarked on a vigorous critique of the American media. They demonstrated by their work how an academic community can bring to bear its expert observations on what has been unilaterally considered one of the most important institutions in a democracy. The commission (Leigh 1974, vii) concludes that the media are the single most powerful influence in modern society and notes the failures of other societal agencies by suggesting that "if the schools did a better job of educating our people, the responsibility of the press to raise the level of American culture, or even to supply our citizens with correct and full political, economic, and social information would be materially altered."

The commission was particularly interested in the flow of ideas and stated (Leigh 1974, vii) that a "civilized society is a working system of ideas. Therefore, it must make sure that as many as possible of the ideas which its members have are available for its examination"; indeed, because of the assigned influence of the media, it is "imperative that the great agencies of mass communication show hospitality to ideas which their owners do not share." Subsequently, communication and media studies in the United States disregarded—by and large—the suggestions of the report and continued on their administrative mass communication research path for another generation when the dominant social scientific paradigm was threatened by the rise of critical communication studies with a return to social criticism as an integral part of media studies.

THEORIZING THE PRESS AND SOCIETY

The latter developments concur with suggestions that a study of communication and media can make sense only in the context of a theory of society; thus, questions about freedom and control of expression, private and public spheres of communication, and a democratic system of communication must be raised to define the conditions of a democratic existence. Also, to understand the importance of communication and media research as a social and political force it becomes vital to comprehend the relationship between economic and political powers in society, their use of communication research as a source of knowledge, and the effect of this relationship on defining the role of the media. It is equally important to address individual concerns for identity and self-respect in the process of societal communication.

This approach also implies that the study of communication and its societal institutions must be placed in the realm of a cultural and intellectual history of society, since the media play a major role in the creation and perpetuation of cultural and social-political traditions. At the same time, they can be understood and explained only in relation to other social institutions, particularly education and religion, and in the context of economic-technological patterns of control.

For these reasons it seems not only worthwhile but important in the context of conceptualizing a history of communication and mass communication theory and research to recall that concerns about the press as a societal institution had a place in the writings of early German and American sociologists; they not only acknowledge the importance of communication but are equally involved in discussing the role of the press as an emerging, powerful agent of collecting and disseminating information in society.

The following chapters constitute an attempt to contribute to the writing of an intellectual history of communication and mass communication theory and research as they relate to the work of American sociology and its roots in German social thought, in particular. German scholarship provides the intellectual and cultural environment for a handful of first-generation American sociologists—whose exposure to political and social thought resulted in early conceptualizations of communication in society—and constitutes at the same time the major source of a German tradition of *Publizistikwissenschaft*. This account will demonstrate the nature of the arguments and illustrate the character of the work in Germany and subsequently in the United States concerning questions of communication and the press in society.

More specifically, the contributions of Karl Marx, Albert Schäffle, Karl Knies, Karl Bücher, Ferdinand Tönnies, and Max Weber—as they relate to communication and media studies—are synonymous with the rise of the social sciences, which includes the first theoretical discussions of modern media. Although primarily known for their scholarship in economic and sociological thought, their ideas about communication and the press are central to arguments concerning a theory of society; they also suggest the need for a contextualized study of communication with particular reference to social and economic conditions, and reflect—in an autobiographical sense—knowledge and experience of these authors with the press and public opinion as dominant political forces in the Germany of their own times. As teachers, colleagues, or contemporaries of American sociologists, they are among the most important sources of modern communication and media theories. Since there is little knowledge about these individuals (with the exception of Marx, Weber, and Tönnies), brief biographical introductions focus on their academic backgrounds and major contributions as they relate to the richness and originality of their thought. Most of the original material appears in translation for the first time.

Among American scholars with similar ideas are Albion Small, Edward A. Ross, and William Graham Sumner. They stand as representatives of a number of early American sociologists whose training or background included encounters with the German social science tradition and whose scholarship—labeled "American science" in Germany—includes references to communication and media and their importance for conceptualizations of a modern age.

As well as reflecting the influence of German or European social thought, their work represents an early attempt to adapt foreign ideas to uniquely American social, economic, and political conditions. It occurs in the historical context of long-lasting and recognized differences in American and German social thought that are based on the nature of political and cultural movements and their specific premises for arguments concerning the role and function of societal institutions, including the press. Hawthorn has characterized these differences, particularly in liberal thought, and concludes that

> philosophical, social and political thinking has proceeded within what are by comparison with Europe extremely narrow bounds, the bounds of an established liberalism. In Europe, liberalism was at first a critical principle, and no sooner had it been established . . . than it itself began to be undermined by what has there generally been understood as socialism. In the United States, on the other hand, liberalism was only ever a critical principle in arguments against Europe. It was established with the new republic, ideologically, if not in fact, and criticisms of the progress, or not, of that republic have always been in its own terms. (1976, 194–95)

Analyses and comparative reviews of conceptualizations of communication and media must recognize these roots of sociological thought to understand their own concrete historical condition. This includes a realization that the tradition of social criticism in the United States—

particularly as it includes the role and function of the press—has never been strong enough to overcome the limitations of its own peculiar development as an intellectual exercise within an established social and political system. Thus a turn to a critical communication perspective occurs much later under specific historical conditions and is the topic of the last chapter.

2

Communication and Change: Karl Marx on Press Freedom

MARX AND THE PRESS

Karl Marx (1818–1883) emerges from his German contemporaries as the most important social theorist to help shape social and political thinking of the twentieth century. His writings informed intellectual discourse well beyond his lifetime, stimulated the imagination of younger generations of social thinkers, and provoked new interpretations that surfaced throughout the twentieth century in numerous reproductions of "Marxism." A history of critical readings of Marx, beginning with Louis Althusser (1965, 1968) and Jean Baudrillard (1973), for instance, not only adds to the presence of Marxist thought but illustrates the challenge of a cultural or political text to contemporary interpretations in light of modernist or postmodernist ideologies. The emerging theoretical narratives constitute a modern literature of explication, founded on the notion of intellectual critique and intended to offer a liberating perspective on the crisis of the state and society. After having defined the political landscape of Europe at the end of World War I, Marx's work continues to inspire new generations of political activists in their struggle for social, political, and economic justice, which has become the goal of numerous liberation movements in many parts of the world throughout the twentieth century.

Consequently, the twentieth-century literature of social thought is, by and large, a response to the writings of Karl Marx and Friedrich Engels, their interpretation of the economic and social conditions of industrialization (and westernization), and their hopes for a revolutionary new social order, which guarantees the conditions for a "good society." Their vision of such an order during the 1840s includes specific ideas about public communication, that is, the role of a free press and the need for a free flow of information as constitutive elements of democratic practices.

For Marx, issues of communication and the press belong to the realm of practical rather than philosophical or theoretical concerns; they constitute the existential dimension of his political agenda. Throughout his life, he remains keenly aware of the central role of the press in the making of a just society and the consequences of censorship for journalistic freedom. His later theoretical work does not specifically address issues of press freedom or censorship, although a case can be made for his interest in communication, that is, "the movement of commodities, people, information & capital" (De la Haye 1980). As a result, the former topics are confined to his early work in Germany as an intellectual, a journalist, and an editor, when questions of communication are related to social and political change and the protection of ideas.

This chapter concentrates on Marx's contribution to issues of press freedom, beginning with his writings as a young journalist and editor of the *Rheinische Zeitung*.[1] Friedrich Engels (1869) observes that after spending "five years in the 'metropolis of intellectuals' " [Berlin] among Young Hegelians, Marx returned to Bonn and Köln to use the *Rheinische Zeitung* "with unprecedented daring" to attack the deliberations of the Rhine Provincial Assembly in a series of six articles. His work attracted much attention. When he became editor at the end of 1842, his activities were heavily censored until the Prussian government shut down the *Rheinische Zeitung* in 1843. Marx resigned immediately. The newspaper had benefited from the widespread public disappointment (also among bourgeois constituencies) regarding promised legal and political changes in Prussia. Moreover, Engels (1967/1968a, 2:17) sees the journalistic accomplishments of the *Rheinische Zeitung* in 1842 as the starting point of a modern German press.

Emerging from his first encounter with authority, Marx realizes—according to Engels (1869)—that civil society and not the state holds the key to understanding the historical process of human development. He concludes that political economy is the science of society and contains the knowledge needed to understand and analyze the evolution of social formations.

Within a few years, Marx moved to France to study political economy and the history of the French Revolution, was expelled, went to Brussels, returned to France, and finally reemerged in Cologne to pursue his political goals by returning to journalism. During this time he contributed to the *Vorwärts* in Paris (1844) and the *Deutsche Brüsseler Zeitung* (1847) in

Brussels. A year later he founded the *Neue Rheinische Zeitung*, which appeared between June 1848 and May 1849 in Cologne; the newspaper lists Marx as "Redakteur en Chef" and six editors, including Friedrich Engels (1820–1895), Heinrich Bürgers (1820–1878), Ernst Dronke (1822–1891), Georg Weerth (1822–1856), Ferdinand Wolff (1812–1895), and Wilhelm Wolff (1809–1864). Marx later dedicated *Das Kapital* to Wilhelm Wolff, who had died in Manchester a few years before Marx completed the first volume.

After Marx's arrival in London, the newspaper was continued as a monthly review from January to October 1850 under the title *Neue Rheinische Zeitung: Politisch-Ökonomische Revue* and printed in Hamburg, Germany. Its appearance was advertised in several German-language publications as a review that "allows for an extensive and scientific examination of the economic conditions, which are the foundation of the political movement as such" (*Berner Zeitung* 1961, 30). Marx's decision to concentrate on writing books was based on the persecution that the newspaper experienced in Germany, its financial difficulties, the lack of collaborators, and the absence of an appreciation of Marx's scientific explanations of the social and political conditions among petite bourgeois revolutionaries (Engels 1961, 34).

In addition, both Marx and Engels contributed articles between 1843 and 1853 without compensation to a number of publications, including "Owen's *New Moral World*, O'Connor's *Northern Star*, Harney's *Democratic Review*, *Republican*, and *Friend of the People*, Jones's *Notes to the People* and *People's Popen*, the *Reforme* in Paris (before the revolution) and a number of journals in Belgium and Paris" (Sorge 1961, 20). According to records of close associates—who dispute the claims that Marx enriched himself while editor of the *Neue Rheinische Zeitung*—Marx spent about 7,000 thalers on "revolutionary agitation" and the publication of the *Neue Rheinische Zeitung* in 1848–1949 in Cologne, "partly in cash from his and his wife's assets, and partly based on 'legal documents' regarding his inheritance." When the newspaper was closed, its inventory consisted of "1. one steam press, 2. a newly furnished composing room, 3. one thousand thalers of subscription fees deposited at the post office. Marx left everything behind, to cover the debts of the newspaper." In fact with 300 thalers, which he had borrowed, Marx paid composers and printers and aided the flight of the other editors (Sorge 1961, 20–21). The last issue of the *Neue Rheinische Zeitung* had been printed entirely in red and contained an editorial notice thanking the workers of Cologne for their participation and ending with the familiar slogan, "emancipation of the working class." It was reprinted several times and was traded as a collector's item for one thaler (Koszyk 1966, 117).

According to Engels,

> freedom of the press of 1848 was probably nowhere so successfully exploited as it was at that time, in the midst of a Prussian fortress, by that newspaper. After the government had tried in vain to silence the newspaper by persecuting it through the courts . . . it had to close at the time of the May revolts of 1849 when Marx was expelled on the pretext that he was no longer a Prussian subject, and similar pretexts were being used to expel the other editors. (1869)

The reason for settling in Cologne (rather than Berlin, for instance) was its prominent position in the Rhine province, not only as a progressive, industrial center of Germany but also because of its previous experiences under the French and the rule of the Code Napoleon, a codex more supportive of a free press, at least implicitly, than Prussian law, since prior censorship removed the threat of criminal procedures against the editors.

The *Neue Rheinische Zeitung* was operated under the "dictatorship" of Marx, whose clear vision and personal confidence made it into the most famous German newspaper of the revolutionary late 1840s, according to Engels (Fetscher 1969, 147). In fact, for Engels the political conditions, and the predicament of the working class in Germany in particular, provide the rationale for the engaged journalism of Marx and Engels. The constitutional prerequisites for a democratic social and political existence, like freedom of the press or freedom of association and assembly, were rights the bourgeoisie had failed to win for itself or for the working class. Now they had become the editorial mission of the *Neue Rheinische Zeitung* in the context of promoting democracy—"but a democracy which emphasized throughout the proletarian character" (Fetscher 1969, 146)—and in pursuit of a strictly political agenda. In his editorial campaigns, Marx emphasizes two political goals: domestically, a united, democratic German republic after the disintegration of Prussia and the breakdown of Austria, and, abroad, the support of revolutionary peoples and a call for war against Russia, the perceived enemy of the revolution. His use of extra editions of the *Neue Rheinische Zeitung* may be indicative of the strength of his political commitment to inform and prepare readers in support of revolutionary objectives.

The result was a revolutionary newspaper that endorsed democratic movements, including revolutions at home and abroad, and advocated change in the face of heavy military and police presence in the city. It was a hostile environment. Engels recalls that there were eight guns, with fixed bayonets, and 250 rounds of ammunition stashed away in the editorial offices of the *Neue Rheinische Zeitung* and that printers were wearing the red caps of the Jacobines, reminders of the French revolution and evidence of a united and determined newspaper staff. The *Neue Rheinische Zeitung* would be difficult to take by force; however, on May 18, 1849, the Prussian government closed the newspaper. Marx was considered a non-Prussian resident and threatened with deportation. Engels reports (1969, 151) that "one half of the editors was under court orders, the other half was non-Prussian and deportable. Nothing could be done as long as an army was supporting the government." At the time of its suspension, the *Neue Rheinische Zeitung* had 6,000 subscribers and, according to Engels, there had not been a newspaper, before or after, that "had the power and the influence and knew how to electrify the proletarian masses like the *Neue Rheinische*" (1969, 152).

In his description of the *Neue Rheinische Zeitung*, Engels characterizes the tone of the newspaper as neither "celebratory, serious, or enthusiastic." Instead, political opponents were considered despicable and were treated with extreme disdain. Individuals, organizations, and institutions could not escape the scrutiny of editorial observation and analysis, while rifts between the petit bourgeoisie and the working class were bridged because "the less we allowed the petit bourgeoisie to misunderstand our proletarian democracy, the more submissive and pliable it became" (1969, 149).

The newspaper represented the hopes of revolutionary movements; Engels reports that when the French revolution of June 1848 was lost, Marx celebrated the defeated insurgents in a "powerful" article. Afterward, the last stockholders of the newspaper withdrew their support. Engels reminisces proudly that "we had the satisfaction to have been the only newspaper in Germany, and perhaps in Europe, to have raised the flag of the trampled proletariat at a time, when the bourgeoisie and petit bourgeoisie of all countries stifled the vanquished with the power of their defamation" (1969, 150).

In the process, both the *Rheinische Zeitung* and the *Neue Rheinische Zeitung* chronicled the official attacks, mounted through censorship and legal proceedings, not only against their own editorial staffs but also against other newspapers in Prussia. Their coverage re-created an oppressive atmosphere of mid-nineteenth-century journalism in Germany and provided the editorial and political context for Marx and his editors in their struggle for press freedom. There was much praise for Marx by his fellow journalists after his series of articles about the press freedom debates of the Rhine Provincial Assembly was published. For instance, the *Deutsche Jahrbücher* notes, "Nothing more profound and more substantial has been said or could be said on freedom of the press and in defense of it" (Marx-Engels Archives 2000, 1).

Marx returned to Paris after the demise of his newspaper career, was expelled in the summer of 1849, and took up residence in London, where he proceeded to discover the vast library holdings of the British Museum in his study of political economy. He continued to publish the *Neue Rheinische Zeitung* in the form of a monthly review as the theoretical and political organ of the Alliance of Communists. Its subtitle had been changed to *Politisch-Ökonomische Revue*, and it appeared from December 1849 to November 1850, when it folded due to financial problems. Earlier Marx had hoped to turn the publication into a weekly or even daily newspaper with the help of financial support from the United States. He writes in a letter (1967/1968, 2:248), "money is only available in America, where all these semi-revolutionaries . . . crack the golden apples." In addition, he became involved with *Das Volk*, a workers' weekly that appeared in London (1859), and was a regular contributor and European political editor of the *New-York Daily Tribune* from 1851, extending his journalistic career until 1862. At that time, the publisher, Horace Greeley, had become disturbed by Marx's views and demanded his dismissal. The editor, Charles Dana, explained to Marx that editorial space was needed for the coverage of the American Civil War, thus ending Marx's productive career (he averaged one article per week) and discontinuing a regular source of income (Christman 1966, xii–xiii).

His association with the press—he also wrote occasionally for other American newspapers and granted several interviews to American journalists—suggests the importance he attached to journalism, its reach and potential effects on readers (for his work as a journalist see Bittel [1953], Hutt [1966], and McLellan [1970]). But he had also become an excellent journalist whose work appealed to American readers. As Christman (1966, xxvii) suggests, "in treating current events Marx was able so consistently to distinguish the real from the illusionary, the important from the trivial, the permanently significant from the momentarily impressive phenomena of his time."

Thus Marx used the press either directly, as a creator of political representations of current European events, or indirectly, as a subject of interviews in later years, when his ideas had begun to spread through various book-length publications and the cause of socialism gained strength in Europe.

The dissemination of his work throughout the English-speaking world, however, proceeded haltingly, extending into the twentieth century. The first substantive work on Marxism (with Engels), *Die deutsche Ideologie* [The German ideology], completed in 1845 to 1846 and published posthumously in 1932, signals Marx's break with the Young Hegelians and his move toward a materialistic conception of history. The work was followed in 1847 by *Misère de la philosophie* [*Poverty of Philosophy*, 1900]—a critical response to Pierre Joseph Proudhon's *The Philosophy of Poverty* (1846)—and (with Engels) the *Manifest der kommunistischen Partei* (1848) [*The Com-*

munist Manifesto, 1883]. Next came *Die Klassenkämpfe in Frankreich, 1848–1850* (1850) [*The Class Struggles in France, 1848–1850*, 1924], *Der 18te Brumaire des Louis Napoleon* (1852) [*The Eighteenth Brumaire of Louis Bonaparte*, 1898], and *Zur Kritik der politischen Ökonomie* (1859) [*A Contribution to the Critique of Political Economy*, 1904]. The first volume of *Das Kapital*—the result of his extensive research in England—first appeared in 1867 in Germany [*Capital: A Critique of Political Economy*, vol. 1, 1886], while volumes 2 and 3 were published posthumously by Engels (in 1885 and 1894 respectively [1907 and 1909]).

According to Engels, *Das Kapital* contains

> the political economy of the working class, reduced to its scientific formulation. This work is concerned not with rabble-rousing phrase mongering, but with strictly scientific deductions. Whatever one's attitude to socialism, one will at any rate have to acknowledge that in this work it is presented for the first time in a scientific manner, and that it was precisely Germany that accomplished this. (1869)

These accomplishments were the result of a lifelong engagement with people and ideas that began when Marx was in his early twenties and started to develop his political strategies of social transformation. The latter involved the circulation of his objectives through the practice of an engaged journalism, which became an instrument of social and political change.

STRUGGLE FOR PRESS FREEDOM

The first half of the nineteenth century in Germany (and particularly the period of the *Vormärz*) produces profound tensions—expressed in attitudes of political despair or utopian hopefulness—as signs of major social, cultural, and political shifts begin to signal a new age of industrial labor, science, and democracy. Golo Mann characterizes this period succinctly:

> From the stagecoach to the railway, the steamship, and the telegraph, from the faith of an earlier generation to unconcealed atheism and materialism, from Goethe to Heine, from Hegel to Marx, from Faust to the *Communist Manifesto*—this is the story of tremendous social and intellectual upheaval. (1968, 52)

It culminates in the unsuccessful revolution of 1848, as Germans attempt to settle their problems with autocratic rule and a host of social and political problems by popular democratic means with major long-term consequences for the cultural and political outlook on unification beyond the immediate desire for a *Rechtsstaat*. Marx becomes a major interpreter of the historical process during the 1840s in Germany; he bases his belief in the possibility of emancipation and the dissolution of society on the dehumanizing experience of capitalistic modes of production and the rise of a Germany that exhibited the worst traits of industrialization.

The early Marx focuses his attention on the idea of freedom—the prerequisite for a democratic way of life—and addresses the specific need for a free press in the context of his professional work as journalist and editor. But the topic of press freedom takes on a particularly relevant and important role with the realization that public communication—accomplished in the institution of the press—and the social and political well-being of society are closely connected; in fact, the condition of communication in society determines the condition of society itself. For this reason, society must rely on the unimpeded workings of a press system to advance its own cause and reinforce progress. But more importantly, perhaps, the press constitutes a general forum for the exchange of ideas among individuals, regardless of their position or reputation but mindful of the quality of ideas. Marx notes that the press is the "most general way for individuals to communicate their intellectual being. It knows no reputation of a person, but only the reputation of intelligence" (*RZ* 139 19/5/42; Fetscher 1969, 94).

His appreciation of newspapers as instruments of public communication and the protection of a free flow of ideas constitutes the relevant dimensions of his journalism, which is driven by the belief that a revolutionary movement must participate in public life and educate the proletariat. For Marx, this means that freedom of the press becomes a necessary condition for expressing and reinforcing (oppositional) ideas and represents a basic requirement of his editorial mission in a political environment in which the idea of freedom had remained a figment of the imagination for most Germans, or at least a sentimental notion; according to Marx, Germans respect ideas so much that they rarely realize them (*RZ* 139 19/5/42; Fetscher 1969, 88–89).

In his arguments, Marx focuses on the political or legal position of the Prussian state rather than on the economic conditions for a free press. Even after his financial backers drop out (for political reasons) and he comes to rely on the financial support of his readers/subscribers, he may still have desired to see the *Neue Rheinische Zeitung* become a permanent fixture in the landscape of the German press. Yet he chooses to ignore the real economic aspects of participation in public communication—as a practical matter of financial support regarding his own newspaper or as a conceptual problem relevant to his own pursuit of political economy as a theoretical explanation—and concentrates instead on problematizing issues of political power and law as expressions of state authority.

His pursuit of freedom is accompanied by the search for truth as yet another objective in Marx's theory and practice of nineteenth-century journalism; it is the pursuit of the real conditions of the social, economic, and political environment that defines the work of journalists and characterizes the mission of the press. In his critique of press practices under Prussian rule, Marx reveals the inconsistencies of reporting when two measures of truth are applied, particularly to the coverage of foreign and domestic affairs. He finds that frequently speculative reports from abroad—open to almost immediate revision—contain "factual lies" that are raised to the level of truth; as such they remain unassailable and uncontested by public authorities, like censors. Domestic reporting, on the other hand, results in condemnation and censorial reproach. Marx asks, What is wrong with attempting to share volatile situations and activities abroad with readers—history in the making—through news from faraway places, while rejecting the representation of similar historical processes in its domestic coverage (*RZ* 8, 8/1/43; Fetscher 1969, 122)? His question is based on the realization that establishing truths may go beyond merely identifying the fact per se to include the process of finding truth; thus, he demands that "the investigation of truth must be honest itself, the real investigation is the unfolded truth whose disconnected parts are combined in the results" (Fetscher 1969, 23).

The belief in a pursuit of freedom and truth becomes the cornerstone of resistance to official attempts to manipulate both, the understanding of freedom as license to act, and the notion of truth as relative and determinable by official public authorities. Consequently, censorship appears as official guidance, disguised in the form of instructions to improve the practice of journalism by proposing definitions of truth.

Censorship of newspapers and other periodical publications was a fact of life in the Prussian state of the 1840s. Koszyk (1966, 89–92) observes that the conditions of the press in Prussia during the 1840s gave no reasons for optimism, although press freedom had increased by 1842. The newspaper landscape is dominated by a servile press, which remains intimidated and ineffective, fearing censorship and termination by the government. Marx relates in one of his frequent and sharp, if not sarcastic, editorial reactions that the "German daily press is the weakest, most lethargic and timid institution under the sun! The greatest injustices could occur before its eyes, or be committed against it, while it remains quiet and secretive; if one would not hear it by chance, one would never hear it from the press" (*NRZ* 246, 15/3/49; Fetscher 1969, 182–83). Newspapers in the Rhine province, in contrast, are moderately liberal, and the *Rheinische Zeitung* emerges initially as a formula for liberal journalism elsewhere only to become—after Marx's rise to the editorship in October 1842—a leading example of a political newspaper in an era of a politicized German press (Koszyk 1966, 98).

At the same time, edicts asserting the power of authorities defined the limits of journalistic practice, including the employment of editors, and reduced the private decisions of publishers to acts of compliance with official pronouncements. Marx ridicules official demands for hiring only "respectable" individuals with scientific expertise as editors, whose "position and character guarantee the seriousness of their activities and the loyalty of their thinking" (Fetscher 1969, 36). He asks whether censors have such expert backgrounds and, if so, why they don't become writers? "What would be better than censorship to end the confusion of the press, when these civil servants—overpowering in numbers, more powerful with their scientific genius—would rise and—with their weight—crush those miserable writers, who practice only in one genre and even then without an officially recognized skill" (Fetscher 1969, 37)?

Who, then, is entitled to be a journalist? Official documents speak of "authorized" and "unauthorized" individuals, suggesting specialization (e.g., the certification of various areas of writing), and Marx wonders about authorizing the cobbler to write only about shoes. He concludes that the result would be a separation of the estates and a fixing of intellectual practices that would end with the creation of authorized and unauthorized readers. He adds sarcastically that it would be "highly expedient that only authorized authors should be permitted to buy and read their own works" (*RZ* 135 19/5/42; Fetscher 1969, 93). As a consequence of such divisions, citizens become both authorized and unauthorized contributors to the press, depending on their profession and what they write about.

Marx exposes the excesses of Prussian rule over the press, including frequent acts of censorship and suppression of information, as well as various suggestions for how to regulate the press, which range from topical restrictions and the establishment of community newspapers to assigning one critical newspaper to each province. He also realizes increasingly that without strict control of the press, the German monarchy would be in jeopardy, if not defeated, because it would mean the rise of democratic principles and practices, including a victory of the working class. As Engels once described it, "freedom of the press, the free competition of opinions, is the release of the class struggle on the grounds of the press. . . . while order means suffocating the class struggle and restricting the suppressed classes" (*NRZ* 283, 27/4/49; Fetscher 1969, 200).

Although Marx articulates his position vis-à-vis issues of press freedom regularly in the columns of his newspaper, the debates of press freedom in the Rhine Provincial Assembly constitute the most coherent and sustained argument—offered in a series of articles written between May 5 and 19, 1842. They provide the political, historical foundation of his arguments concerning a free press in the context of a larger commitment to individual and collective social, political, and economic freedom.

Marx begins with some general observations about personal relations to press freedom by suggesting the importance of knowing what it means to labor under unfettered conditions of freedom; uninhibited personal communication, the ability to express and share ideas, and access to the means of communication, like the press, become desirable elements of a free existence. These observations also assume an educated citizenry, the presence of an intellectual milieu, and cultural or political competencies that warrant protection, such as the struggle for the emancipation of the working class by committed writers and political activists.

His own experience as well as his knowledge of intellectual working conditions elsewhere (e.g., in France, Holland, England, Switzerland, or the United States) and the practice of journalism specifically also reveal the depth of his interest and provide a measure of his concerns, which he expresses eloquently when he writes that "one must have loved freedom of the press, like beauty, to be able to defend it. I feel that the existence of whatever I really love is necessary and needed, and without it my own being is neither fulfilled, satisfied, nor complete" (*RZ* 125, 5/5/42; Fetscher 1969, 49). Marx suggests here a close (if not loving) relationship between press freedom and a full intellectual life—grounded in the proximity of freedom and life in general. Love anticipates commitment; thus, it would be difficult for anyone to fight for a free press without a sense of commitment, since those who never desire freedom of the press as a necessary condition of their own intellectual lives, and whose rationality prevents an emotional attachment to the notion of a free press, will treat this issue like any other "exotic" phenomenon—as a removed, external episode beyond the boundaries of their own existential interests.

But Marx insists on the centrality of the press in the pursuit of freedom, and he maintains that the "press, in general, is a realization of human freedom. Where there is a press, there is also press freedom." He implies that freedom is ever present and assailed only when it is someone else's freedom. Thus, since "every kind of freedom has always existed, either as privilege or universal right," the question of press freedom becomes a question of whether it is a privilege or a common right, or, as Marx proclaims, "whether press freedom is the privilege of specific individuals or the privilege of the human mind" (*RZ* 132, 12/5/42; Fetscher 1969, 69).

Censorship, on the other hand, constitutes critique as official monopoly, resists an open exchange of ideas, and opposes any notion of criticism (or the process of reflection and articulation) that is inherent in the idea of intellectual work and the practices of a free press, in particular. Censorship contradicts the very character of the press; it does not emerge from the idea of freedom—which is part of the character of the press to provide access to divergent ideas—but promotes consent by suppression.

Press laws are expressions of freedom calling into question specific press practices; censorship, on the other hand, punishes freedom. Marx insists that press laws, for instance, consider freedom a normal condition of the press. Consequently, breaking these laws suggests a violation of such a freedom; thus, legal codes are the "bible of freedom of a people" as "press laws are the legal recognition of press freedom." Marx considers press law a right because it constitutes a positive existence of freedom and must be present, although it may never be applied. Censorship, however, like slavery, cannot become legal, although it may be present as a law (*RZ* 132, 12/5/42; Fetscher 1969, 77). Thus censorship is not a law but a police order. Yet even in this form, it is a poor regulation because "it does not accomplish what it sets out to accomplish, and it does not want to succeed in what it achieves" (*RZ* 135, 15/5/42; Fetscher 1969, 79).

In fact, censorship has detrimental effects on society, since every uncensored publication, regardless of its quality, is an extraordinary event and produces martyrs, while press freedom eliminates the aura of fame surrounding a print product in the hands of censors. Moreover, a censored press is demoralizing, since it is inseparable from hypocrisy, the source of its problems. Marx notices that under a system of censorship, the government "hears only *its own voice*, knows that it hears only its own voice, and is yet fixed on the delusion of hearing the voice of the people and demands that the people fall for the trick." As a result, the relationship between people and politics deteriorates and journalism becomes disillusioned. Both people and the press must live with and by lies. He concludes that "since people must consider uncensored publications lawless, they will get used to considering lawlessness as free, freedom as lawless, and lawfulness as unfreedom. Thus censorship kills the public spirit." Indeed, censorship is the unrelenting attack on the rights of private persons, and on ideas, in particular (*RZ* 135, 15/5/42; Fetscher 1969, 83–84). But above all, "censorship does not avoid the struggle, but makes it one-sided, turns an open struggle into a hidden one, and turns a struggle over principles into a struggle between a non-violent principle and power without principle" (*RZ* 12/5/42; quoted in Koszyk 1966, 11).

The presence of censorship creates instant problems for writers and intellectuals, who are identified with language and the expression of ideas and whose activities extend across cultural or political borders. Marx addresses the problem of authorship—and influence—from outside Germany, reminiscent of his own existence as an expatriate intellectual during the years leading up to his editorship of the *Neue Rheinische Zeitung* and suggestive of the concrete conditions of intellectual life in Europe. Under such historical circumstances, Prussian authors have a choice: they may either publish their ideas under the threat of censorship at home or move beyond the borders and publish them under the specific conditions of a particular state. In either case, authors are under surveillance by the Prussian state. Indeed, Marx notes that publications abroad draw more objections from authorities because they have not been scrutinized by domestic censors and are therefore liable to contain injurious material.

Censorship, however, also breeds defiance and helps strengthen the resolve of authors in their critiques of authority. Its consequences are flaunted like a badge of courage. For instance, Engels writes at one point (1967/1968b, 2:421) that although censorship is annoying, it is also honorable: "an author who turns thirty—or writes three books—without the marks of the censor is worthless. Scarred warriors are the best. One must be able to tell that a book emerged from a fight with the censor."

In the context of debating censorship and freedom, Prussian authorities also created the specter of "good" and "bad" newspapers, thus producing images of either a supportive (good) or jealous (bad) press. Marx, on the other hand, wants to differentiate between a rational and moral (free) press and the shameless, "perfumed miscarriage" of a (censored) press, calling into question the official perspective of the ruling power. Moreover, he concludes that "the free press remains good even when its products are bad because these products are deviations from the nature of a free press." At the same time, "the censored press remains bad, even when its products are good, because these products are only good insofar as they represent the free press within the censored press, and insofar as it is not in their character to be products of a censored press" (*RZ* 132, 12/5/42; Fetscher 1969, 72–73).

Official differentiations (good or bad) or characterizations (real or false) imply definitions and intentions that remain unanswered. Thus Marx wants to know the meaning of a "real" press and which one represents reality or a favored reality. How are these distinctions made, who makes them, and where is the voice of the press in these deliberations about its own very existence? Differently expressed, labeling is a challenge to press freedom, and confronting the existence of the press or its conduct constitutes an interrogation of freedom as such. Marx adds, "Whenever a specific form of freedom is rejected, freedom in general is rejected and can only lead a quasi-existence, and pure chance rules the activity of unfreedom. Unfreedom is the rule, and freedom is the exception to chance and arbitrariness" (*RZ* 139, 19/5/42; Fetscher 1969, 98).

Marx addresses the relationship of press and people or nation as a crucial connection between the spiritual and material spheres of everyday life. Being an integral part of society also means that a free press not only represents ideas and ideologies of people but also reflects engagement and participation. This also means that the German press—as a young press—is a growing institution, united with the people and thinking and feeling like the people. Therefore, this press is "like life, always expanding, never complete. It stands among the people, truly feeling its hopes and fears, its love and hate, its pleasures and pains." Marx concludes that because of its proximity to the people, the press reflects their real life with all of its natural contradictions, trials, and errors. Because of its tender age (as a press for the masses rather than special interests), this press is liable to make mistakes, overstate, exaggerate, and even distort events, only to learn from its practices. These are shortcomings and yet people recognize their own condition in the flawed performance of their newspapers and know that they will eventually rise to represent their moral spirit. Indeed, Marx concludes that attacks on the people's press constitute a political acknowledgment and a significant initial recognition of "its presence, its reality, and its power" (*RZ* 1, 1/1/43; Fetscher 1969, 117).

Thus Marx frequently uses the term *Volkspresse* (people's press) to refer to newspapers as representative examples of social, cultural, and political movements and mirrors of societal growth and intellectual advancement with all of their imperfections, failures, and successes. The press of this type functions neither as an authoritative instrument of elitist control nor as a publication for and by the people (such as *Le Prolétaire* [1878–1884], a weekly produced exclusively by manual laborers in Paris; see Engels 1967/68c, 1:144). Rather, it constitutes a public sphere that accommodates the voice of the people—the working class—with its own tolerance for contradiction and dissent. The idea of *Volkspresse* implies a special relationship between people and the press that finds its expression in the editorial attention paid to the interests of people and suggests a specific nurturing, protective role for newspapers in the process of public communication. It is located, particularly, at the level of community and in the notion of collective self-determination and reflects a conception of freedom as autonomy.

Specifically, Marx proposes that the free press is a public institution that unites people, confirms their self-confidence, and provides surveillance. He declares quite polemically that

> a free press is the ever present, vigilant eye of the people's spirit, the embodiment of a people's trust in itself, the communication link that binds the individual to state and world, the embodied culture that transforms material struggles into spiritual ones while idealizing their crude material form. It is the people's outspoken self-confession, whose redeeming power is well known. It is the spiritual mirror, in which a people discovers itself, and insight is the first prerequisite of wisdom. It is the public spirit, which may be

> delivered to every cottage cheaper than coal gas. It is multifarious, ubiquitous, and omniscient. It is the ideal world, which emerges from the real world only to return to it as an enriched spirit, newly charged. (*RZ* 135, 15/5/42; Fetscher 1969, 80)

Marx repeats his understanding of the role of a responsible press in his first court appearance as editor of the *Neue Rheinische Zeitung* in 1849, when he concludes his defense (against a libel charge) that "it is the duty of the press in its own milieu to represent the oppressed" and to confront the specific executioners of social and political power. Reflecting on the conditions of the time, Marx suggests that his newspaper has no choice but to attack. "At this moment it is the first duty of the press, to undermine all foundations of the existing political situation" (*NRZ* 221, 14/2/49; Fetscher 1969, 175).

The important emancipatory role of communication is confirmed and reinforced by subsequent editorial comments in response to debates about the poster law. This time Engels writes that posters keep the revolutionary spirit of the working class alive: "Posters change every street corner into a large newspaper, in which the passing worker notes the events of the day, comments on them, or finds opinions expressed and debated, and where they meet, at the same time, people of all classes and opinions, with whom to discuss the posters, where they have a journal or a club at no cost" (*NRZ* 283, 27/4/49; Fetscher 1969, 199). Extending the idea of press freedom to posters as collective vehicles of public communication, his arguments are reminiscent of the extensions of the public sphere with the introduction of posters during the Russian revolution, their use by German working-class movements of the 1920s and by the Chinese Communists in the form of wall newspapers a hundred years later.

Differentiating between the "idea" of press freedom and its concrete historical existence, Marx refers to the conditions of freedom in a number of countries and finds that the United States enjoys the "natural phenomenon" of a free press in its purest form. Yet he concludes that Germany actually furnishes a more significant historical basis for press freedom because literature and, with it, intellectual growth constitute the real historical determinants of a free press (*RZ* 135, 15/5/42; Fetscher 1969, 83). In the meantime, however, he also reminds his readers that "Germans know their state only through hearsay, that closed doors are not made of glass, that a secret state is not a public state, and thus one must not blame newspapers for the mistake of the state, which is the mistake newspapers try to correct" (*RZ* 8, 8/1/43; Fetscher 1969, 122).

Instead, the historical context often arises from remarks about commerce and the definition of the press as a business; elements of trade rather than literature are the constituents of a working model of the press and decide the ways in which the press is conceptualized. Indeed, some of his contemporaries (e.g., Schäffle and Knies) work with a commercial model in their discussions of the press. Marx takes this argument to its logical conclusion by suggesting that even if the press is viewed as a commercial enterprise, it must be considered more significant than any other business, since it involves intellectual labor *(Kopfarbeit)* rather than activities defined as physical labor *(Arm- und Beinarbeit)*. He declares that "the emancipation of arm and leg becomes humanly significant with the emancipation of the head" (*RZ* 139, 19/5/42; Fetscher 1969, 88).

Consequently, commercial freedom cannot be press freedom, since "every particular sphere of freedom is freedom of a particular sphere, just as a specific way of life is the way of life of a particular nature" (*RZ* 139, 19/5/42; Fetscher 1969, 90). Marx insists on separating discussions of freedom that relate, if not combine, different spheres of human activity and therefore rejects the idea that press freedom is a category of commercial freedom. For instance, the carpenter who demands freedom for his craftsmanship cannot be given the freedom of the philosopher. In fact, "the first freedom of the press is not to be a business," according to Marx. He continues that if the press is seen as a business, it is an object assigned to the sphere of printers or booksellers rather than writers (*RZ* 139, 19/5/42; Fetscher 1969, 92).

The discussions of real or potential threats to press freedom not only are a reaction to the concrete historical situation of authoritarian control over public communication but also reflect an interest in protecting personal freedom and intellectual independence through appropriate organizational guarantees. Indeed, Engels writes (in a letter to August Bebel) years later that dependence, even on a workers party, "is a tough situation." He thought it actually hopeless for anyone with initiative to be an editor of a party newspaper. He had agreed with Marx since the beginning of their editorial collaboration never to accept such a position, but "to have a newspaper which was also financially independent from the party" (Fetscher 1969, 234).

Although the editorial work of Marx (and Engels) was overshadowed by economic and legal issues of survival, the latter condition, in particular, offers a constant challenge to Marx and results in a series of assaults on Prussian rule over intellectual labor (and political expression). It is, indeed, a journalism of confrontation that characterizes the publication of both the *Rheinische Zeitung* and the *Neue Rheinische Zeitung* during the 1840s.

AUTONOMY AND PRESS FREEDOM

These theoretical and practical contributions to placing press freedom in the historical context of revolutionary consciousness, political struggle, and commitment to a proletarian democracy define the intellectual position of a young Karl Marx in his first encounter with the authority of the state. They also constitute the sophisticated response of a politically motivated, dedicated individual to the conditions of freedom in German society. Consequently, these writings reflect not only his intellectual abilities and professional determination but also his firm belief in the importance of freedom as a spiritual and political sphere. The latter is contained in and preserved by the anticipated transformation of capitalism into socialism; and it is confirmed and strengthened, no doubt, by future victories of the working class, which will lead to the complete self-realization of the individual in a communist society. This freedom in the sense of independence explains his insistence on freedom of the press and its importance for the success of socialism, a social order that, according to Erich Fromm (1961, 69), permits the return of individuals to themselves, and a world in which the individual "is no longer a stranger among strangers," but at home in his or her world.

Thus, in his consideration of press freedom, Marx focuses on the notion of autonomy when he separates the practice of journalism—as intellectual labor—from the institutional existence of the press—as commercial enterprise; he identifies news work, as well as editorial practices in general, with freedom of expression that belongs to those working as journalists, while the economic concerns of the press are to be addressed by different requirements. Freedom of the press must be understood as a (desirable or ideal) professional prerequisite for intellectual labor. By privileging the latter, Marx creates optimal conditions for the practice of journalism, since the press—as an institution—has no control over editorial functions (news work as such) but serves journalists as a medium of public communication. Therefore, press freedom equals freedom of expression as an individual or collective right governing the relations between journalists—and intellectuals generally—and public and private authorities, including the owners of the press itself. Indeed, his writings on press freedom are aimed at the emancipation of news workers from the ownership of the means of communication, that is, from domination by publishers and stockholders.

Implicit in his arguments for press freedom is a belief in the importance of ideas and their consequences for the well-being of society. Marx writes from the vantage point of an intellectual who lives from the power of his words and relies on the need to communicate freely. He understands the potential effects of the press—or any other medium, including books—because he believes that the world can be changed by the force of ideas. Thus an intellectual life—the quality of ideas, their disclosure, and dissemination—contributes immeasurably to the cause of society. But since theories come to life only in practice, beliefs need implementation. Marx is prepared to act, and his own work as journalist and editor illustrates the necessary relationship between ideas and actions. As a result, intellectual labor—and the process of communication in general—must be protected without fail for the sake of progress and the potential of change.

Together, his understanding of press freedom and the power of ideas reinforces the role of journalists as intellectual workers and secures their place in society. But since Marx addresses specifically the necessary conditions for an emancipatory journalism and its part in the implementation of a revolutionary course, he empowers journalism as a subversive activity in the historical context of his time. To this end, he contributes to various publications and combines his vast and detailed knowledge of current global political and economic developments with skillful interpretation and professional delivery to produce an argument for the creation of specific conditions that will lead to individual freedom and protect creativity.

Thus most of his comments on the state of press freedom are addressed to the concrete political situation of the press (including his own newspaper) rather than to the rise of capitalism and its consequences for the development of a free press, or to a theoretical or constitutional debate, based, for instance, on the democratic experiences of press freedom abroad. In fact, the notion of commercial power and its effects on the future of journalism in Germany are more clearly expressed by some of his contemporaries, such as Knies or Schäffle. They in turn seem to be less focused in their own theoretical work on the political realities of their times and their consequences for the press than Marx, who is preoccupied with the role of his political journalism as a vital strategy of a larger political mission to liberate the working class.

Consequently, his writings provide ample evidence of threats to his own journalism, but they also shed light on the relations between government and the press generally, the nature and extent of censorship, and the concrete consequences for the existence of a critical press in Germany, whose editors and journalists could only look elsewhere—to England and the United States, but also France—for models of a free press and an autonomous practice of journalism. Indeed, in his arguments for a free press Marx draws on the experiences of journalism in different countries and introduces concrete examples of how freely journalists operate in other press systems, including the U.S. system. He also considers what press freedom means in the political and philosophical context of the respective societies without being idealistic or blind to specific problems, including the subsumption of labor under capital in those societies. For instance, writing about the French press, he notes that it is not free enough because it is subjected to oppressive material conditions—the requirement of large bail bonds—which propels newspapers into the sphere of commerce and destroys their independence (*RZ* 135, 15/5/42; Fetscher 1969, 83). Little could he know, on the other hand, that only a generation later, socialism in the United States suffered from state censorship and persecution, especially during and after World War I, when First Amendment guarantees were turned into a privilege (by the Supreme Court) for those defending a particular vision of democracy.

Marx treats press freedom as a necessary condition for a democratic society and (together with freedom of association and assembly, for instance) as a political goal. He demonstrates through his editorial practice, including the actual infractions and his numerous court appearances, the concrete foundations of his theoretical discussions of the nature of a free press and the location of press freedom as an unalienable right among other freedoms in the catalogue of human rights. His theoretical writings are tied into the political agenda of emancipating the working class.

Indeed, press freedom is a prerequisite condition for competing political beliefs and struggling ideologies in the public sphere. It reinforces conflict and is a crucial element in defining hegemony, which relies on communication and exchange. Press freedom suggests access not only to contesting ideas but also to the public discourse of society, which is strengthened by the potential of participation. Furthermore, protecting the process of public communication encourages alternative constructions of reality by confirming the merits of different social, political, or cultural forces. At the same time, however, press freedom works only for those who have the means of communication at their disposal (e.g., access to the media or sufficient public or private support to sustain the financial burden of a publishing enterprise). Speaking about the role of capital in the rise of the bourgeoisie to power, Engels (1967/68d, 2:57) once remarked that "freedom of the press is a bourgeois privilege because printing requires money and buyers of the product, and these buyers need money, too."

Marx is keenly aware of these conditions, as editor and publisher of a newspaper whose specific political goals differentiate between the emancipation of the bourgeois classes and the working class, but whose articulation of press freedom reflects the influence of nineteenth-century liberalism. The latter championed the protection of the individual (politically and economically) and promoted freedom of thought, speech, and press—or cultural production—in a bourgeois state. Marx employs the ideology of an enlightened, liberal bourgeoisie, whose assistance he sought in the fight against Prussian authority and in accordance with his long-term political strategy. He embraces liberalism only to undermine it with his insistence on press freedom in the service of an emancipatory struggle of the working class. According to Engels, the political interests of communists in Germany at the time were best served by supporting or collaborating with the bourgeoisie in its fight for power without falling for its promises to the proletariat—and to overturn the regime of a victorious bourgeoisie as soon as possible (1967/1968e, 2:14).

Nevertheless, Marx's writings on freedom and the communication of ideas, as well as those against censorship and the authority of the Prussian state, contain the vocabulary of mid-nineteenth-century liberalism—with references to democracy, freedom, and the role of the press, for instance—and reflect the idea of the state as a facilitator of individual happiness. He uses the language of liberalism to particularly address pertinent issues regarding freedom of the press in ways that could help enlist bourgeois support for his specific political agenda, a strengthening of the working-class movement. But liberalism as a doctrinal aspect of capitalism does not embrace the totalizing approach of socialism; the latter insists on the emancipation of working people, equality, and classlessness in the spirit of a perfect communal existence and certainly in opposition to capitalist individualism, which specifies and categorizes the conditions of freedom and subordinates the individual to state or bureaucracy. Marx rejects the rather narrow (liberal) position that exchange relations (i.e., economic relations) are compatible with freedom, since genuine freedom is self-determination. Instead, the earlier Marx follows a Western, humanistic tradition in his own intellectual practice by constructing the individual as independent, productive, and nonalienated human being, while his political objectives help prepare the foundation of socialism as it would evolve from his later writings (and the work of Engels).

Furthermore, Marx understood that, as a determinant of political processes, the press produces and reinforces specific ideological positions. In fact, it becomes an instrument of propaganda, agitation, and organization, as Lenin would announce two generations later in his instructions to the communist press, at a point in history when the era of a Russian bourgeois press comes to an end. However, Marx does not theorize these functions; he merely generates and applies the power of the press based on his intellectual strength—as well as the tenacity of his editorial staff—to pursue his political mission. Indeed, his writings on press freedom expose considerable differences between his own understanding of a socialist press and the appropriation of his ideas by Lenin, which may serve as evidence of the misinterpretation and (deliberate) misrepresentation of Marx by Soviet-style communism in the 1920s and beyond. While his critique of capitalism includes, by necessity, a radical reconfiguration of the press and the role of unrestrained intellectual labor, Soviet communism treats the press (or intellectual practice) in the spirit of capitalism, that is, at the expense of genuine human emancipation and in favor of state-directed goals, and it promotes socialism by decree. Rosa Luxemburg (1976, 256), for instance, is among those who revisit the original ideas of socialism to demand not only public control but also "the most unlimited, broadest democracy and public opinion."

Marx appreciates the potential effectiveness of the press to assist in educating the working class and reinforcing a nascent political movement. His journalism explains distant events (in India, China, Russia, or the United States) in terms of close-by, relevant affairs; thus, he applies historical thinking in his conclusions about the forces of capitalism elsewhere to encourage criticism and participation of the proletariat in the process of public communication. But his journalism is not merely the expression of a socialist ideology. It is also the practice of translating theoretical thought into the language of everyday life, in which ideology becomes a material force with a potential of rallying the masses.

Marx shares with contemporary German political economists (e.g., Schäffle and Knies) an understanding of the press as a pivotal institution in modern society, but he also knows about its potential as a social and political means of persuasion and therefore as an attractive, if not indispensable, weapon against political authority and for the rule of democratic ideas.

But he also comes down on the side of press freedom in ways that produce a sharp contrast to later "Marxist-Leninist" interpretations of the role and function of the press in socialist societies. For instance, the bureaucratic subordination of the means of communication in Soviet-style socialism results in the management of thought and the repression of the public discourse, even among supporters or sympathizers. Hence, press freedom turns into a privilege, which is protected, reinforced, and perpetuated by specific (political) interests. As such it is reminiscent of earlier bourgeois claims of press freedom with similar consequences for public access and participation. Marx, on the other hand, had a clear sense of the importance of ideas and their weight in the war against all forms of suppression and control. Most important, he sees freedom as a prerequisite for the success of socialism, whose goal it is to generate circumstances under which the individual overcomes alienation from work, from others, and from nature. The result is the return to the self and, therefore, to independence. Freedom of the press, as a means of providing public surveillance, information, and thought to articulate (political) alternatives and promote the idea of choice, remains central for advancing the independence of individuals in the social realm. Indeed, when Marx insists that "freedom remains freedom, whether it expresses itself in printer's ink, a parcel of land, consciousness, or in a political meeting" (*RZ* 139, 19/5/42; Fetscher, 1969, 99), he also suggests the various manifestations of freedom as well as the consequences of its denial by those in power.

Marx also reveals in these early writings on press freedom and public communication his thinking about the social (or cultural) concept of the individual; by privileging expression (and the role of the press) Marx acknowledges the centrality of communication in the process of self-realization. The individual does not exist except in terms of social relations; praxis is cooperative and existence interdependent. Thus, when individuality is realized through interaction, language and communication become the means by which individuals realize their being and engage in cooperative activities that constitute the essence of society. Human existence is an ongoing social process fueled by the potential of communication. These nascent ideas are confirmed throughout his writings in later years. Their contemporary relevance, particularly as they pertain to the future of journalism, however, seems clear: to sustain democracy requires freedom of expression and the protection of the public sphere, including the media, particularly from those forms of censorship that arise with the control of intellectual labor by those who own or influence the public means of communication.

Implicit in these discussions of press freedom, and in his struggle for survival as a critical voice in the sea of bland and conformist Prussian journalism, is a belief in the power of the press to influence and lead people. Newspapers are more than conveyor belts of a new industrial information retrieval system. They reproduce ideologies, create sentiments, and reflect the spirit of the people. In addition, a free press also represents cultural progress with its unlimited potential as a source of human emancipation. As a contributor to the rise of social criticism in Germany (which may have begun with Hegel's critical philosophy of history), Marx examines freedom within an institution (the press) to measure human progress. But perhaps more importantly he comes to realize and acknowledge the potential roles of freedom and communication in the overthrow of the old order—after having emerged from the radical intellectual milieu of the Young Hegelians, who increasingly addressed social problems.

In fact, for Marx, communication is freedom because socialism creates the conditions of a new social order in which individuals realize themselves; self-realization, however, depends on the production of ideas and—ultimately—consciousness by individuals who live in communication with their surroundings. To communicate under these circumstances means the realization of personal freedom and autonomy. For this reason, the process of communication can be secured only by a social order that advances the emancipation of the individual—including the right of communication—and charges the press with providing institutional support for the self-expression of a conscious existence.

Marx writes on freedom of the press with moral conviction and political determination; he demonstrates the power of his intellect and offers an early glimpse at the logic, style, and persuasive force of his later projects. Unlike later theoretical works, however, his thoughts on freedom of the press emerge from the front line of a concrete, existential struggle (beyond the survival of his newspaper in a climate of official mistrust and hostility) as a personal challenge to an individual in his roles of journalist and political activist. His journalism mediates between intellectual forces and material conditions—or between philosophical thought and a proletarian reality—to reveal a powerful and noteworthy polemic of an extraordinary mind.

3

The Nerves of Society: Albert Schäffle on Symbolic Communication

CONCEPTUALIZING THE SOCIAL BODY

Albert Eberhard Friedrich Schäffle (1831–1903) is the most important German contributor to an organismic theory of society, which has its roots in the writings of Herbert Spencer and Paul von Lilienfeld. His work as a social theorist reflects a variety of personal and professional experiences in business, politics, and academic life that marked his distinguished career.

After formal schooling in his native Württemberg, Schäffle became a journalist at age nineteen. In the course of his duties as a foreign affairs editor for the *Schwäbischer Merkur*, he felt a need to further his education and specifically to engage in a systematic study of economics, law, politics, and technology. Subsequently he read the works of Friedrich List, Bruno Hildebrand, and Karl Heinrich Rau (economics); Robert v. Mohl, Johann Kaspar Bluntschli, Karl Zachari, and Heinrich Matthias Zöpfl (constitutional law); Christian Reinhold Köstlin and Hufnagel (criminal law); and Anselm Payen, Karl Karmarsch, and Eduard V. Hartmann (technology). In his autobiography Schäffle (1905, 43) also admits that his newspaper career provided him with the best possible education, since he was forced to express himself in writing promptly and on a wide range of subjects. The result was his acquisition of extensive knowledge in a number of academic disciplines, including the ability to read original French and English sources. He left his editorial position in 1855 rather critical of publishers who did not seem to recognize the intellectual capabilities of journalists and their expertise in particular fields. But he remained active as a publicist through his acquaintance with Johann Georg von Cotta, whose *Deutsche Vierteljahrsschrift* became an outlet for his ideas on economic and fiscal matters.

In 1860 Schäffle accepted a professorship at the University of Tübingen in political economy and shortly thereafter became editor of the *Zeitschrift für die gesammte Staatswissenschaft*, a position he occupied until his death. He continued to publish regularly in academic and popular journals and newspapers, where many of his contributions—often meant to be practical—were concrete reactions to specific political events.

In addition to his university teaching and his work as an economic and political writer, Schäffle served as a state representative to Württemberg's Chamber of Deputies and contributed to the work of the European tariff union. He left Tübingen in 1868 to accept a similar university position in Vienna, Austria, but resigned after three years to join the Graf Hohenwart cabinet as a secretary of commerce, a post he had held for less than a year when the government collapsed.

At age forty Schäffle returned to private life. Unable to secure a government appointment or return to a university position, he devoted his time to writing and speaking on economic, financial, and political issues in his native Württemberg. From there he participated in the political life of Germany.

Schäffle's major theoretical work is *Bau und Leben des Sozialen Körpers* [Structure and life of the social body], published in four volumes between 1875 and 1879, followed by a two-volume edition in 1896. The project represents a considerable theoretical effort to conceptualize sociology as a complete description of reality. Focusing on the organizational, functional, and developmental aspects of society, Schäffle offers a systematic view of social life as a starting point for an explanation of social phenomena. In this light, *Bau und Leben des Sozialen Körpers* becomes the basis for combining practical experiences with theoretical insights from his lifelong confrontation with economic and political problems.

Bau und Leben des Sozialen Körpers reflects Schäffle's conviction that a discussion of economic and political affairs cannot advance without an understanding of human interaction. Consequently, he develops an organismic perspective to explain social conditions through a series of analogies, while acknowledging differences between social and organic bodies and rejecting criticism of reducing a social phenomenon to a biological fact in his development of a science of sociology. In fact, Schäffle considered the writing of *Bau und Leben des Sozialen Körpers* a liberating and successful experience of formulating his later ideas; he cites Alfred Espinas, Friedrich Ratzel, and Albion Small among his contemporaries who understood and appreciated his intentions (1905, 31) and expresses hope that others would find this work stimulating despite the fact that at times he may have appeared strange and difficult to identify among his contemporaries (1905, 132).

Schäffle recognizes the influence of Auguste Comte, Herbert Spencer, and Paul von Lilienfeld, in particular, on his work, although he never identified society with an organism, or social movements with the biological struggle for survival. Instead, his discussion of the function of political economy, for instance, emphasizes the importance of psychological and moral considerations. Defining socialization in terms of the production and consumption of external goods, he places the individual at the center of any economically controlled process and argues that people with their moral lives must not only satisfy material wants but also attempt to realize their potential as human beings. Like Small, he feels that

> personal self-preservation and self-development of human beings—i.e., their conscious moral life—depends significantly on the acquisition and use of those external goods not furnished gratuitously by nature. Either universally or . . . for particular members of society, many goods are accessible only as a consequence of human co-operation, i.e., only mediately—and in comparison with human want—only to a limited. i.e., insufficient degree. (Small 1924, 299)

Small adds that "this limited availability of means of satisfaction or use is the occasion of a peculiar regimen of production and of use. The aim of the same is: with a minimum of personal sacrifice to secure a maximum of realization of human purposes; in other words, at minimum cost to a maximum of utility, and, thus, to insure the amplest possible provision for the entire personal life."

Since individuals instead of material goods become the focal point of Schäffle's economic theory, their necessary presence provides guidelines for the subsequent treatment of social, political, and economic problems. He becomes known as a reformer who engages in a search for more equitable solutions with propositions concerning the development of public property and a planned economy—without joining the socialist cause, however.

The basis for understanding the systematic nature of social life and the complexity of the social system may be found in his 1873 essay, "Güter der Darstellung und Mittheilung," which documents his appreciation of symbols, tradition, and communication in society; it also provides an opportunity to describe these elements as constituting a psychic mechanism of the social body that mediates collective sensations, collective stimulations, and the internal relationships of a collective consciousness. Consequently, Schäffle's views on communication and the press must be read as an explanation of the existence and survival of society in the context of an anti-individualistic approach to the study of social systems. His contribution to the study of communication and media phenomena in society, therefore, relies heavily on ideas presented in "Güter der Darstellung und Mittheilung" and *Bau und Leben des Sozialen Körpers.*

THE BINDING FORCE OF COMMUNICATION

Schäffle does not offer a unified theory of communication but returns throughout his writings to the fundamental importance of communication as a binding force in society. This observation also informs his statements about the press and suggests the significance he attaches to the notion of communication in his theory of society.

In developing his organismic understanding of the social environment, Schäffle compares the nervous system in the animal world to the communication system in human societies. He describes the existence of nerve cells, ganglions, and nerve centers in terms of constituting an extensive network throughout the body and suggests the existence of a similar phenomenon in the social world, but differentiates between individual and institutional elements of the communication system.

Accordingly, individual members of society and their respective nervous systems—with which they receive, internalize, and disseminate impressions and suggestions—constitute the first element resembling "cells." In this role, individuals act as observers and reporters of events, disseminators of value judgments, and participants in the public decision-making process. "Individuals and entire corporations, councils, public authorities, and meetings function as professional organs of knowledge through observation, research, reporting, supervision, and control, as social organs of consciousness through evaluations, valuations, criticism, judgments of taste, expressions of appreciation and condemnation, and, finally, as executive organs through decision-making processes, orders, instructions, prohibitions, agitations, etc." (Schäffle 1881, 1:353).

The second element—which approximates the function of nerve centers—consists of societal institutions for the dissemination of ideas. Schäffle refers to them as external institutions for communication and suggests that "the presentation, the production of symbols and their acquisition belong to individuals, who are capable of thinking, feeling, and acting. Only the finished product of the presentation falls into the realm of communication" (1881, 1:353).

The activities of creating and internalizing symbols result in messages that consist of a variety of symbols, such as oral presentations, gestures, songs, musical productions, signs, drawings, writings, printed matter, art exhibitions, stage and opera productions, pictures, paintings, and other works. But symbols can only be carriers of ideas; they still must be transmitted. This means that "the path, the space through which this carrier of ideas will take its course and flight, must be prepared in the most appropriate way as an institution for external communication and transmission" (Schäffle 1881, 1:353).

Schäffle connects these two basic elements—the production of symbols and the means of external communication through appropriate institutions—with the presence of technical, economic, and other protective measures. They surround the process of social communication, not unlike muscles and bones that protect nerves throughout a body. Thus social "nerve centers" consist of professional and nonprofessional intellectual workers, symbols, translators, and other technical means concerning the physical plant of these enterprises. For example, besides books, catalogues, and librarians, libraries also need "technical-mechanical installations and a labor force, regular support, accurate safety devices, and a solidly constructed building" (Schäffle 1881, 1:353).

In discussing the role of individuals as contributors to the cultural production of society, Schäffle proposes a comprehensive, participatory model of intellectual labor. Accordingly, everyone, at least to some degree, adds to the final outcome and all intellectual activities consist of the sum total of individual efforts to contribute to the intellectual atmosphere of society. In fact, individuals are in touch with each other—and the social environment in general—through various avenues of communication. They are collection points of communication networks and are tied into the social structure in a variety of ways, depending on the degree of individual versatility. Schäffle refers to the "multipolarity" of each individual and suggests that the rise of civilization results in an increasingly denser and more integrated communication network. In other words, "each new book, which is read by an individual, each newspaper subscription, and each link with a social circle increases participation by dozens and hundreds of connections—and often from one day to the next" (1881, 1:355). Implicit in these observations is the importance of language as a prerequisite for participation in society. Schäffle is confident that individuals are capable of acquiring a vocabulary that matches their intellectual goals and can be extended to include foreign languages and cultures. Indeed, language becomes an instrument of intellectual growth that permits the development of relationships with others and with the social environment at large.

Symbols—and the process of symbol making—are unique features of human civilization; they are external reflections of internal processes to be divided according to their personal or material nature. While the former include words, language, sounds, songs, and gestures or facial expressions, the latter ones consist of writings, prints, pictures, monuments, and sculptures.

Since the external presentation of ideas involves the use of the body and is a common characteristic of all personal symbols, Schäffle stresses the subjective character of the symbolism of language, song, dance, and gesture. Their culmination in language constitutes the most powerful and influential means of social communication. In fact, the spoken word as the "ur-symbol" of ideas will always remain the most important and, at the same time, the most immaterial and inexpensive means of achieving intellectual cohesion in the daily affairs of society.

Language, according to Schäffle, is the outcome of a historical process that reflects a world of ideas and remains the shared property of all members of society. This view implies a commonality of certain ways of thinking and feeling to achieve a sense of mutual understanding; that is, specific words, proverbs, songs, and stories elicit similar emotional and intellectual responses from all members of a culture. Therefore, language remains the most treasured possession of individuals, and the suppression of a native language or dialect, for instance, constitutes a crime comparable to murder and mayhem committed against a people and its culture.

Schäffle also recognizes the importance of nonverbal communication and considers gestures, for instance, an appropriate example for expressing ideas in a language for the eye rather than the ear. He observes that the

> slightest movement of the body is enough to produce this type of personal symbol. The medium of communication is the light which surrounds us—according to the hypothesis of the natural sciences—the vehicle for communicating these thoughts is the ether. In terms of its simplicity, cheapness, originality and durability, mimicry resembles language. . . . However, mimicry is as unique as language is universal. Its collection and publication through mediating objects, analogous to written and printed words, is impossible. . . . But the individuality of mimicry makes it most useful for artistic presentations and the communication of idealistic feelings and values. (1881, 1:358)

Indeed, theater and dance represent specific forms of artistic communication; their expressions of feelings and values have an almost universal effect on society as statements of common, shared experiences.

Schäffle recognizes the potential effectiveness of personal symbols and stresses their "intimacy, ardour, and immediacy" but also acknowledges their disadvantages for communicating over distance and time. Furthermore, since the production and consumption of symbols often occurs alone and in isolation, a high degree of motivation, peer pressure, and small group interaction are essential elements of an effective production and consumption of personal symbols. Their uses become less effective with the emergence of large audiences distributed over vast areas. Nevertheless, personal communication becomes institutionalized in the form of regular communal events or festivities with the establishment of markets and fairs, school and church activities, and the work of traveling artists and musicians.

Schäffle acknowledges that "the beginnings of any civilization encounter great difficulties with the establishment, protection, and technical assistance of personal symbols. Language and the art of speaking are hardly developed. Knowledge and the art of presentation belong to the few" (1881, 1:361). People, at that time, are not very receptive to religious or scientific talks and presentations, and there are no external means to help unite an audience for the benefit of a presentation, especially when traveling actors run into obstacles, such as prejudices, legal dilemmas, uncertainties of transportation, and differences in languages and dialects that must affect style and content of their presentations.

Symbols in their material form—their increasing numbers, varieties, and uses—mark significant cultural advancements, and their collection and distribution suggest notable economic progress. Specifically, "the invention and introduction of the alphabet, mathematical representation, chronometric representation of time, money as the symbol of value . . . contributed to leading humankind to the fine arts and crafts, technology and business, and to knowing and feeling in the context of a moral and religious life" (Schäffle 1881, 1:362).

This development established a tradition that was documented in a variety of material symbols that could now be gathered and transmitted for the benefit of future generations. Personal symbols (e.g., words) could be equated with material symbols (e.g., letters), gestures with pictorial languages of paintings and sculptures, and artistic and scientific works with material representations of specific ideas and decisions. Consequently, communication with the aid of material symbols suggests permanency and the capability of widespread circulation. Scientific knowledge, for instance, may be gathered and disseminated, while the same process of committing ideas to a fixed form of writing or printing governs the private and social affairs of individuals. Represented by scrolls, pamphlets, and books, knowledge becomes the content of a thousand-year-old tradition.

Furthermore, the printed word provides a record of observation and reflection in the modern world. Schäffle sees press and literature as "organs of criticism of contemporary activities" and technologies of unification (1881, 1:363). At the same time, he notes the dangers of neglect that come with modernization and the demise of traditional practices. He warns that it would be a mistake to ignore the meaning of personal symbols in the context of technological advancements:

> The spoken word and gesture belong to what is by far the largest component of the communication of ideas. . . . Most expressions of ideas occur and end within a smaller circle and belong to the moment. . . . the need for material symbols of longer lasting quality and with wider distribution is added . . . with an ascending civilization. (1881, 1:367)

However, other dangers lurk in the process of introducing universal education. He notes that when "writing, reading and arithmetic . . . become the first elements of universal education. . . . training in oral presentation and the communication of ideas, feelings, and intentions are often neglected due to false educational methods" (1881, 1:363).

Material symbols contain the possibility of remarkably efficient production, communication, and consumption, although the original production (the first issue) is far less economical than the mass production of symbols. As a rule, the former becomes a highly individual effort, regardless of whether it is a personal effort to record a private experience or a business transaction; although unique, individual cooperation to produce a message or describe a situation is always needed. This is the creative stage in the process of communication beyond which the art of mechanical reproduction is capable of achieving the highest degree of effectiveness; it also raises the quality of reproduction in processing material symbols.

Schäffle considers the original work raw material for the communication industry. "These industries reproduce the manuscript in literary publishing houses, drawings, designs, pictures, models, prints, and photographs in art publishing houses—often with the intention of only providing accessibility to reproductions" (1881, 1:364–65). At the same time, increasing education and wider distribution contribute to lowering the cost for the production of originals and the process of copying and reproducing originals in large numbers with the result of attracting even more consumers.

These technological and industrial advancements raise economic issues and lead to a political economy of communication. Schäffle is aware of the most fundamental and obvious differences between symbolic and material goods, which rest in the fact that the former can and will be reproduced and disseminated without raising the kinds of economic problems in society that occur with the production and consumption of material goods. Using the analogy of food production, Schäffle refers to the real potential of increasing the amount and distribution of intellectual "food" at any time, whereas food production, for instance, may be affected by population explosions or limitations in production cycles.

Schäffle is aware of the interaction between communication technologies and other forms of technological progress, or of dependence on industrial delivery systems in a modern society. He emphasizes the importance of traffic and cites advances in communication technologies, including the institution of postal services, which are involved in the exchange of material symbols among individuals and organizations; they also enhance the uses of material symbols in society. Consequently, he urges sociologists to recognize the importance of material symbols because their production, consumption, and adoption are key to realizing the "tremendous effects of social communication on one hand, and the growing simplicity of its means on the other" (1881, 1:368).

Schäffle calls the system of personal and material symbols and their interconnections the "psycho-physical mechanism" of the social body. He argues that without an understanding of this communication mechanism, individuals will be unable to grasp the functions of a social and intellectual life in society. Specifically, he notes that "each individual as receiver and sender is woven into the social body through thousands of communication links each day and each hour of the day." Similarly, he describes the press as a "nerve center" that connects readers and "involves a complete system of conduits which run back and forth endlessly" (1881, 1:369).

These developments have consequences; for instance, the "texture of the social nerve centers displays—at least in an educated society—infinitely more communication links than an organic nervous system." Schäffle projects a massive and highly complex communication apparatus embedded in cultural practices that is infinitely more intricate than a purely physical, organic nerve system. Thus "each of the numerous words of a language creates at least a community of two—or perhaps of millions of people through reading a newspaper or a book—in thoughts, feelings, and decisions" to constitute a "mass of social communication and tradition which occurs in oral, written, and printed form, in all kinds of artistic productions, social circles, and business relationships, and with immense paper consumption" (1881, 1:369).

Earlier in his career, Schäffle had engaged in a concentrated and rather specific discussion of the symbolic process while focusing on issues of material production and consumption; his 1873 article became the basis for considering personal and material symbols in *Bau und Leben des Sozialen Körpers*. It acknowledges that the material goods of society—which represent its morality and economic wealth—may be divided into

> presentations, representational goods, signs, and symbols. The latter are—because of the social nature of the individual—often also the means of presentation for other goods of expression and communication. They are, in a

real sense, useful goods, organs, and instruments which are not merely signs or mediators of ideas, but means of production and consumption and of symbolic, not purely ideal use. (1873, 1–2)

Schäffle offers various ways of differentiating cultural and social goods; for instance, speeches, books, and art are specific examples of the means of symbolic communication, while food, clothing, and shelter are means of sensual pleasure. They could also be differentiated and classified as means of entertainment and means of subsistence, and they form the basis for a wide-ranging discussion of communication and the means of communication in society.

From the beginning, Schäffle stresses the definite need for communication, which coexists with a need for *Gemeinschaft*, and its sustained development as a spiritual and political idea. Since knowledge, values, and plans of action can be communicated only through symbols, communities must acquire and advance their communication technologies to enhance the quality of symbolic goods and foster the growth of all forms of communication. Schäffle foresees increasing societal needs to communicate and enter into dialogical relationships—concerning not only scientific or factual matters but also feelings, fantasies, and matters of personal taste. He also anticipates increasing requirements for decision making in the process of communication in a society, whose potential for growth—in terms of culture, religion, art, science, or economics—must rest on the production and consumption of symbolic goods. Specifically, he concludes that "progress of association among people, the expansion of a cultural community—specifically the growth of a moral community in the ideal cultural areas—depends on developing a symbolizing technique, adequate supplies of steadily improving symbolic goods, and the expansion of all forms of communication for an intellectual intercourse involving knowledge, recognition, and decision," although expressions of feelings, judgments of ideas, and criticisms are equally important (1873, 6).

Schäffle understands the emerging problems of harnessing the flow of communication in advanced stages of development and the need for coordination and control in production processes, including the means of presentation. He sees symbols—and their control—as the foundation of creating a social system in which tradition, transportation, and commerce are fully developed (1873, 9).

Commercial pressures, consequently, lead to specific forms of presentation (i.e., to the development of media), and commerce favors progressive cultural environments with established media systems. Economists therefore must understand symbolic processes and increase their knowledge of symbolic goods because of their economic impact on society. Moreover, symbolic goods contain collective and individualistic elements in their deployment throughout a culture with specific economic effects. Schäffle states that their "communistic definition of uses and their extremely individualistic creation have significant economic consequences for symbolic goods in the societal processes of production, transmission, compensation, and consumption" (1873, 14). He provides a listing of examples for a multitude of symbolic goods involved in the successful conduct of commerce and industry, where communication is the key to efficient and profitable business transactions. With the evolution of cultures, the production and consumption of symbols increase simply because of improved utilizations of time and space. Literature as a time-binding force contains the traditions of a society, which are preserved and carried forward into the future, while other similar devices, such as public lectures or newspapers, bridge physical distances with their capabilities of transmitting ideas. In fact, commenting on the power of the printed word, Schäffle sees the press and literature becoming organs of contemporary criticism and organizers of people and ideas. But the economics of material symbols also affect the use of personal symbols in society. Since the latter are based on books, newspapers, and similar media, individuals are capable of reproducing their truths and expressions of feelings frequently and almost anywhere.

The production of symbols, important for the growth of civilization under any circumstance, may be studied in terms of the production of original symbols and their reproduction for mass consumption. Indeed, Schäffle sees a close relationship between the making of symbols and progress. He argues, for instance, that the production of original symbols is closely tied to an expansion of society, which, in turn, will support the rise of talented individuals. But he insists that the creative act remains a personal contribution that cannot be subsumed under a theory of mass production. At the same time, the production of original material symbols requires the existence of scientific and creative talents and their training and education as they emerge in and through society. Consequently, collecting and disseminating surviving literatures and arts of the ages becomes not only culturally important but also economically meaningful for the education of artists. Since only material symbols can be transmitted and preserved over time—either in original or reproduced form—their development becomes a prerequisite for progress and future growth.

Newspapers may serve as examples of media that carry a variety of symbols reproduced for the benefit of their readers. In fact, they frame issues of reproduction in terms of useful consumption, reflecting the goals of an industry that tries to organize the reproduction of symbols in an economically feasible and profitable manner, while advancing the needs of society for the reproduction and circulation of original symbols among a general public. Since the creative process is stimulated by (the potential) of fame and financial rewards, it results in an increasing production of original symbols and their wide circulation through mass reproduction.

The task of reproducing material symbols, however, does not require creative talents but relies on the fundamentals of education. Schooling becomes an important cultural institution, and Schäffle describes the purpose of elementary education—with its emphasis on reading, writing, and arithmetic—as providing a foundation for preserving and transmitting symbols. Consequently, political economy considers elementary schools effective institutions, since they produce through their "teaching of writing a prerequisite for the most fruitful production, through teaching of reading a prerequisite for the most prolific use of material symbols in everyday life, and through both a mediator for a productive creation and acquisition of useful goods" (1873, 26). The resulting economic interpretation of schools as an aspect of social life, however, is not based on questions of feasibility or profits. Instead, education serves processes of production and reproduction of communication, including consumption; in fact, the uses of symbolic goods tend to be maximized through the reproduction and dissemination of original material symbols.

When Schäffle insists that reproduction is necessary for achieving an economically most efficient level of consumption, he concentrates on the publishing industry which—as a modern phenomenon—combines the efforts of promoting original works and their reproduction. "Economically speaking, the production task of publishing industries consists of bringing forth the best possible products in the best possible form for preservation and dissemination at the lowest cost" (1873, 34).

In this connection, Schäffle shifts to traffic in symbolic goods and suggests that discussions regarding material symbols—such as mechanically reproduced presentations—should be considered under notions of tradition, transportation, and personal transactions. They relate to the collection and storage of symbols, which are essential activities of societal institutions, including museums, schools, universities, and private or public libraries, and a result of realizing that the preservation of symbols constitutes the prerequisite for an emerging tradition. Aware of past difficulties of preserving information (e.g., during antiquity), he emphasizes contemporary efforts and the importance of maintaining continuity while commenting on the strength of existing traditions; he also acknowledges the advantage of public collections, from an economic point of view, which are preserved in institutions such as "the British Museum, the Glyptothek in München, or the Gallerie in Dresden" (1873, 40).

With technical and bureaucratic improvements in the ability to collect and store symbolic goods come better ways of transmitting symbols; the postal system, for instance, represents a beneficial and efficient organization for the transmission of news and information. Commenting on a variety of ways in which symbolic goods are disseminated among organizations, groups, and individuals, Schäffle observes that the technology of transporting symbolic goods has also led to economic considerations of their use and consumption.

Finally, personal transmissions of symbols and the commercial activities of publishing houses, or even free publications, are additional means of dissemination. Books, newspapers, and public announcements are among the potential carriers of important information—organized for the purposes of successive uses by large audiences—for which they receive special economic considerations. The latter include speculative approaches, for instance, manifested in consignments, advance payments, or on-approval purchases, which constitute modern business practices of the newspaper industry or publishing houses.

Discussions of the production and distribution of communication also raise questions of costs and cost efficiency. Schäffle recognizes problems inherent in assessing costs at the level of private exchanges of information, conversations, or personal messages, but he suggests, nevertheless, that a cost-benefit argument could focus on the degree of personal satisfaction gained through communication with others, since the highly personalized nature of communication precludes any standardization of values attached to interpersonal exchanges. He notes that another type of communication that receives no attention—except in connection with business transactions—may be found in business planning, correspondence, bookkeeping, and similar communication practices that are typically subsumed under general expenses and included in the sales price of a product.

On the other hand, the communication of symbols may be tied in to an economic system with specific institutional practices. For instance, theatrical productions, books, or newspapers may be utilized as sources of information or entertainment only after payment of an admissions fee or a set price. Indeed, many symbolic goods are offered in the marketplace, often in competitive situations, as commercial properties or objects of commercial speculation, by institutions that specialize in the reproduction of symbolic goods and their distribution in society. At the same time, Schäffle stresses the idea that the production of symbolic goods must not be viewed solely as a speculative venture—based on the initiative of business interests—but also as a public effort aimed at advancing culture and society.

A unique phenomenon in the marketplace of communication is the dissemination of so-called free symbolic goods. Schäffle creates awareness of a problem nowadays related to commercial television as "free" entertainment. He refers to traditional institutions (e.g., education, religion, and politics) as sources of symbolic goods that are frequently advertised as being available at no cost to members of society, and he offers a differentiated response by suggesting that

> the mission and the church disseminate their symbols, sermons, religious instruction, bibles, tracts, and hymn books free or at very low cost. This also happens with the profane symbolism of political life; appeals, posters, etc. are distributed free to the masses during political agitation. The real or assumed intrinsic value of communication must be appreciated only through communication itself. (1873, 45)

In fact, these symbolic goods bear indirect costs of production that must be absorbed by individuals, groups, or organizations. In the field of education, for instance, the question whether state, community, or individual citizens will cover the cost of producing symbolic goods frequently becomes a significant issue with serious political consequences. A substantial amount of symbolic communication, however, is produced with commercial interests and direct and full remuneration in mind. Schäffle cites specifically symbolic goods with private or personal values—among them university-level lectures, musical productions, and literary and artistic publications. He also notes the peculiar effect of transitions from an original to its reproduction, since the latter condition accentuates the "communistic" nature of symbols in their collective use and application. "Once published, the work allows for widespread acquisition of its intellectual content; the private 'property' of this content ceases to exist with the first copy. This means . . . that the imitator is freed from the cost of producing an original, experimental presentation and paying an honorarium" (1873, 46).

Since the consumption of symbolic goods remains a key to the development of society, Schäffle argues for a communication system that maximizes the use of symbols by individuals. Therefore, he envisions a system in which access to information and enactments of regulations for the use and protection of symbolic goods become priorities among economic considerations of communication; he implies that any good administration of libraries, collections, or schools—to maximize the consumption of symbolic goods—follows these principles of access and protection. But it is schooling and private or public education that must help perfect an individual's capacity to produce and consume symbols by emphasizing practices of reading, writing, drawing, and mathematics.

Aside from the symbolic communication represented in spoken and written languages and literature, Schäffle identifies architecture and the applied arts as other forms of symbolic practice that join symbols and technology in a "symbolizing-organizing" manner. They are examples of practices that contribute substantially to the satisfaction of societal needs and—with rising education—will produce incentives to introduce more aesthetically designed consumer goods. "Since each product represents the realization of a prescribed idea, once they circulate, useful products of some originality may become symbols, whose ideas may be imitated and generally acquired" (1873, 66).

Schäffle concludes his discussion of the economic aspects of communication—as cultural practices involving the exchange of original or reproduced symbols in the service of societal needs and gratifications—with an observation about the effects of industrialization and mass markets on the process of communication. He suggests that "increasing cheapness, simplification, and distribution of a rational, linguistic use of symbols—in oral form during earlier cultures, in written-typographical form culminating in the present culture and its rising population—had to and will continue to exert a most radical and beneficial influence on the moral and intellectual developments of the societal organism" (1873, 69).

Considerations of media and the economic consequences of industrializing the reproduction of communication necessarily lead to issues of influence and control in mass society. Schäffle relegates questions of media effects to social-psychological explanations and particularly the relationship between masses and their leaders. Based on the premise that social organisms must be coordinated by intellectual centers, which represent the leading elements in society, he addresses questions of leadership and domination of the masses and their reactions to leaders as corresponding to notions of "active" and "passive" sides of authority. Thus intellectual and spiritual practices of social organisms occur in symbolic interactions between leaders and their masses, where questions of authority are typically settled by birth, tradition, or intellectual superiority, and where individuals, families, rank, class, or professional institutions act as carriers of authority. But the latter are only one part of the spiritual and intellectual activities that lead from individual to collective movements. Public opinion and media influence, therefore, constitute part of a reactive mechanism that is employed by the masses. The power of a collective mind, however, emerges only from a mutual exchange between leaders and their followers; such an exchange is based on the existence of certain conditions that affect the proper functioning of the social system. Thus the quality of leadership and its size, intensity, and skill in triggering appropriate reactions to influence the masses are as important as intellectually and spiritually strong and vital people who are capable of releasing new energies on appeals to their feelings and convictions.

For instance, a favorable international climate and the advancement of communication technologies provide ideal conditions for increasing the size of mass appeals; the spread of socialist propaganda around the world suggests the magnitude of political campaigns in modern times. But to arouse the masses requires skills in selecting the opposition press, for instance, and demonstrating a considerable degree of perfection in the high art of stimulating and guiding the reactions of the masses.

In this connection, Schäffle singles out notions of the public sphere, the public, public opinion, and the press as homogeneous elements in the effective exchange of ideas that characterizes a well-functioning social system. He asks,

> What else is the much debated public sphere, but an intellectual openness to social knowledge, appreciation, and decision, mediated symbolically through words, writing, and print to the masses or at least to interested, special circles? What else is the public but a social mass, open, receptive, and reactive to the organs of social and intellectual activities with whom they share knowledge, appreciation, and decision making? What else is public opinion, but the expression of opinion, value, and disposition of a general or special public? And finally the press—is it not the real transmitter in an intellectual exchange between the leading instruments of society and the public? (1881, 1:433)

Since the press and the public are of universal importance to the intellectual life of society, Schäffle assigns responsibilities for a systematic treatment of communication and media to the social sciences and offers a meaningful rationale for their study and analysis with an implicit indication of media studies as a legitimate academic concern. An understanding of communication in society is based, in particular, on a series of concepts that constitute the foundations of a social system and the source of specific cultural practices.

According to Schäffle, the public sphere (*Öffentlichkeit*) emerges as a site of exchange of personal and material symbols in the social body—regardless of distances—and is based on openness, that is, on the possibility of disseminating ideas beyond the boundaries of certain groups or organizations. It is absolutely necessary to preserve the public sphere as a battleground for ideas and ideologies and a source of social and political decisions that are expressions of an active and participatory community. Positive law and regulations secure the existence of a public sphere and concomitant basic rights—including freedom of the press and speech, the right to petition the government, and rights bestowed by open records and meeting laws—and create possibilities for an exchange of information and assistance in the daily activities of social and political organizations. He observes that

> often publicity is seen as an evil, and its most effective form, a free press, as an arbitrary concession to liberal legislation. Even though one deeply de-

> spises the contemporary corruption of the press, one would have to say that the above statement is confining but completely true. The public sphere per se—excused where degenerated and abused—is neither an evil nor a necessary evil, but a social-psychological necessity. (1881, 1:447)

In fact, the public sphere cannot be suppressed, and Schäffle anticipates its revival under the most difficult conditions of society: "Prohibit all newspapers, and the public sphere will choose public streets; scatter all groups gathered for small talk in public places, and the public sphere will move into taverns; close them and the necessary exchanges of symbols will occur in private salons, family or business circles, and among normally cooperating masses of society" (1881, 1:449).

In other words, abolishing the public sphere is a task compared by Schäffle to removing the nervous system, resulting in the mutilation of the social body. Thus church and state have yet to be successful in their attempts at such an operation, which would undoubtedly weaken the spiritual powers of the people, if not damage the spiritual bonds between leaders and masses, resulting in society's general decline into passivity and impotence, particularly in crisis situations.

On the other hand, there are strictly private matters that must be left outside the public sphere (e.g., marriage and family affairs) which are the concern of those directly involved; also, there are laws—restricting press coverage of private affairs and suppressing profane or obscene publications—that provide the necessary protection of individuals. But even within the public sphere there remain undisclosed occasions or stages of thought and preparation, since not all thinking is constantly exposed to public scrutiny. "Neither governments, parliaments, courts, or parties, not even editorial offices work like publicly displayed machines under glass covers, nor do they place themselves behind a megaphone to invariably think, feel, reflect, and plan aloud" (1881, 1:449).

According to Schäffle, the public or audience (*Publikum*) consists of those who appear "publicly" on streets and public thoroughfares; but the public also refers to specific groups of people—without legal or organizational boundaries—who participate in intellectual exchanges with specific individuals or institutions, such as the press. His idea of the public embraces the notion of people interacting freely and without force with those who provide intellectual and spiritual stimulation; he implies the existence of more than one public at all times, its number depending on a particular identification with leaders. There are also specific publics of scientists, writers, poets, preachers, journalists, and politicians. But the "essentially free and intellectual relationship between one public and the other public for whom it represents the public, is established through an informal exchange of personal and material symbols, namely through the press" (1881, 1:451). For Schäffle, the public is basically passive and receptive; it is an object for outside stimulation rather than an aggressive or imparting force. There is one exception, however: when the public expresses a mood that may provide feedback for those formulating new or additional strategies, for example, public speakers, politicians, and speculators who investigate public sentiments in preparation for political or commercial campaigns.

These sentiments are described as public opinion *(Öffentliche Meinung)*, which is a public reaction to specific ideas, decisions, or feelings expressed by leading individuals or groups. Despite the fact that public opinion has often been held in low esteem, it is extremely important for discussing social actions, since it seems almost impossible to act without or against public opinion on social, political, or commercial issues, for instance, which need public participation for their success. In this context, the press constitutes a primary cultural mechanism for channeling the flow of ideas and opinions. Accordingly, newspapers represent "the most powerful means of influencing public opinion by intellectually active members. In this role the press is a superpower. Belletristic literature, the tribunal, the forum, the eloquence of profane and sacred language, and even the social conversations of salons, clubs, and pubs, as psychophysical foundations of public opinion, must yield to the daily press and retreat in their importance to second or third positions" (Schäffle 1881, 1:452).

Interestingly enough, Schäffle sees the value of public opinion not in representing the opinions of the masses but in corresponding to the true necessities and the pure nature of the social body. Therefore, a good opinion—which is also a public opinion—has real power, whereas even good private opinions cannot become powerful. Consequently, to be effective, actors in political, cultural, or economic life must act "through the people for the people."

Public opinion is not always a single, unified reaction; it can and often does consist of a multitude of reactions, some commonly running counter to others, depending on the seriousness of national, class, or religious differences within a society. Also, public opinions may be manufactured by manipulating the press until the public believes in what it hears or reads and adopts those ideas as its own creation.

Schäffle warns against underestimating public opinion in the service of promoting ideas or attitudes. "Those who want to be effective must count on public opinion to replace an artificial or falsified public opinion with a natural, widely popular, and healthy public opinion" (1881, 1:455). Also, the importance of public opinion does not wane because it cannot be fully grasped or measured. Schäffle suggests that those situations, in effect, often lead to various claims by members of the dominant elite to know and understand the opinions of the people, however, without substantial proof.

Public opinion emerges as a backdrop, or choir, in the social drama, set against the leading roles played by individuals or small groups that constitute the dominant power in society. Public opinion deals with matters developed in the minds of others; it is incapable of producing innovative ideas, or even recognizing them, before they are presented, for instance, by those who popularize discoveries. Schäffle comments on individuals in the chorus of public opinion, whose attitudes and behaviors are reactive rather than innovative; in fact, people who

> cheer earlier accomplishments and erect monuments to honor past achievements are often those who face the aspirations of their contemporaries with indifference or hate. They place wreaths at the feet of older martyrs of human progress and keep a rock ready in their other hand to hit the struggling genius of their own age. As a rule, public opinion in its role as a choir is neither appointed nor able to completely understand the first sign of new ideas at the threshold of public consciousness. (1881, 1:456)

And finally, the daily press—as a constitutive element in the conceptualization of the social system—represents the most powerful institution for the exchange of ideas between people and their leaders. Schäffle characterizes the press and its journalists not in terms of representing a creative intellectual or political power but rather of being an instrument that modifies and transmits messages. The press is a "conductor" or "condensator" of intellectual currents and seeks the company of government, political parties, and organizations as well as contacts with the public. Although prestigious newspapers may have some influence on segments of the leadership or the public, more often than not newspapers suffer from a loss of credibility. They need feedback to gain some measure of their editorial position vis-à-vis the masses, and they constantly look for justifications in their coverage of mass meetings and other events, which may help measure the amount and type of their public support. Elections, in particular, seem to offer a chance for periodic public measurements of opinions regarding a host of political and practical questions.

In their various manifestations, ranging from special interest journals to the local press and prestige newspapers, these media represent a large, interconnected system for collecting and transmitting ideas and, as such, serve as an organ of public opinion. Although other media (e.g., tribunals, theater stages, and public forums) may serve a similar function, the press remains without competition—except among its own representations of journalism—when it comes to the regularity of its service and success in reaching specific publics. It is an organ of public opinion.

The power of the press to identify and define contemporary movements and ideas in society is a function of its regular and frequent access to the public and its use of suitably prepared material to fit the intellectual requirements of its readers. Neither public speakers, preachers, nor teachers reach as large an audience and as frequently and with such a variety of materials as the press. At the same time, Schäffle dismisses the influence of the press on scientific work and adds that it has not contributed to great new ideas; instead, the press has emerged as the strongest means of stimulating and regulating its social environment on a daily basis. In this context, the press constitutes an indispensable instrument for the destruction, change, or creation of public opinion, and a necessary forum for those who want to preach, lie, judge, terrorize, excite, or alarm the masses. For these reasons, newspapers are desirable properties, and the press frequently is targeted by a variety of interests (e.g., politics, finance, and religion) for purposes of speculation and propaganda. After all, "with the help of the press one 'makes' public opinion at least for the day" (1881, 1:460).

As a "maker" of public opinion, the press becomes the first power in the state because "the domination of opinions, judgments and dispositions of various social masses and classes is the key to successful social action and exertion of power" (1881, 1:460). For this reason, it comes as no surprise that governments purchase newspapers and encourage corruption, even on an international scale. For instance, financial interests own newspapers and pay for their services; political parties, expecting success, must support their press; and those who want to profit in the marketplace must influence the buying and consumption habits of the masses. It becomes obvious that benefactors and detractors, or the good and evil forces in society, are compelled to use the press as an instrument of persuasion. As a result, media become victims (or willing instruments) of manipulation, which suggests that all avenues of public opinion—including the press—are subject to corruption and falsification.

Referring to a series of prominent comments by Ferdinand Lasalle (1825–1864), Johann Wolfgang von Goethe (1710–1782), Friedrich Wilhelm Joseph von Schelling (1775–1854), Johann Gottlieb Fichte (1762–1814), and Georg Friedrich Wilhelm Hegel (1770–1831), Schäffle considers the continuing influence of a corrupt press system on the spiritual and psychological well-being of society. He is convinced that the degeneration of the daily press is related to social-psychological dysfunction in society. For instance, he notes Fichte's description of the "ideal reader," whose reading of book reviews—instead of books—had a narcoticizing effect on his mental disposition; he lost his power to think but gained an opinion that gave him security (1881, 1:462).

But Schäffle also recognizes that neither the press nor journalists alone are to blame for the mental decline of society and identifies two major causes that he denounces for corrupting the press and affecting the roots of a nation's health; they are the "one-sided mechanical centralization in the state and monopolistic exploitation of the daily press for purposes of speculation by financial interests" (1881, 1:463). In fact, the press is easily controlled and manipulated, since journalists, who think, feel, and live for the day, are often not used to serious intellectual work or are incapable of it. Schäffle feels rather strongly that "except for some stylistic skills, the journalistic trade requires just a minimum of thorough education" (1881, 1:464).

These are favorable conditions for those who seek to corrupt the press, but Schäffle blames in particular leaders who misdirect the press and abuse its facilities, as well as people who choose to tolerate a bad press. In other words, society is responsible for the quality of its media. He concludes that "in the long run, a nation will have the press it deserves and will be responsible for its own downfall if it continues to put up with a poisoned press" (1881, 1:464). Since a weak or inferior press is due to a general deterioration of society, neither police intervention nor legal protection under a universal right of freedom of expression will help improve press practices. This condition leads to increasingly mechanical rather than natural reorganizations in society, for instance, when centralization breeds powers that use the press for their own purposes and exert a corrupting influence on journalists.

However, Schäffle traces the corrupt nature of the press to the economic organization of society rather than to any particular political condition. He notes that for the most part the influential metropolitan press is in the hands of banking and stock market interests; since it has been turned into a profitable investment, it risks complete enslavement by financial powers. Schäffle attributes "this primary cause of press corruption . . . to control by a degenerated form of capitalism. The evil is intensified by the fact that the reward of speculative newspapering depends on advertising and its readers" (1881, 1:465). These economic conditions must also have a devastating effect on the work of individual journalists, who become members of a proletariat—degraded and on the block, like intellectual slaves—and servants to press baronies and their backers (e.g., stock exchange and banking interests).

The deterioration of the media situation is particularly alarming because the press remains—for Schäffle—the most pervasive instrument of social communication; it covers all areas of social and political life, including the privacy of individuals, under the guise of exploring the shape and content of public opinion. Although journalists function primarily as modifiers and mediators between leaders and followers (or the public) rather than as originators of creative ideas or political opinions, they do continue the creative process in an indirect fashion. They are in constant need of contact with those who furnish new artistic or intellectual stimuli and with the public, whose support they constantly seek to legitimize their own work.

Schäffle's suggestion for improving the newspaper industry becomes part of a general economic reform by which the press will be freed from financial speculation and advertising control to regain its freedom and operate independently. Rejecting ideas of establishing a government press monopoly or centralizing journalistic activities under official supervision, he aims for an economic reconstruction of society that minimizes or even destroys the potential for corruption. His reform ideas are radical suggestions for freeing the press from the influence of private capital with a takeover by publicly owned corporations. Organized into production and delivery systems with specific duties, media organizations would be able to operate newspapers free from financial speculations and advertising pressures and keep government out of literary and journalistic activities. In addition, he argues for serious attempts in socialist states to avoid the centralization of printing industries and pleads for the establishment of various types of production facilities, capable of offering their services to any organization, party, or individual—and for the same rates. Even better, "it should be up to any organization or party to maintain their own printing plants. The production and delivery of manuscripts, as well as fixing their exchange value, would be a private matter among individuals, parties, and organizations, such as public [scientific and other] institutions" (1881, 3:520).

His reform plans are based on the need to protect individual and collective freedoms of expression; Schäffle feels strongly that these freedoms can be guaranteed only when the production and dissemination of ideas remain absolutely free and undisturbed by capitalist or bureaucratic efforts to organize these activities for purposes of financial gain or political control. Given these circumstances, journalism will recover its natural form and flourish with renewed vigor. Without advertising constraints journalism once again becomes the subject of "parties and organizations, and scientific, political, and religious propaganda" (1881, 3:520–21). Profits from the sale of press products, on the other hand, would be distributed among writers to benefit the journals and newspapers for which they work. Under such a system, journalism would rise to new heights, and "an end would be put to the official claptrap of a centralized-communistic state that narcotizes the people, and to the liberal bunk of the monied aristocracy that has the same effect" (1881, 3:521). His observations anticipate the consequences of media systems operating under communism in Eastern Europe and capitalism in the United States over half a century later, when "the same effect" helped distort information and handicap the work of journalists.

Schäffle considers advertising a waste of economic resources, although he continues to advocate the establishment of advertising sheets, or shoppers, financed by large institutions in society, while political debates dominate the party press. He also envisions a better-educated public that is able to follow the arguments of experts and critical minds, and he hopes for a general improvement of the image of journalists and their morale. At the same time, however, he realizes that these developments—necessary for the welfare of society—must be viewed as historical processes. For his own time, Schäffle expresses a more pessimistic outlook when he concludes that "on the basis of the current social order, the corruption of the press will increase rather than decrease. . . . Nowadays the journals are and must be business enterprises and speculative ventures if they want to survive competition without subsidies" (1881, 4:69). In support of his own critical assessment of the press, he cites the sober conclusions of a cultural historian (Friedrich Anton Heller von Hellwald) who had observed earlier that

> the press is a simple business, aimed at maximizing material gains and operating by the standard that all's fair for the trade. . . . Nobody thinks of defending a principle that could be injurious to the moneybags because one wants to do well and make excellent profits; great newspaper publishers who think of themselves as businessmen must know the advantages of supporting A or fighting B; but for the good of the newspaper these roles are changed very calmly overnight. (1881, 4:69–70)

COMMUNICATION, POLITICS, AND THE PRESS

Schäffle's *homo symbolicus* holds the key to his organismic theory of society, which treats communication as a necessary condition for the development of civilization and the progress of humankind. Personal and material symbols and their interconnections constitute the mechanism of the social body that directs social and intellectual activities. Schäffle stresses the importance of individual, creative contributions while acknowledging the dynamics of an economic environment with its own demands regarding the production and consumption of symbolic goods. Thus the notion of communication emerges as an early and central concern among economic theorists and begins to play a serious role in their assessments of societal expansion. The press appears as a transmitter of ideas and leader of the public and occupies a major role in advancing the causes of society, despite its dependence on economic and political forces that are apt to corrupt or misdirect journalistic practices. For these reasons, Schäffle advocates the need for substantial press reform, suggesting a separation of advertising from information and opinion to improve the quality of newspaper coverage and strengthen professional ethics among journalists.

The degeneration of journalism, however, must also be traced to the specific conditions of the social sciences. According to Schäffle, the social sciences have been unable to provide the necessary insights based on the kind of evidence produced by the natural sciences, for instance. There is a definite need for information that can only be derived from social scientific inquiry. In fact, sound and positive insights from the social sciences "would have put an end to the charlatanism of government, the cult of verbosity in the press, the deception of audiences, the contamination of journalism with literary scum, and the paid sophistry and rhetoric" (1881, 1:466).

In this context, Schäffle simply echoes Comte's hope that progress in the social sciences could end the corruption of the public spirit, aware, of course, that "sociology, because of the nature of its subject matter, can never attain the positive reliability of the natural sciences in the treatment of objects" (1881, 1:466). His observations suggest a rather firm opinion that human nature and the organization of society introduce highly subjective elements to a systemic approach to social life and would never preclude the communication of false or deceptive materials for the benefit of individual power brokers or special interest groups in society.

His representations of the public sphere, the public, public opinion, and the press link social and political theories with a general theory of communication—anticipating the interdisciplinary nature of the field of communication studies, for instance—and reflect his own knowledge of the natural sciences, economic theory, and history. This knowledge is firmly grounded in a practical understanding of contemporary events, particularly as they relate to press practices in the political process of his times. Although pessimistic about immediate changes, Schäffle nevertheless articulates the potential for change by proposing new press practices to help maximize the communication of information for the benefit of a modern society.

4

The News of Society: Karl Knies on Communication and Transportation

ECONOMICS AND INFORMATION

Karl Knies (1821–1898) is one of the founding fathers of the German historical school of economic thought. He joins Wilhelm Roscher and Bruno Hildebrand in their criticisms of the classical school and in attempts to describe the economic behavior of individuals in terms of their association with diverse groups in society, while carefully stressing the limited applicability of generalizations based on observations of varied economic activities among people.

Knies was born and raised in Marburg (Hessen), where he became a *Privatdozent* at the university in 1846, lecturing on history and political science. After a teaching assignment at the polytechnic institute in Kassel, he became a teacher at the Kantonschule in Schaffhausen (Switzerland) in 1852. Three years later he was appointed professor of cameralistic sciences at Freiburg University (Germany), where he headed a reform committee for elementary and middle schools. In 1861 he became a member of the lower house of the Baden parliament, and from 1865 until his retirement in 1896, he served as a professor of political sciences at Heidelberg University.

Throughout his career Knies published widely, mostly monographs and books on economic and political topics but also articles in scholarly and popular journals. Among his most important works are *Die Statistik als selbständige Wissenschaft* (1850); *Die politische Oekonomie vom Standpun-*

kte der geschichtlichen Methode (1853 [1883]); *Der Telegraph als Verkehrsmittel* (1857); and a two-volume work, *Geld und Kredit* (1873–1879).

His work reflects the concerns of German political economists about the protection and development of the state. Thus questions of economic policy, within a larger study of the social environment, are often raised in the context of assessing technological advancements and their effects on society. His monographs addressing railroads (*Die Eisenbahnen und ihre Wirkungen,* 1853) and the telegraph (*Der Telegraph als Verkehrsmittel,* 1857) are examples of treating specific economic problems in light of technological developments. Members of the historical school stress the unity of social life and describe the interconnections of individual social processes; indeed, an organic view of society constitutes the basis of their theoretical propositions.

Gustav von Schmoller, a later representative of the historical school, offers the following description of Knies's approach:

> The most essential requirement from his point of view is war against mere abstraction and premature and false generalization—common among older economists. . . . The connection between national economy and other aspects of national life, dependence of economic systems on intellectual and material elements of periods in which they arose, and emphasis on the collective character of social phenomena, are his major concerns. In addressing these issues, he displayed rare foresight, calmness, prudence. (Scott 1933, 277)

Political economy engages in a study of the historical realities of the economic world, according to Knies, whose own work stresses the interdependency of the economic and cultural spheres of society; it is based on an understanding that the sum total of all economic subsystems does not constitute the total economic structure of society, since it omits social and societal processes. Consequently, the task of economists includes observations of a variety of historical manifestations within nations that yield information about common social and cultural expansion. Indeed, "the economic conditions and developments of peoples constitute only one close link with the total organism. In reality political economy is neither isolated nor complete in itself, but it is the economic side of the life of the people" (1883, 141). In his definition of society as a growing and expanding organism, he recognizes the importance of process as a definitional aspect of society and its consequences for a scientific approach to the study of economic questions. Indeed, "economic conditions, too, participate in the general and uniform movement and development . . . in a continuing movement—because the evolution of life is a continuous process" (1883, 143).

Having privileged a social- or cultural-historical perspective on economic issues, Knies addresses the difficulties of historical research, ranging from a lack of data to problems of interpreting statistical materials and limitations of pursuing comparative analyses. He also expands on the prerequisites for a critical research perspective. "Unprejudiced critical research must admit or even stress the fact that mistakes and deceptions easily occur during the collection and arrangement of economic facts . . . because so much material must be obtained from 'interested parties,' who may not only make wrong judgments but also act under the spell of an 'optical illusion.' " Unlike natural science experiments—which either succeed or fail—critical research faces the reality that the "task of verifying and completing factual accounts is made more difficult by the fact that . . . direct insights into 'position and movement' of intellectual-personal elements of those interested in economics are impossible." Consequently, considerable disputes arise and persist concerning the reliable and complete collection of facts (1883, 495).

These observations are based on an understanding of economic facts as combining material and personal factors. Specifically, Knies recognizes that an individual's economic environment consists of an interaction between material and intellectual and/or spiritual dimensions, and he cites Schäffle, who had suggested that "without a psychological explanation there is no truth to political economy or politics." According to Knies, this was a flat admission that theorizing "an evolution of society based on a mechanism of external events—which is a logical consequence of a positivistic sociology—must lead to showings and results that are objectively false" (1883, 253).

As an economist and critical social scientist, he was particularly interested in identifying and defining developments regarding quantitative and qualitative methodologies. For instance, he realized that qualitative differences could not be described numerically and that the spirit of movements or traditions could not be reflected or explained adequately by mere aggregates. His appreciation of contemporary situations in light of past experiences provides a rationale for using statistical materials combined with historical observations. In a sense his work reflects his own dictum that "the method of investigation used by an academic discipline—reasoning and conclusion—is closely related to its overall character. It is for this reason that the progress of a science, in general, certainly affects its current methodology, while, on the other hand, any significant improvement of a method of investigation has a most profound influence on science" (1883, 453).

Knies's interest in communication or symbolic interaction remains ill defined, although *Geld und Kredit*, a work of considerable theoretical importance for contemporary economic thought, addresses the symbolic nature of money in the context of interpersonal communication, without, however, advancing a theoretical framework for symbolic transactions. Money is defined by Knies as serving particular economic conditions in which a commodity "turns into 'money' because it is used to function as a 'measurement of values,' 'means of exchange,' and 'legal tender' " (1885, 23). In *Der Telegraph als Verkehrsmittel,* on the other hand, he elaborates on the impact of technology on symbolic communication with an emphasis on the economic problems of the press. Advancements of technology, expansions of a national economy, and developments in transportation and communication in Germany become catalysts for discussing the role and function of "mass" communication. Recognizing the significant impact of technological change, in particular, on societal communication, he concludes that "to enable and to facilitate communication is synonymous with eliminating the earlier degree of isolation of a country" (1885, 94). Consequently, the press becomes an important means of transporting information through time and over vast distances; his interpretation of the press, however, stresses the mechanical, vehicular functions of the medium at the expense of more commonly expressed social, cultural, or political notions of newspapers in society.

COMMUNICATION, TRANSPORTATION, AND THE PRESS

Knies bases the progress of technology and transportation on the fundamental idea that individuals need and seek contact with others; in fact, most earlier efforts in education and training are aimed at perfecting an individual's ability to function as a social being. "From earliest childhood on, our efforts are directed at making ourselves proficient in social intercourse, to accept others and communicate to others; these efforts, large or small, presuppose a mutual exchange of means with which to satisfy human needs" (1857, 1). Thus individuals have always tried to overcome natural barriers that prevent their intellectual growth and physical expansion by turning to communication as a process that helps break down their isolation, embracing not only "the celebrated inventions of the alphabet, printing, etc., but nearly everything coinciding with the history of the individual as a social being" (1857, 4).

The idea of transportation emerges as a particularly important aspect of his view on communication, since it yields an appropriate opportunity for Knies to introduce his economic approach to understanding the processes of socialization and acculturation. He defines transportation as "an act of moving objects from their original place to another place with the help of force, while the means of transportation are the sum of all necessary instruments to make the move" (1857, 4). Different types of material goods need specific kinds of vehicles for transportation. For instance,

Knies indicates differences among objects, people, and news, their need for different means of transportation, and different time requirements associated with the transmission of different objects. Thus experience tells us that "faster transportation is more desirable for individuals than goods, and it must be even faster for news than for individuals. This situation has always found its expression in the institutions of transportation" (1857, 6).

In this context, the flow of information and communication in society becomes the site of extended discussions that yield historical insights and offer contemporary observations about the press. For instance, the history of transmitting news has its beginnings in interpersonal contacts when information passes directly from source to intended receiver. Inherent in this basic model is, in all likelihood, the most accurate or trustworthy manner of communicating ideas, since content and audience are controlled solely by the source. Furthermore, this type of personal communication invites a dialogical relationship in which the mutuality of receiving and dispatching information invites immediate decisions. But face-to-face communication also lends itself to instant manipulation of messages (if so intended by the source) with the possibility of instant recognition by the receiver. Knies proposes that the peculiar nature of direct communication links continues to be most appropriate for specific kinds of news dissemination—even in the presence of advanced communication technologies and regardless of their disadvantages concerning time and division of labor.

A more advanced system of transmitting news and information arrived with the employment of messengers whose oral presentations replaced the intimacy and accuracy of source-to-recipient communication. Although freed from the physical constraints of direct communication, the source/sender sacrifices specific advantages of interpersonal contacts, as Knies indicates. "The intellectual and moral qualities of the messenger and confidence in personal loyalty are all important when more significant news is involved. . . . The gates are opened to misuse when information strictly meant for a second individual is also communicated to a third one" (1857, 8). Yet under most favorable conditions, this system of news dissemination does not constitute a substantial change from earlier models of interpersonal communication; such change came about only with the invention of optical and aural systems of communication capable of covering greater distances at faster speeds. These primitive technologies of communication—forerunners of the telegraph—supplied a genuinely new dimension of social communication. News could be received indiscriminately by miscellaneous individuals within the reach of the signal, which replaced the need for personal contacts with the originators of information or their messengers. Knies assigns this type of news communication to instances when relatively little information needs fast and widespread dissemination, and he acknowledges its increasing importance as a public communication system, unless the latter was engaged exclusively for messages decipherable only by specific private groups or individuals.

With the introduction of written communication, news dissemination was to be organized according to principles that combine the advantages of earlier systems with new technologies. For instance, to make the process less expensive, news could be kept secret, and the task of transmitting messages could be left to intellectually less qualified individuals. Knies observes that the "use of the written word provides the same accuracy and security that oral communication guaranteed all participants in the dissemination of news. In one respect even more so, since what is offered is not only an exact formulation of the respective expression but also a durable and fixed one. *Littera scripta manet*" (1857, 13).

Printing advanced the progress of news dissemination for and among large numbers of individuals, resulting in specific types of news transmission and a tremendous growth of form, frequency, and quantity of messages, including other types of print products (e.g., lithographs) or the use of pictures on handbills.

At this point in the history of news dissemination, transportation becomes a significant issue and leads to the development of occupational roles (e.g., news carriers) and the establishment of institutions (e.g., postal services). But no other technological advancement influenced news traffic more greatly than the construction of railroads across countries and regions. They "promoted in many ways a faster means of transportation . . . indeed, they initiated it. . . . The goal was reached with the invention of the electric telegraph, which turned out to be well suited for the transmission of news with a speed that surpassed by far the efficiency of a locomotive" (Knies 1857, 18).

Knies locates the invention of the telegraph within a series of related scientific discoveries over long periods of time; in fact, he relates science and economics by suggesting that the advancement of science acts as a stimulus of economic progress. For instance, he describes how developing technologies provide inexpensive telegraph lines and a coded "language" that allows for the most efficient and precise expression of words and ideas.

Technology supports the need of individuals to remain in communication, while news furnishes a vehicle for ideas and becomes one of the forms in which individuals express their relationships. According for Knies, news "belongs to intellectual thought communication, which occurs between persons and differs from other forms . . . by . . . being between individuals who are physically separated." He also renders a modern definition of news when he observes that "news is the communication of an event that occurs away from the location of the recipient" (1857, 44).

However, actual distances are immaterial, since the conditions are met when news is actually transmitted. A more important criterion is the form of publication. Knies differentiates between books and newspapers, for instance, assigning the former to an educational mission, whereas "news follows the daily events, is part of the events, part of the day with attendant occurrences" (1857, 45). Since he separates historical accounts from contemporary phenomena, his definition of news focuses on spatial rather than temporal elements of social communication; in addition, he acknowledges that news is short-lived: "once announced, its traces are lost again, or its account becomes history, a registered fact, or its vehicle becomes a document for argumentation, a means for refreshing one's memory of past experiences" (1857, 47).

The purposes for using specific kinds of communication technologies—ranging from oral communication to telegraphic transmission—increase with the growth and complexity of a social and cultural existence beyond specific, newsworthy events that affect the lives of individuals or organizations; for instance, Knies contemplates the idea of transmitting "moods [that] want to find their expression and feelings, problems and suspicions, happiness and sorrow, love and hate. . . . Who can count all the forms in which individuals search for each other and meet?" (1857, 48).

Knies distinguishes among uses of news when he observes that news satisfies the needs or interests not only of readers or audiences but also its originators or sources. Differently expressed, news presentations in editorial sections of the press and commercial information in advertisements contain different interests in the process of communication itself, depending on the intent of their creators; an exchange of business correspondence, on the other hand, serves all parties who share an equal interest in the outcome of their communication.

Since increases in news communication are strongly assisted by decreasing illiteracy rates, literacy statistics may help determine the limits of participation in the exchange of information. Advanced cultures produce and maintain a more cohesive and well-developed system of news communication—partly because of high literacy rates among their populations and partly because of sophisticated technologies of survival, including specific efforts aimed at perfecting the transmission of news and information. The latter systems are actually based on economic considerations; thus, the transmission of news remains a service operation. It is financially supported either by those seeking to satisfy their curiosity or by others whose social and economic livelihood depends on news. Knies recognizes the discriminatory potential of news communication—and thus anticipates the emergence of future conditions of participation in the exchange of information—when he observes that "not only those who cannot write or read but also those who cannot pay, e.g., the extremely poor—those who lack disposable goods for a relatively superfluous service—are excluded from the communication of news" (1857, 55). Since the number of individuals affected in such ways differs with the degree of wealth in society, rising prosperity, availability of disposable income, and access to reasonable or cheap means of transmission may actually help improve social and economic conditions for increased news communication.

There are also noneconomic considerations that affect the spread of news communication. For instance, Knies realizes that increasing rates of communication also imply physical mobility and estrangement in the changing environments of modern societies. He stresses the importance of recognizing specific psychological needs of physically separated individuals, since separation alone does not necessarily meet the conditions for communication. For instance, emigration had brought about an increase in long-distance communication based on family ties or close personal relationships, resulting in an exchange of letters by members of certain social classes, who under normal circumstances would never have resorted to this type of communication. The arrival of letters signals a special event in villages or small towns, and individual residents act as if they had communal rights to share their contents. Similarly, relocating or traveling individuals remain in touch with their communities through letters, although they may return eventually to tell their stories. War experiences, in particular, increase the flow of written communication dramatically.

More generally, Knies suggests that modern civilization is an outcome of ways of life that affected the communication patterns of individuals within and beyond specific cultural or political boundaries to include different nations. For instance, during the Middle Ages people lived relatively isolated lives in their respective communities, often quite removed from outside events. Governments too operated at a distance and in ways seemingly unrelated to the people. With continuing improvements in communication, however, all regions of a nation became interrelated and even inseparable, leading to reconsiderations of individual, independent states as parts of larger and closely connected organizations of states. At that moment, people routinely experience events in distant places and become interested in the fate of other nations.

More important, perhaps, is the effect of information networks on the organization of bureaucracies, especially after international news had become a considerable aspect of information exchanges between governments and their representatives. Also, the centralization of modern government bureaucracies acts as a lever of domestic news communication.

Knies notes the cumulative effect of producing and storing information at each level of government. "Small mountains of official news accumulate from towns to county seats, from county seats to provincial capitals, and from provincial capitals to the capital" (1857, 59). In addition, the modernization of the social and political existence of individuals is accompanied by the need for public information, including the development of innovative forms of disseminating public and private communication. The press, among other institutions, not only relies on these services but establishes a dependency that becomes a potential threat to its freedom.

Knies proposes that the improvement of the postal service, for instance, is in itself an indication of the demand for more communication with other parts of the world. But it also positively affects the dissemination of newspapers. Low postal rates help secure a fast and regular stream of information between correspondents and their editorial offices; regular and far-reaching postal delivery also enables newspapers to rely on reasonable rates and distribution without delay. Knies recognizes the vulnerability of newspaper circulation under these conditions and warns that changes in postal policies pertaining to newspaper delivery could result in serious setbacks for the press. "Besides a real death penalty (i.e., the suppression of a newspaper) there is a milder form, the lifting of postal privileges. We hope that this will never be implemented against a newspaper that has not been forbidden by the state" (1857, 103). The elimination of postal privileges would be regarded a restriction, if not prohibition, of a particular newspaper. Thus the post office emerges as a public institution whose services must be available to every newspaper—not just a few privileged ones. Underlying these concerns is a recognition that purely economic factors—which remain crucial to the survival of the press—are not confined to the relationship between private and public interests but also affect issues of freedom of expression.

Knies pays considerable attention to advertising, since the press turns into the most important vehicle for the transmission of commercial messages; indeed, place and significance of advertisements become major elements in the contemporary discourse about functions of the press in a modern, industrialized society.

Advertisements explain specific circumstances under which commodities are bought or sold; they also stimulate business by suggesting the availability of goods in the marketplace. Knies confirms the role of newspapers in the dissemination of commercial messages by focusing on the idea of knowledge and information as expressions of power. Based on the insights of politics and science that knowledge is power, he adds that " 'knowledge is sales,' according to those who offer material goods, personal services, etc.," and he elaborates that " 'knowledge is production,' according to those who sense a need they cannot satisfy, because they cannot see its source'' (1857, 49).

Knies recognizes the importance of advertising also in the context of supply and demand as guiding free market principles when he addresses production and consumption of industrial commodities in terms of the needs for speedy and inexpensive dissemination of information in an industrial process. In addition, advertisements are also important sources of information about the economic and cultural conditions of society. They are, in fact, the cultural documents of a society that offer valuable insights into the life of communities. Knies proposes that advertisements be used not only by social or cultural historians but also by politicians who want to learn about the conditions of their own localities, towns, or regions. He notes that the advertisements are excellent guides (except in cases where they are restricted) ''to the communication of recognized facts because an advertisement appears naive and not conscious of its power as historical evidence while submitting to contemporary controls'' (1857, 50).

As well as informing potential consumers about supply or demand, advertisements also lead directly to the source of goods and services and therefore save time and effort. Consequently, advertising exposes those who advertise their commodities to the public and frequently enough in competition with others. For Knies, the advertisement ''provokes more competition; whoever participates must be confident to win or possess the goodwill of a target audience on an open battlefield and against competitors'' (1857, 51). At the same time, there is a realization of abuse in competitive situations when advertisements are introduced, especially by those unwilling to submit to fair play and honesty in business transactions. But even under these circumstances, prices remain competitive.

Advertisements stimulate consumption and production, and the effects of commercial communication are considerable and important to an economic system. Knies acknowledges the power of persuasive communication when he describes the exposure to advertisements in everyday life. ''The goods we imagine are as stimulating as a stroll through warehouses and stores when our unwillingness to shop turns into exiting with loaded shopping bags'' (1857, 52). Industrial and commercial interests are quite aware of the impact of advertising, and its effectiveness explains, at least in part, the amount of attention business has paid to advertising and it accounts for huge sums spent on disseminating commercial information.

In addition, the consequences of advertising support for newspapers and magazines are more subtle than immediate financial gains. For instance, ''free'' deliveries of the press or printed materials such as shoppers (based on advertising revenues) raise questions about the real cost of disseminating press products. Knies observes that recent experiments have been conducted "to deliver newspapers and handbills to thousands of customers without charge—relying on advertising revenues," and he wonders how confidence could be raised "by the fact that deliveries were really made to thousands of recipients at no cost" (1857, 52).

Since product and service advertising compete for specific markets and groups of consumers, placement strategies within publications or in different types of media become crucial for business interests. Thus "locally limited purposes can only be served by local newspapers; advertising for worldwide communication, however, can only be meaningful in newspapers with large circulation" (Knies 1857, 53). It is equally important to realize the time constraints of advertisements, since their usefulness or effectiveness may well be limited by seasonal considerations—when certain goods may be in more demand than others—or economic conditions—when financial resources may or may not be available to execute purchasing decisions.

Knies argues that the press shares a basic problem with advertising, namely, the realization of the widest possible distribution with the goal of saturating the market by reaching all relevant segments of the public. However, he also recognizes that readers must pay for their news or share in the cost of gathering it, and he compares the sale of news to other business arrangements. Commodities are regularly sold to an identifiable group of customers, whose routine purchases form the basis for production and marketing decisions. These decisions concerning the printing and circulation of newspapers are also based on the awareness that sheer numbers of subscribers do not significantly raise labor costs. Knies suggests that "even the largest increase in customers raises the total labor and the production costs only by a very small margin, while the expenditure for 100,000 or 100 customers remains the same for the rest" (1857, 60). Consequently, publishers and editorial staffs prefer to operate with the largest possible base of customers, a fact that has invited considerations of forming industrial concerns for fast, cheap, and efficient services and has projected the industrialization of journalism into the twentieth century and beyond.

Knies acknowledges that the transmission of news has become an important business in modern society as well as a career path and a livelihood for many. Journalism evolved into a profession that serves the production of news (and opinion) as short-lived commodities but also feeds on the need for individual recognition, excitement of being involved in the daily affairs of society, and feelings of power and influence. Professional journalism constitutes a practice that rewards individuals mostly with the intellectual satisfaction of personal interests.

Given the pivotal role of journalists in the dissemination of news, it becomes tempting for third persons to pay (regularly or in isolated cases) for obtaining certain news items before they reach the public. Knies notes that the reception and reading of news alone by particular groups of readers can be of tremendous importance to news sources, since news not only describes daily events but may also influence the mood of readers and their decisions.

Journalists play a powerful role in the construction of reality; at the same time, by offering representations of the world, they expose their own ideological perspectives. Knies proposes that the editorial selection process of the press provides clues about how journalists try to manipulate ways of perceiving the environment. Although the most important events of the day can hardly be ignored and omitted, other incidents, however, often receive qualitatively different treatments. Knies observes, "Not only books can receive the 'silent treatment,' but also news that is forgotten sooner or later." Thus news can be presented in a variety of ways and without editorial comment; Knies adds that "all this does not really diminish the truth even when editors follow their own mood without any further reflection" (1857, 61). On the other hand, he expects readers to recognize the different treatment of public events, particularly by a partisan press.

The wide dissemination of news and its potential effects on readers challenge the moral responsibility of those in charge of the press, particularly in times of civil unrest, when public opinion and the influence of the masses are felt by the government. The existence of a party press with its biased reporting of public events makes it even more necessary to insist on a high degree of professional ethics, especially when readers have no access to other sources or refuse to consult them. "The moral responsibility of leaders in news communication can only grow in light of the fact that recipients, subscribers, stay with newspapers of their leanings—in many cases with those of their party. The known one-sidedness makes a balancing reply impossible" (1857, 62).

Although editorial decisions—including definitions of what constitutes matters of public interest—remain in the hands of journalists, the latter depend on the interests of their readers. Thus editors may find it more convenient to yield to public taste and give readers what they want than to follow the dictates of their own taste or intellectual preferences. Yet there is a mutual influence—flowing from readers to newspapers and from journalists to their publics—in every case and even under different cultural circumstances, according to Knies; he admits, however, that obvious differences exist in types and forms of news communication in different countries and during different periods of history—albeit with a shared incipient trend toward homogeneity in news production. Thus Knies can say that "la gazette c'est le peuple, c'est le temps . . . in view of the contrasts between present and past, between German, American,

English, and French newspapers, although powerful and regular worldwide communication has led to some adjustment" (1857, 62–63).

A prerequisite for the dissemination of news is the people's interest in public affairs. Earlier years and the Middle Ages witnessed the isolation of individuals and their communities, which had an unfavorable effect on regular news dissemination. The rise of the modern European state coincided with the rise of the press, and newspapers became important elements in the formulation and perpetuation of public policies and ideologies. Their evolution occurred under culturally distinctive circumstances that dictated attitudes toward the press and affected their content, size, and general treatment as a cultural artifact. For instance, Knies finds that "in England, to read a newspaper belongs to the category of 'necessary expenses' for the manual laborer; in the North American Union there appear more German newspapers than in our beloved fatherland" (1857, 63).

In addition to satisfying particular social or political needs by providing readers with information through daily reports and commentaries, newspapers also help create needs. The state in its modern democratic phase could hardly tolerate citizens who have no interest in public information. By reporting regularly about public life and events of the day, newspapers have become part of the foundation of the state. Knies argues that most countries having large populations spread over wide territories and metropolitan centers of political and cultural life need communication networks to enable individual and collective participation in the affairs of the state. Thus newspapers become the carriers of politically and culturally vital information and the means by which individuals share in the life process of society. Unless newspapers reverse their original roles, they work almost instinctively, aiming to publish information about matters of public importance concerning the state. Times of political and social stress or peace and order produce variations in newspaper circulation and information needs, as newspaper subscriptions either rise or fall. In other words, it is the political that defines and drives the press in its efforts to serve its customers.

The production of newspapers also reflects the prevalent system of developing large-scale enterprises to keep up with a growing economy. Knies sees these changes as a result of increasing sales combined with business strategies to raise production costs and amend current offerings, such as more and improved news services, specialization among reporting staffs, and diversified coverage. For instance, in smaller newspapers world news coverage becomes more selective in response to an extensive foreign news coverage by a larger, metropolitan press, while coverage of community affairs and regional events characterizes the unique position of the local press and remains the primary task of small-town journalism.

But newspaper readers continue to demand other types of information or services. Knies mentions the popularity of the feuilleton in many newspapers—offering novels (in installments), anecdotes, and other feature material—the creation of special sections, and the inclusion of review articles on literary and artistic matters, expertly written editorials, and morning, evening, and extra editions. Following the tastes or preferences of a majority of readers, newspapers include religious news or economic and business reports; elsewhere reader demands lead to the creation of a press that caters exclusively to special interests. Once institutional participation is assured and the prospective readership is large enough, many business enterprises engage in the publication of their own newspapers or journals. Increasing pressures for more or better coverage, according to Knies, are accompanied by the fact that people demand "very much for little money" (1857, 66).

As a result of the modern press system, as well as the increasing need for information services, newspapers confront conditions similar to those faced by any other vendor of commodities. Price increases lead to selective purchases, and regarding newspapers Knies finds that "the higher the price for one copy without increasing its quality appreciably, the smaller the circle of customers must get" (1857, 66). Newspapers, however, need appreciable circulation figures to survive. Indeed, one of the major concerns of newspaper enterprises is the distribution of its products to all segments of society, including low-income groups; consequently, prices must be kept down.

The need for newspapers differs from the need for life-sustaining commodities such as food. Knies refers to cultural or historical differences when newspapers become dispensable or are even unfamiliar to some people, while others welcome them as necessary means of survival. For instance, he speculates that "if an individual reads a newspaper once a week—as he eats meat once a week—it will happen on his day of rest [with a Saturday or Sunday edition]. It is curious to see how much different tastes of readers and the diversity of required spices . . . contain an analogy to the consumption of material food" (1857, 66–67).

Underlying these descriptions of the role and function of newspapers, however, is the fact that news communication remains an ephemeral service. Knies wants his readers to understand that yesterday's newspaper is practically worthless for the daily business of society, although he recognizes the value of newspaper collections as historical documents and sources. He refers to news as a commodity and insists that "it must have a certain intrinsic value. But the intrinsic value alone is not inherent in the object itself; it can only be there if and as long as a human need for news exists" (1857, 67).

Personal relationships between senders and receivers are a crucial point of departure for a theory of news communication, according to Knies, who adds a material element to the definition by suggesting that "all inter-local exchange of commodities tends to be accompanied by news communication, even demands it" (1857, 68).

In earlier times personal contacts with customers, visits to markets in different parts of the world, and attendance at local or regional conventions or fairs were common occurrences. But contemporary conditions require contemporary methods of reaching potential customers. Consequently, newspaper advertising and business correspondence, in particular, become primary means of disseminating product information, availability, and cost, resulting in contacts and sales without face-to-face interaction. This development gains even more importance with the expansion of markets and business connections into distant countries, increasing competition, and fluctuating market prices, which produce additional occasions for exchanging written communication. Knies feels that letters are often more appropriate than conversation for certain types of information, particularly when people prefer unhurried communication; it is in letters rather than speech that they can use the most delicate and also the worst expressions. Letters may be more efficient for business transactions than oral communication because they must be based on firm prior decisions, and they provide documentary evidence concerning any specific decisions (1857, 72).

The arrival of the telegraph introduces a new dimension of public communication—time. It constitutes an important aspect of conducting business because promptness and reliability of a transportation system are crucial for executing transactions. News, in particular, more than most other material goods, thrives under conditions of speed between production and dissemination (or sales).

The telegraph is a technological development that meets conditions of fast and continuous services, not only for newspaper publishers but also for readers, whose information needs are a prerequisite for conducting business and exchanging material goods. Knies describes the capabilities of the telegraph in terms of simultaneous news communication from one specific site to various destinations or vice versa. "This has been made possible, and for the first time, only because the time needed to bridge these distances is = 0" (1857, 243).

Indeed, Knies concludes that the capability of the telegraph surpasses the potential of the human nervous system, since the body operates with a nervous system that differentiates between physical and psychological reactions, whereas the telegraph is used to serve all functions regardless of their content. He notes that "in comparison to our body we must say that the central organ in the network is an ambulatory one. . . . the telegraph must appear to us like the eye and the ear with which regions and countries perceive what is going on in the world." As a result of the telegraph, events are experienced simultaneously around the world, not unlike a single sensation racing through the body. For Knies, the telegraph has "an overpowering strength to unite a compounded social body" (1857, 244).

Although the effectiveness of the telegraph is not always noticeable in the day-to-day operation of news communication, it nevertheless exists and must be taken into account by producers and users of information. Knies suggests that economists, historians, and politicians, in particular, have an obligation to consider the contributions of the telegraph to the cultural, social, and political life of society. They must bear in mind the effect of the telegraph on the lives of millions of people, especially when combined with the realization that news affects the behavior of individuals.

COMMUNICATION AND COMMUNITY

Knies realizes the centrality of communication in society and offers a brief but succinct discussion of its characteristics and potential in the evolution of modernity. His conclusions frequently anticipate late-twentieth-century social scientific findings and qualitative assessments of news or commercial information, including the place of advertising in the context of social and political communication.

Knies argues that the significance of communication arises from a persistent need to perfect the individual's ability to function as a social being. Communication establishes the bounds of community, offers proximity, and empowers the individual in contacts with others. The maturation of the social environment, or the "social organism," according to Knies, coincides with improvements in social communication. The latter includes a system of occupational roles and institutional activities dedicated to the collection and dissemination of information, which constitutes the culmination of a long history of public communication.

Such a history is embedded in an interdependence of the economic and cultural spheres of society; in fact, Knies articulates a modern cultural studies perspective with his insistence on the interdisciplinary nature of inquiries into the state of social communication and advances a methodological perspective that reflects a contemporary approach to qualitative communication research. His discussion of news communication as a means of creating and satisfying individual and collective needs, for instance, or his awareness of the relations between economic status, or class, and participation in social communication resembles current critical concerns of media studies.

At the same time, Knies combines economic insights and a cultural critique in his historical treatment of communication and media systems. He acknowledges the information function of advertising, not unlike the role of news and other information services. But he looks with suspicion on the rise of advertising as an economic necessity of a modern press system, fully aware of the social, cultural, and political consequences of commercial messages for the press itself and for society.

Since newspapers—and media in general—occupy a central position in society, their practices demand close scrutiny, including knowledge about political leanings, uses and misuses of commercial and noncommercial information, and work habits of journalists. Knies realizes the dilemma of newspaper enterprises caught between the economic necessity of advertising revenues and society's need for a source of trustworthy and credible information. Consequently, he argues for the highest standards of education and professional ethics among journalists. But he offers no specific solutions for solving issues of supply and demand or raising professional standards that would help regulate the press and provide socially or politically viable ways of preserving the institution. In fact, the invention of the telegraph with its enormous technical capabilities and its social and political consequences further complicates the conditions of institutional communication. By providing fast and continuous service, the telegraph facilitates almost instantaneously the unification or solidarity of a social system through shared mediated experiences and accessibility to large quantities of information by a society still ill prepared for the onslaught of news. His view of communication technology, however, is not deterministic. Knies presents a remarkably modern perspective on communication by providing the outline of a social or cultural history of communication that contains a contextualizing approach to the impact of new technologies (e.g., the telegraph and the modern press) on the idea of progress. Steeped in organismic notions of society, his theoretical writings privilege a totalizing view of communication as a central element in the life of modern societies.

5

The Linkages of Society: Karl Bücher on Commerce and the Press

INTRODUCING THE STUDY OF JOURNALISM

Karl Bücher's (1847–1930) contribution to the discussion of communication and the role and function of journalism in society occurs in the context of his economic theory of development, his emphasis on exchange as a modern criterion for defining economic phenomena, and his analytical approach to investigations of social and political institutions.

He was born in Kirberg near Wiesbaden, Germany, and attended the universities of Bonn and Göttingen, where he majored in history, political science, and classical philosophy. As a teacher and private lecturer, he gained his early professional experience in Göttingen (1869–1872), Dortmund (1872–1873), and Frankfurt (1873–1878) before he joined the editorial staff of Leopold Sonnemann's famous *Frankfurter Zeitung* as an expert on economic and social policy questions. At that time he had published widely on historical topics, ranging from medieval labor conditions to the position of women in the Middle Ages and medieval tax ordinances, and had started his major work on the organization of guilds in the high Middle Ages.

Bücher resigned from the *Frankfurter Zeitung* after only two years in a dispute over the publisher's attitude toward outside business interests. Unable to secure a similar position elsewhere, he turned to an academic career with the intellectual and financial support of Albert Schäffle. He continued his studies at Munich and subsequently held university appointments as professor of statistics at Dorpat, Russia (1882), political economy and finance at Basel, Switzerland (1883–1890), Karlsruhe (1890–1893), and Leipzig, from which he retired in 1917 after establishing a university-level institute for the study of the press and the education of journalists.

In his economic theory of stages, Bücher describes the advancement of Western society in terms of the role and function of exchange. He identifies three major stages of economic development from antiquity to modern times (when the idea of exchange becomes more pronounced), ending with contemporary society's dependence on an exchange economy. He also argues that human progress can be defined by the way in which production and consumption—as basic social activities—developed into separate functions over time, identified with distinct groups or organizations in society. Transportation and communication become increasingly important in an economic system that is based on the exchange of goods and services to the point where state and private enterprises help develop and maintain communication systems to maximize their efficiency and effectiveness. Thus newspapers and journalism play major roles as carriers of information and become necessary objects of study and research by economists and others interested in the workings of a modern society.

Bücher's contribution to the literature of sociology consists of a treatise on work and rhythm (1909), which traces the relationship between work, play, and the underlying principle of rhythm. He criticizes previous studies that had differentiated among play, sports, body movements, and work as separate types of activities and goes on to describe rhythm as a basic human phenomenon across a wide range of civilizations and stages of human development.

His brief encounter with journalism—including his refusal to compromise his position on newspaper ethics—provides the biographical background for his scholarly interest in the workings of the press and its participation in the social and political life of society. Since he was also concerned about the education of journalists, he offered a course at the University of Basel dealing with the history, organization, and statistics of the press system, arguing that it was extremely important for students planning a public career to have an opportunity for journalism studies in the context of their university curricula. At the same time, he suggested that universities should acknowledge the importance of the press in society by offering appropriate courses on journalism. He restated these ideas later at the University of Leipzig, arguing that it is the duty of the state to provide for the education of editors with public funds, since editors hold positions similar to those of civil servants, while newspapers are like judges, who must make important and difficult decisions every day.

Bücher reiterates Schäffle's theoretical discussions of the press and society, stressing the transportation function of newspapers and their role as links among various segments of society. He sees journalists as moderators and participants who serve leading factions of society in the process of social communication. In his plan of study for educating journalists (Jaeger 1926, 103–6), published in 1916 at the University of Leipzig, Bücher's institute (Institut für Zeitungskunde) is identified as a coordinating center for various academic disciplines with unique course offerings in newspaper-oriented topics and research. The publication mentions specializations in political, business, and literary journalism, describes the existence of several historical, statistical, and contemporary affairs courses regarding the press, and concludes that the creation of the institute expresses the belief (of the University of Leipzig) that newspaper journalism as a profession must be ranked alongside theology, law, education, and medicine.

Earlier Bücher had asked members of the International Statistical Institute to consider compiling a statistical work on political newspapers in individual countries. His recommendations were accepted during the eleventh meeting of the organization in Copenhagen (1907) with a plan to collect information about the national and local density of newspaper units, circulation, regularity of publication, subscription, and advertising rates (Bücher 1908). He had already completed similar statistical accounts for Germany at Leipzig together with his students, among them Hjalmar Schacht, who completed a statistical analysis of the German press (Muser 1918). In addition, the events of World War I provided new incentives for the study of the press and propaganda.

Bücher places the study of newspapers in the context of a historical treatment of the growth of civilization and the development of cultural and social institutions. He does not want to establish a separate "discipline" of journalism but tries to suggest the need for cultural historians and economists to learn more about the press. He singles out the role and function of advertising and statistical compilations of newspaper practices as examples of information that forms the basis for an understanding of press systems and their location in society. His lecture courses at Basel and Leipzig were designed to provide knowledge rather than initiate a new science of the press. He observes that "the sociological study of newspaper journalism, which has hardly begun, may furnish the building blocks for such a science; but we are still a long distance away from that point today" (1915, 67).

Bücher actually supplements Schäffle's work by adding his own systematic, historical study of newspapers as social institutions to Schäffle's theoretical claims. He applies his knowledge of statistics to the treatment of the press as a vehicle of societal communication while maintaining the perspective of a professional economist and economic historian. He had addressed the problems of journalism in modern industrial societies rather early in his career, beginning with a collection of essays entitled *Die Entstehung der Volkswirtschaft* (1893), which contains a hitherto unpublished paper, "Genesis of Journalism," in which the author traces the development of journalism and its contribution to contemporary society (1901, English edition).

Commenting on the lack of scholarly attention paid to press studies, Bücher offers multiple perspectives by noting that journalism could be studied "from the standpoint of political history, literary history, bibliography, law, and even philosophy" (1901, 215). But he adds that political economists should find the study of journalism most directly related to their concerns, since newspapers as commercial entities must maintain important societal functions identified with economic activities.

TECHNOLOGIES OF COMMUNICATION

Bücher ranks newspapers—together with postal services, railroads, and the telegraph—among the technological means of society that connect and draw its members closer together. Accordingly, he notes that

> the newspaper forms a link in the chain of modern commercial machinery. . . . Yet it is not an instrument of commercial intercourse in the sense of the post or the railway, both of which have to do with the transport of persons, goods, and news, but rather in the sense of the letter and circular. These make the news capable of transport, only because they are enabled by the help of writing and printing to cut it adrift, as it were, from its originator, and give it corporeal independence. (1901, 216)

Bücher distinguishes between letters and newspapers as means of private and public communication, adding that the publication of newspapers presupposes some common interests in information about public affairs or commercial and trade activities. The latter are based on a political organization of the people, or what he describes as a "certain community of life interest" (1901, 217). Given expanding political and commercial interests, increasing travel, and a rising curiosity about the world in general, newspapers appear to serve information needs that in earlier times were quite unnecessary, since they could be satisfied by oral communication or written messages. Bücher explains that circulating written materials became necessary only after Roman supremacy "had embraced or subjected to its influence all the countries of the Mediterranean" and "members of the ruling class who had gone to the provinces as officials, tax-farmers, and in other occupations, might receive the current news of the capital" (1901, 218). He also suggests that "Caesar, the creator of the military monarchy and the administrative centralization of Rome, is regarded as the founder of the first contrivance resembling a newspaper."

In fact, Bücher traces the development of news communication through the ages, from organized information services in the twelfth and thirteenth centuries to publications with limited numbers of readers throughout the next 400 to 500 years, until the age of technology with rapid transmission capacities for the widespread circulation of news and information. During this evolutionary process, organizing and handling the collection and transmission of information resembled the existing system of commercial exchanges and trade centers. Newspaper writing and the collection of news were often practiced by large traders in Germany and Italy, for instance. Bücher notes the relations between wholesale trade and newspapers. "Like the Nuremburg merchants . . . some large trading houses in other localities had also organized an independent news service. Especially prominent were the Welsers and Fuggers" (1901, 230). Their newspapers regularly featured news from all parts of Europe, the Middle East, and places such as Persia, China, Japan, and America, consisting of political information. But they frequently reported about harvests, noted prices, and sometimes also contained advertisements and long listings of Austrian firms with information about how and where merchandise could be procured in Vienna.

Discussing the relationship between written news sheets and printing technology, Bücher reports that the production of written news sheets as a business could not be traced beyond the invention of the printing press; he insists that the widespread use of written news sheets was not a result of particular censorship pressures, but rather an answer to the economic question of finding "sufficiently large circles of readers to guarantee the sale necessary to meet the cost of printing" (1901, 238). With the end of the sixteenth century, the development of the press underwent radical changes, based, according to Bücher,

> on the separation of news collection from news dispatch (post), and on the commercial organization of the former into correspondence bureaus and telegraph agencies. To the telegraph agencies have fallen the duties of the earlier postmasters and news-scribes, but with this difference, that they no longer labour directly for the newspaper readers, but supply the publishing house with half-finished wares, making use in such work of the perfected commercial machinery of modern times. (1901, 239)

These changes are accompanied by a change in the role and function of publishers, whose duties go beyond supervising the production and sale of particular products, because news—unlike books or pamphlets—does not form one single theme or subject matter. Instead, "news-items were brought together, taken from different sources, were of varying reliability. They needed to be used judicially and critically: in this a political or religious bias could find ready expression'' (Bücher 1901, 239). The process continues and intensifies with the rise of political consciousness, the establishment of political parties, and the beginnings of a party press in Europe. Newspapers become instruments that support or shape public opinion, and Bücher sees the rise of editors as a result of these influences, while newspaper publishers now became dealers ''in public opinion as well'' (1901, 240). Throughout these periods of change, however, readers remain powerful determinants of newspaper content.

The introduction of advertisements complicates the public service features of newspapers. For Bücher, this means that private interests and trade provide the press with opportunities to sell its readers to those willing to pay for advertising space. He observes that ''in the same paper, often on the same page, where the highest interests of mankind are, or at least should be represented, buyers and sellers ply their vocations in ignoble greed of gain. For the uninitiated it is often difficult to distinguish where the interests of the public cease and private interests begin'' (1901, 241).

Looking at the modern newspaper as it presents itself to society, Bücher calls it a ''capitalistic enterprise, a sort of news-factory in which a great number of people . . . are employed on wage, under a single administration, at very specialized work'' (1901, 242). Instead, he emphasizes the complexity of the modern press and the problems of mass circulation and competition in the marketplace that determine the type and quality of news. ''The simple needs of the reader or the circle of patrons no longer determine the quality of these wares; it is now the very complicated conditions of competition in the publication market.'' Under these circumstances, consumers, or newspaper readers specifically, ''take no direct part; the determining factors are the wholesale dealer and the speculators in news: the governments, the telegraph bureaux dependent upon their special correspondents, the political parties, artistic and scientific clique . . . and last but not least, the advertising agencies and large individual advertisers'' (1901, 242–43).

Bücher elaborates on the economic production aspects of newspapers in the context of discussing the collision of intellectual labor and capitalism. He expresses doubts about the commercial press as supplier of news when he suggests that

> each number of a great journal which appears to-day is a marvel of economic division of labour, capitalistic organization, and mechanical technique; it is an instrument of intellectual and economic intercourse, in which the potencies of all other instruments of commerce—the railway, the post, the tele-

> graph, and the telephone—are united as in a focus. But our eyes can linger with satisfaction on no spot where capitalism comes into contact with intellectual life; and so we can take but half-hearted pleasure in this acquisition of modern civilization. (1901, 242–43)

He concludes that it is difficult to believe that the newspaper in its present form of development constitutes the final answer to the need for news.

A few years later, Bücher renews his discussion of newspapers when he addresses the role and function of the modern press in a collection of articles on the press (1926). He summarizes the historical developments of newspapers and suggests that they are cultural phenomena which arose from the social, political, and economic needs of societies to unite segments of the population distributed over large areas, share common interests in events outside national or social and cultural boundaries, and maintain and establish new social and economic relationships. Despite different types of newspapers—including a mass-circulation or party press—these newspapers share common economic features as enterprises, "which produced advertising space as a commodity that could only be sold because of an existing editorial section" (1926, 21). This characterization of the press emphasizes the overriding economic interests that had changed newspapers into business-oriented, commercial actors.

One of the noticeable trends in newspapering during the nineteenth century is the expansion of news coverage, with increasing editorial attention paid to all spheres of social life. Consequently, the output of news creates more interest among readers; according to Bücher, " 'wer vieles bringt, wird manchem etwas bringen' " (who offers much will offer something to many a person) becomes a motto of the press (1926, 21). It also characterizes a practice that resulted in more subscribers, more advertisers, and, ultimately, in the rise of independent, mass-circulation newspapers. The latter constitute a national threat, according to Bücher, because their "far-reaching influence makes them profitable objects of political, literary, and speculative-financial corruption, and a favorite hiding place for open or veiled advertising" (1926, 52).

He also criticizes developments in other European countries and implies that expansions in Germany were neither unique nor more alarming than those abroad. Thus the rise of newspaper monopolies and the domination of major news agencies by a few industrial interests are the result of modern technologies. On the other hand, he also notes the democratizing effects of technological progress on culture and suggests that "modern means of communication—especially the telephone, wire services, and correspondence bureaus—support this development which, without doubt, works to the advantage of maintaining depth and diversity of the national culture while also preventing the rise of an all too powerful press oligarchy" (1926, 52).

Despite the growth of the press and its expanding overage, Bücher feels that its effects as a cultural messenger are limited and of rather secondary importance. He follows Schäffle's ideas and reconstructs the press as a conduit—a transmission belt—between the intellectual currents of the people and their leaders. There are differences, however. During earlier times, newspapers provided these services for respective authorities. Later they perform a similar task to satisfy intellectual demands, and most recently the press exerts political and social influence in the form of political propaganda. Bücher places the work of editors and journalists in the context of larger cultural, social, and political forces in society and sees a limited role for journalism in actually making intellectual or creative contributions to society. In fact, the

> active, leading elements from which those currents flow are found outside and not inside the press. Editors and contributors do not fit into an independent, creative, and leading role. They are organs of adaption. . . . Their work is primarily one of molding ideas. They forge the metal—which is discovered by the creative, intellectual work in politics, science, arts, and technology—into small coins for circulation. They disperse intellectual impulses—which emanate from political and cultural centers—among the masses and collect their reactions to return them to the centers of intellectual movements. (1926, 53)

In describing these editorial processes and the role and function of journalists, Bücher implicitly presents his ideas concerning public opinion. In fact, the press is an organ of public opinion and is involved in collecting and formulating ideas that originate with the people. At the same time, he acknowledges the possibility of newspaper influences on public opinion. For instance, the press may be used to publicize individual or institutional judgments or ideas as reflections of mass sentiments in the public sphere. "A well-known trick of demagogy consists of presenting subjective ideas and special interests as ideas and interests of the people" (1926, 53).

It would be incorrect, however, to assume that the press creates public opinion. Bücher differentiates between existing general sentiments and ideas that are always alive in society, and emerging dispositions based on particular events. In the latter case, people's opinions become "public" with their appearance in newspapers. Indeed, newspaper coverage often amplifies those opinions because journalists succeed in formulating and expressing them most effectively. It is the ability to detect and describe the moods and opinions of the people that marks the success of the press.

Bücher stresses the importance of mass appeals in modern society and the need to capture the imagination of the masses in ways that assure the stability of the economic, social, and political system. Although he recognizes the importance and effectiveness of face-to-face communication, Bücher remains convinced that the press—with its built-in capability of reaching the masses regularly and repeatedly with the same messages containing the same ideas and suggestions—is more effective and that its effects are longer lasting than any other form of communication. As a result of massive and regular coverage of public events, editorial opinions, and critical judgments, readers begin to see newspaper stories as reflections of their own impressions of the world. But the emphasis on timeliness and competition for supplying news and opinion among daily newspapers prevent most readers from drawing their own conclusions. The construction of news is a highly subjective, biased task involving journalists and editors, and—as Bücher explains—the reader "has no time to form his own judgment, compare it with an independent judgment, and correct his own. Everything is predigested for him; news is mixed with judgments, opinions, and feelings in each column, and each small item in the newspaper. . . . Finally, a view presented by one or a few members of the press turns into a common view, a moral opinion into mass morality" (1926, 55).

Despite increasing education and the spread of knowledge, Bücher feels that the masses remain incapable of making critical judgments concerning daily press coverage; on the contrary, they follow newspaper leadership blindly, thus expressing confidence in the press. Under these circumstances, the press has to realize the great danger of misleading the masses. The modern newspaper as a business enterprise with substantial financial investment, in particular, provides opportunities for profit-oriented publishers to sell out to special interests or political parties. In fact, it may be impossible for the press to resist financial and business interests that typically operate through their involvement in the business and advertising sections of newspapers.

On the other hand, Bücher recognizes and describes positive aspects of the press related to the accumulation of enormous amounts of cultural and social information that may help bring nations closer together through mediated participation in various aspects of societal life. Ideas and events become objects of a shared experience and contribute to creating a common spirit. "The fact is that newspapers attract everything that lends itself to arousing public interest, maintains and stimulates culture" (1926, 57). At the same time, there is danger in the effectiveness and efficiency of the press as an interpreter of foreign customs and ideas. Bücher warns that the press could easily be used to aid special interest groups with hostile propaganda and defamation of national character. For instance, in an article written at the outset of World War I, he describes these dangers more closely when he attacks the power of news agencies, in particular. Referring to damage caused by the publication of one-sided materials over longer periods of time, Bücher calls these assaults more vicious and serious than any battlefield attack. Large news agencies with global connections have access to many newspapers; when their news dispatches are reprinted without criticism by most newspapers, they contribute to the spread of public opinion. The activities of wire services frequently promote a first impression and consequently create a homogeneous image of the world.

Bücher notes that the "men who sit at the controls of the far-reaching press apparatus know only too well how critical the first impression of telegraphic news transmission is. They don't have to report falsehoods; in the manner in which they suppress disagreeable events and report whatever is favorable to them one finds a continuing influence on public opinion in favor of their employers and against us" (1915a, 13). Consequently, Bücher argues, international news agencies prepared the way for disseminating lies and distortions that contributed to a general atmosphere of distrust. He criticizes press systems everywhere for having neglected their duties to serve the truth and fight attempts to manipulate news coverage through censorship or monopoly ownership.

Since the press is always forced to reduce the contents of ideas and feelings for its readers to a common level of understanding, the danger of superficiality as a by-product of the modern press and contemporary life will always exist. Bücher observes a new generation, "which tastes everything but enjoys nothing in a leisurely way," and concludes that "a general intellectual lethargy prevails that cannot be forced to be alert by even the most powerful typographical means (such as sensational headlines)" (1926, 57). Consequently, it comes as no surprise that newspaper reading finally becomes a business; Bücher refers to clipping services used by politicians and others as early as 1870 in England, and later in France and Germany. The steady demand for these services led to the establishment of an industry with branches across Europe.

As a scholar and historian, Bücher recognizes the importance of newspapers as sources of information and argues that the press constitutes perhaps the most important source for future historians, who would extract—with care and understanding—a sense of the cultural currents of the times quite accurately and minutely from old newspapers. Although archives and collections have been established in several countries, Bücher also asks that each country designate one location for the collection and storage of complete sets of newspapers, particularly because the press is a source of life-long education. Newspapers, according to Bücher—although time-consuming to read, competing against books, and overflowing with information—constitute the only reading material for many individuals. There is "a large segment of the population that would have no opportunity to read without a newspaper," and he refers to "those subscribers of local newspapers, who will be enabled to participate—in a modest way to be sure—in a cultural exchange, and be lifted above the drab routines of work and a marginal existence by the newspaper that guides them to discover events around them and expands their vision" (1926, 59).

Bücher recognizes specific disadvantages that come with the introduction of a new (mass) medium and its widespread use at the expense of earlier, traditional methods of information seeking or entertainment. For instance, the more educated members of society could be prevented from reading other materials, notably books and magazines, because of the amount of daily information offered by the press. Consequently, magazines, in an effort to compete against the daily press for current information, begin publishing more frequently (e.g., offering monthly instead of quarterly and finally weekly editions) with more information and more articles competing for the same space. Scholarly publications, too, are affected by these developments, and monographs are increasingly replacing book-length publications. He anticipates that "the book as a form of publication will be preserved only in the compendium, the textbook, the encyclopedia, and similar aids for scholarly education and professional work" (1926, 60). There is a similar trend in fictional literature, where magazines and newspapers also replace the book. Newspapers often act as midwives for publishers who even waive prepublication rights for the press to run chapters or sections of books before they are available in print. Together with publicity pieces composed by publishing houses, they constitute the basis for much of what readers would ever know about these books. Thus book reviewers act as agents for publishing houses and perform tasks that complement the work of clipping services when they "assume the professional task of reading books for the public and furnishing extracts—the shorter the better" (1926, 61).

The reason for most of these observations and predictions, however, is Bücher's interest in the economic conditions of society and the ways in which the press contributes to the welfare of society and the maintenance of the economic system. As a conduit, newspapers organize the stream of information into intelligible parts that contribute to up-to-date knowledge about the world and provide the basis for political and economic decision-making processes. Bücher is convinced that all kinds of information, besides purely economic or business-related news, help create the necessary understanding for engaging in the reality of day-to-day practices. Thus science, technology, and politics are equally important sources for news coverage, along with stock market trends or industrial growth.

Finally, there is the need for advertising, a "child of the capitalistic age" (1926, 61), which supports the quantity and diversity of social communication offered by the press. Bücher admits that only advertising revenues enable publishers to improve their products and reduce their prices. While recognizing the dangers of subversion by economic interests, Bücher submits that historical conditions have helped merge demands for news and information with demands for access to potential customers and subsequently produced advertising columns:

> One can always admit that the fantastic organization of political and economic news services could not have been accomplished without the rich resources of the advertising section, and that our newspapers would be less abundant, less educational, not as cheap and, therefore, less widely circulated without it. . . . The historical reality of combined public and private communication can hardly be changed, it does have the advantage of economic expediency. (1912, 530)

A few years later, when Bücher confronts the question of press reforms in a number of publications, he maintains that editorial and advertising matters warrant separate consideration because of their different functions. He argues that newspapers serve public interests in their news coverage but private interests in their advertising columns, and he repeats his suggestion that editorial contributions serve to make space more attractive to advertisers. Indeed, he concludes that "the editorial section is an annoying, expensive element of the organization, and it is carried only because without it, there would be no subscribers and therefore no advertisers. 'Public interests' are addressed by newspapers only insofar as they do not obstruct the profit motives of publishers" (1922, 12).

The dilemma of the press had been the subject of discussion and reform movements before. Karl Marx once proclaimed that the first freedom of the press is not to be a business, and others, including Albert Schäffle or Karl Knies, recognized the shortcomings of an emerging mass-circulation press without effective controls to protect the interest of people in a free and open flow of communication. On the other side of the Atlantic, Walter Lippmann (1920, 1922, 1925) had begun to write about the press and public opinion in light of the increasing role of journalism in the construction of social and political realities and the rising perplexity of the public vis-à-vis the complexities of a modern life.

In an article about the future of Germany's press, Bücher mentions the possibility of treating the press legally as a public utility (not unlike the railroads, another important transportation link in society), with the goal of nationalizing newspapers to achieve a clear separation from business interests. Later, he also develops a plan for creating community-controlled advertising sheets, which would contain entertainment, some news, and other features and be distributed without cost to households.

Bücher's suggestions echo Ferdinand Lasalle's call for separating the information and advertising functions of newspapers. In the context of his political commitment, Lasalle had advocated that advertising be located in federal or communal registers or gazettes, since the corruption of the liberal press resulted from its involvement with advertisers. He explains the need for a separation of these functions by suggesting that

> as far as the press represents intellectual interests, it may be compared to a public speaker or preacher. . . . as far as it carries advertising, it is a public announcer. . . . In a social-democratic state there must be a law that prohibits the publication of any advertisement by a newspaper and assigns advertisements to official gazettes published by the state or by communities. (1930, 335)

Along similar lines, Bücher develops his argument that capitalism had successfully organized intellectual energies to produce newspapers that could be exploited for commercial gain. The effects on social and cultural aspects of life would be eliminated by a system of communal advertising gazettes. Bücher uses the analogy of transportation as a general interest of society to explain that "advertising is a creation of transportation, like the postal service, telephone, and railroads, and cannot be left in the hands of private concerns." Thus he concludes that the "transfer of advertising to operate under public administration follows considerations similar to those of the last generation in connection with the nationalization of the railroads: it intends to protect the general interest, which is tied to transportation" (Groth 1948, 291–92).

Although none of these plans succeeded and questions of "socializing" or nationalizing the press were soon dropped, Bücher had still hoped that his proposals would help create a more responsible while economically healthy press. Specifically, he had drafted a bill for consideration by the Bavarian legislature that would have set up and maintained an official community press, based on the observation that since the German press was basically local, advertising and official announcements would provide a solid economic foundation for a community-oriented press system.[1]

He explains his intention of creating an advertising monopoly for the benefit of counties rather than the state government, consistent with the observation that most advertising in the German press is based on a local choice for its placement. At the same time, regional and national advertising could be continued in special publications; in no case would the political press be allowed to carry advertising, however. Size of the circulation and frequency of publication were to be determined by the size of the county. Bücher envisions the free distribution of these publications. Realizing that readership of a newspaper carrying only advertising and official announcements would be low, he adds an editorial section, divided between news agency and feature materials, and designed to educate and entertain readers. To reduce production costs, editorial sections would be assembled centrally and delivered to newspapers in the form of boilerplate. For a set fee these newspapers could reprint announcements from other newspapers, whereas announcements originating in their own counties would be carried free of charge.

Aware of the consequences for a privately owned press, Bücher suggests that such newspapers would compete with official newspapers for local information and feature materials; in addition, they could carry more news and add their political components to the presentation of information. Although privately owned newspapers would be significantly more expensive than they were before the reorganization of the press, Bücher feels that the few wanting to continue reading them would also be able to afford the higher prices. His proposal effectively establishes a separation between information-rich and information-poor citizens and reflects a condition achieved two generations later under the excesses of late capitalism.

Transportation and transmission of information are social and cultural forms created by society, and Bücher's proposal is designed to maximize these forms of communication for the benefit of the general public. Thus he expresses less concern for private enterprise and the profit motives of newspaper publishers than for the establishment of an independent forum to serve the best interests of local communities. Accordingly, he argues that the

> county would gain control over its own areas, like public streets and water systems. The state would have the opportunity to achieve the best for informing and instructing the population, which would breathe a sigh of relief if it could be freed from the pressures of a sensational and business-oriented press. What is new in the world would be communicated to the poorest households day after day; in addition, advertisements would acquaint them with what could become economically useful, and their curiosity concerning local events would not remain unsatisfied. . . . It is obvious that whatever remains of the contemporary newspaper press would gain a new basis. Freed from the pressure of the business interests of the publisher, editorial staffs would represent their own convictions and have no other goal but to serve the common good. (1926, 426–27)

The result is an idealistic picture of the relations between media and society, or the purpose of news consumption, that ignores the attraction of entertainment and the power of sharing the mediated realities of news and advertising—even at the beginning of the twentieth century.

But press reform also addresses the role and function of journalists. Bücher's observations about editorial labor are influenced by the conditions of news work during World War I and the potential for societal growth at the end of the conflict. He comments on the war's impact on newspapers, which are also central agents in the development of a modern, postwar society. Thus "the great upheaval of social values as a result of this war cannot go unnoticed, especially not by the daily press. With the tremendous influence it gained on the intellectual life of peoples, the press becomes a measure of their culture and a criterion for the development of future goals" (1915b, 106).

Journalists play a major part in shaping the press. Although Bücher often defines their work as a messenger service between societal leaders and their followers, he does not underestimate the intellectual status of journalists and the importance of their professional role. "One cannot think highly enough of the work of the genuine journalist. Such an abundance of judgment, available knowledge, experience and political tact, presence of mind and humor, creative talent and word usage utilized each day by the press of a country would be difficult to measure" (1926, 62). At the same time, he realizes that journalists often abandon careers as authors and writers and waste their talents in exchange for the privilege of remaining in constant communication with large numbers of readers. There is social and political power and the potential of influence connected with their positions and the ever present danger of abuse.

According to Bücher, journalists occupy a function between civil servants and businesspeople. With the former they share "the necessity for a comprehensive education without respect for the position with its built-in influence, title, and social status." With the latter they are "incorporated into a capitalistic enterprise without participating directly in its profit and success" (1926, 147). But he also differentiates between professional journalists employed by large newspapers and others, whose work is mainly confined to the small-town press. Among intellectually and morally qualified editors and those with editorial positions on smaller newspapers are many who depend on the interests of their publishers. Since journalists are not licensed, and their profession is not regulated, they are subject to external and internal manipulation and control. Bücher observes that while "no one would want to change this situation . . . one must not overlook the dangers caused by this condition. This means, then, closing both eyes when talking about the profession of journalists and obtaining special rights; of course, they are useless because the good ones don't need them anyway, and they cannot be granted to the others because of the danger of abuse" (1926, 143).

He sharply attacks the wide practice of anonymous contributions with their negative effects on the moral and intellectual climate in newspapers—including the dependence of journalists on their publishers—and argues for more signed articles, to help identify good journalists who could assemble their own circles of readers and move into independent and critical positions on their editorial staffs.

Specifically, the question of anonymity (i.e., identification and publicness of writers and their work) is tied to issues of professional integrity and freedom of the press. Bücher offers a historical review of the principles of anonymous journalism that "advanced across the continent from England and gained ground with the spread of representative government everywhere" (1926, 110). These principles were based on the argument that the press represents an anonymous public opinion and must communicate ideas in the same manner. Questions of press freedom and anonymity are not contradictory but constitute necessary and related issues. The opposite would be true only in a social system in which an individual's right of free expression or freedom of the press conveys a duty to publicly stand behind one's statements (Groth 1930, 4:185).

Bücher argues that the trend toward anonymity in the process of public communication also supports inaccuracy, carelessness, and perhaps irresponsibility in the act of writing. Consequently, anonymity easily breeds a kind of journalism that will not be respected by its readers. Furthermore, "anonymity must lead necessarily to a superficial, uncritical treatment that will attempt to hide the lack of expertise behind the use of slogans and invite frivolous demagoguery, ignorant criticism, after the fact, and flippant, personally offensive polemics" (Groth 1930, 4:190).

Bücher is convinced of the negative aspects that accompany the use of anonymous articles in the press, but he agrees that exceptional circumstances may warrant an anonymous approach to news writing. More specifically, "news and explanations, whose sources or mediators have justified reasons to remain hidden, need not be excluded entirely. They would be able to continue appearing under the responsibility of the managing editor (and not a straw man), but be limited to exceptional cases in which the existence of a higher public interest in publication should be demonstrated together with the fact that it could not be done in any other way" (1926, 159).

Bücher observes the increasing amount of impersonal news dispatches and warns against the dangers of sinking to a level of mediocrity that cannot be in the best interest of journalism and its public. At the same time, he raises the professional consciousness of journalists by reminding them of their public position and the specific responsibilities that come with news work. He summarizes these ideas related to journalistic ethics in his memoirs, concluding, "There must never be a lack of awareness of speaking to a large circle of readers and of being responsible for their thought and desire in public matters" (1919, 231).

His statement reflects a belief in the professional freedom and intellectual integrity of journalists as basic conditions for the exercise of journalistic duties amid constant threats to the development of professional responsibilities. His comments are made in the context of real or imagined economic pressures to convert newspapers into mass production enterprises that compile and package information for public consumption, while journalists, joining these organizations, quickly become minor functionaries in a commercial system. His description of joining an editorial staff reflects the alienation of news work and the fate of news workers as industrial labor. Bücher notes that it is

> like entering a lion's den: many tracks lead into it, none of them leads out of it. The talent and competence of an editor is known to the publisher, and his professional fate continues to depend on him. He has no opportunity to distinguish himself: day after day his intellectual work disappears in the anonymous pulp of news content. He slaves with his pen like the cottager with hoe or sickle for the powerful squire. There is no advancement for him; and when he loses his position, he is lucky if he is allowed to start again someplace else. (1926, 146)

Bücher also realizes that there are no laws or regulations that protect individual journalists, except their own ability to resist internal and external influences and their own moral code. Journalism is not a calling for the weak or undetermined and not a course of action for just anyone, "especially not for those with weak characters, for individuals who can maintain their internal balance only in a secure, professional situation." The continued pressures of daily routines destroyed many journalists, and Bücher adds that, surprisingly, "despite all of it, this class embraces a very large number of valuable and unique individuals, which outsiders would not guess easily" (Groth 1930, 1:147).

Bücher does not support demands for regulating entry into the profession, however. Based on the peculiar economic circumstances of newspapers in Germany, he feels that any attempt to develop a system of qualifications would fail in light of the diversity of types and economic conditions of the press. Instead, he strongly believes in a sound education for journalists and relates experiences of former colleagues, whose university education did not prepare them adequately for newspaper careers. They had argued that reporting and editing can be learned, to some degree, in laboratory situations and suggested that courses dealing with the history, organization, and contemporary problems of the press will help students focus on the prospects of engaging in news work after graduation.

Initially, however, Bücher is less passionate about creating a university-level program of journalistic studies, especially after observing such programs in Switzerland and the United States. He is sure that an attempt to introduce journalism as a science would be met with skepticism, if not hostility, by the academic community, simply because journalism is not a science. Instead, the education of journalists could be accomplished only in connection with established university disciplines, leading to an integrative, multidisciplinary approach to news work that recognizes and reflects the many facets of professional involvement in the affairs of society. He concludes that

> indeed, there is no such science. One may treat the history of newspapers as part of a general history of culture. One could organize facts about the organization and technology of the contemporary press. The political economist must try and understand the position of advertising in modern-day economics, and newspaper statistics cannot be ignored by cultural statisticians. But to construct a special science of journalism out of these elements that satisfies demands for the unity of such a science is unnecessary and impossible. (1915a, 66–67)

Still, when he develops a curriculum for journalism education at the University of Leipzig—where an institute becomes the center of his experimental program—it is based on the idea that a combination of existing courses of study in the social and natural sciences and journalism (*Zeitungskunde*) would be sufficient for preparing future journalists. Subsequently, Bücher organizes a catalogue of courses for students who want to specialize in political, business, or literary journalism from available lectures and seminars. In addition, he institutes a foundation course and adds several specialized courses to introduce students to the details of news work. Specifically, the foundation course is designed to acquaint students with relevant source materials, the workings of the press system, and a scientific treatment of the modern press, while specialized courses dealing with news work are to be conducted by practitioners. Bücher prefers the employment of practicing journalists because "with quick changes in newspaper technology, only individuals who benefit from immediate daily experiences can teach useful aspects, while my own, older observations together with my scientific studies may be sufficient to organize the main course" (1915a, 68).

A plan of studies, issued by the University of Leipzig in 1916, for instance, states that students of journalism need a three-year, university-level education whose details are to be determined by their specializations. The extensive curriculum reflects Bücher's own interests and education in history and political economy. Thus the requirements for political journalists read like a comprehensive social science course.[2]

Despite Bücher's success as an organizer and a defender of the professional education of journalists within a university setting and as an investigator of press practices, his major contribution is in locating journalism within political economy. Thus his discussions of journalism and the press must be seen as part of a much broader attempt to explain the development of economic systems, such as the rise of national economy with its growth of production and the creation of physical and political conditions that improve communication among people and result in the establishment of a press system (1924, 14).

He notes that commercial communication had been highly developed in primitive economic systems and could be identified with the beginning of any economic history. He adds that this type of communication had "enjoyed the fullest development that we would naturally associate only with the highest culture, namely, the communication of news. It forms indeed the . . . kind of trade for which primitive peoples have created permanent organizations. We refer to the courier service and the contrivances for sending verbal messages" (1901, 77). Bücher, like Schäffle and Knies, returns to the significance of understanding symbolic communication and describes the elaborate system of creating symbols, signs, and the means for transmitting intelligence in a number of primitive societies.

A related concept that is central to the study of human evolution is mobility; indeed, migration provides a key to explaining social, economic, and cultural histories. For instance, cultural advancement is closely tied to "a new period of wandering," and Bücher describes the nomadic nature of early agriculture, early trade, and even early industry "that free themselves from household husbandry and become the special occupations of separate individuals and are carried itinerantly." Likewise, he notes that "the great founders of religion, the earliest poets and philosophers, the musicians and actors of past epochs are all great wanderers," and he suggests that even today, "the inventor, the preacher of a new doctrine, and the virtuosi travel from place to place in search of adherents and admirers—notwithstanding the immense recent development in the means of communicating information" (1901, 347).

With the continued advancement of society, producers of goods become stationary, however. "The Thespian carts and the resident theater mark the starting and the terminal points of this evolution" (1901, 348). When the amount of fixed capital grows, it affects the conditions for economic development. In recognizing "capital as the creative influence in a modern national economy" (1901, 310), Bücher addresses the importance of the entrepreneur who sets agendas and directs consumption in modern society. In fact, Bücher anticipates the rise of a consumer society from market conditions and under the reign of commercial interests; accordingly, the contemporary "entrepreneur determines what we shall eat and drink, read in the papers and see at the theater, how we shall lodge and dress. That means everything. For a great part of the goods we consume, the right of self-determining is taken away. And since uniform production on a large scale is most advantageous to the manufacturer, there is operative in the sphere of consumption an increasingly active process of uniformization" (1901, 310). His comments imply the total determination of physical and intellectual needs and their satisfaction by an economic system and suggest the need for effective means of persuasion.

In fact, the idea of advertising emerges from these conditions of entrepreneurial control and occupy a central position in Bücher's discussion of the role and function of the press, including the contributions of journalists to what he basically considers a commercial enterprise. Bücher notes, in passing, that the social sciences so far had neglected advertising as a modern phenomenon, and he reports about the efforts of the German Foreign Office to collect samples of advertising messages from many countries to provide valuable raw research data.

For Bücher, advertising is a tool that constitutes a social selection process through which individuals seek to become successful, while camouflaging their real intentions with suggestions that their efforts will benefit the general public. He states quite emphatically that deception is part of the definition. For instance, he describes attempts to present advertising messages in the form of news stories, since the latter easily convey the impression of being trustworthy editorial matter. He excludes display advertising and other matters clearly identified as advertisements, however, and notes similarities between advertising and propaganda, although their goals differ significantly. "Propaganda wants to recruit followers for an idea or institution but precludes efforts to obtain material gains. Advertising, on the other hand, always serves to obtain customers and, through them, an increase in profits" (1926, 243).

Focusing on the notion of "customer," Bücher traces advertising from the economic conditions of the Middle Ages—where it rested in the personal relationship between producers and consumers—to modern times. The early period is characterized by its emphasis on the "production" of customers, which continues until the liberation of trade and commerce, when the era of production separates customers from producers and demands a new form of communication through which both parties can meet to satisfy their respective needs. Later—and throughout the current age of mass production—producers are separated from consumers by distributors, individual sales outlets, and the triumph of retail trade. However, the loss of personal ties results in a loss of moral responsibility, which had also characterized the relationship between production and consumption before it disappeared from the marketplace.

Advertising becomes fully recognized as a means of communication when other means of distributing goods remain insufficient. Bücher systematizes the study of advertising based on five categories: retail sales, outdoor, indoor, newspaper, and demonstration. He considers (under each of these headings and in succession) store customs of marking sales items, newspaper advertisements in all kinds of print publications, and live demonstrations of goods and descriptions of articles and their usefulness.

Finally, the press had come to depend on commercial support through the sale of advertising space to such an extent that the periodical press, for instance, would not be able to exist without it; high production costs guarantee neither reasonable prices for readers nor profits for publishers. Advertising provides the necessary subsidy and ensures the continuation of the press. But publishers sell not only white space and a percentage of the printing costs to advertisers but also the power inherent in a published periodical.

Whether we like it or not, advertising "is a necessary component of the capitalistic system of the economy, and who can say whether it will not survive that system?" (1926, 256). According to Bücher, consumers benefit from the free enterprise system, which lets them participate in all aspects of economic progress, and advertising helps raise capital necessary to enter and remain in business. Indeed, it seems to have promoted the rise of big business. Advertising as a historical necessity constitutes an unavoidable development, and hence "it is unproductive to get excited about it" (1926, 263).

THE PRESS IN MODERN TIMES

Bücher provides by far the most extensive discussion of the press in modern times. Influenced by Schäffle, he formulates the practical consequences of his theoretical views and offers possible solutions to the dilemma of contemporary newspapers, including the education and training of journalists. The press remains a cultural phenomenon created by specific social and political needs to formalize social communication. But it is also an economic enterprise that sells opportunities for communication in the form of space as a commodity, and therefore it identifies logically with the interests of the business community.

But such an alliance is potentially dangerous and morally troublesome in the eyes of media critics. Bücher clearly recognizes the dangers of abuse by economic and political powers, not only vis-à-vis a trusting public but also as a threat to the careers of editors and journalists, testing their personal integrity and raising questions about their professional responsibilities. For these reasons Bücher supports separating the advertising and news functions of the press to promote editorial independence and raise the credibility and trustworthiness of newspapers.

In a more general way, Bücher anticipates the rise of a consumer society and understands the workings of communication—and advertising in particular—in the process of leveling tastes and directing purchasing decisions to accommodate the industrial-commercial interests in a modern society. As a political economist, he must recognize the historical necessity of advertising as an outcome of general economic developments, but he continues to insist that only an independent press with its undiminished news function can contribute effectively to the well-being of people and the advancement of society. His solution, which is tentative at best, lies in the education of journalists and their rise as independent, expert observers through an interdisciplinary course of study that also involves the press as a social and cultural institution without calling for a separate scientific discipline. It reflects his own approach to understanding the practice of journalism and his professional experience, which is informed by an economic perspective and tampered by his interest in social communication. It also demonstrates the need for a multidisciplinary approach to the study of the press as a determinant of social, economic, and cultural movements in the modern world.

6

The Mirrors of Society: Ferdinand Tönnies on the Press and Public Opinion

SIGNS, LANGUAGE, AND COMMUNICATION

Ferdinand Tönnies (1855–1936) shows a lifelong interest in the study of social and political problems, but he is equally committed to securing the place of sociology in the university setting. His major contribution in theoretical sociology begins with the publication of *Gemeinschaft und Gesellschaft* in 1887.

Tönnies was born in Oldenswort, Schleswig, and studied at the universities of Jena, Leipzig, Bonn, Berlin, and Tübingen between 1871 and 1877 to acquire an extensive background in philosophy, history, ancient languages, and archeology before he concentrated his studies in the social sciences. His *Habilitationsschrift* in 1881 qualified him for a university-level teaching position, but he was not appointed until 1913, when he joined the faculty at the University of Kiel. At that time he had already published several works besides *Gemeinschaft und Gesellschaft* (1887), including *Hobbes' Leben und Lehre* (1896) and *Die Sitte* (1909). He resigned after three years at Kiel to devote his time completely to study and writing for scholarly and popular journals. His second major work, *Kritik der Öffentlichen Meinung*, was published in 1922, one year after he had returned to a teaching position at Kiel. The completion of his third major book, *Einführung in die Soziologie*, appeared in 1931, two years before he was forced to resign from his university post as a result of Hitler's rise to power. At that time he also relinquished his position as president of the German Sociological Association (Deutsche Gesellschaft für Soziologie), which he had founded in 1909 together with a number of colleagues, among them Georg Simmel (1858–1918), Max Weber (1864–1920), and Werner Sombart (1863–1941).

His philosophical studies led Tönnies to the writings of Thomas Hobbes, Herbert Spencer, and August Comte. He also became interested in the organismic theories of Spencer and Albert Schäffle, which stimulated his curiosity about the biological sciences. He also took great interest in the philosophy of law, particularly as represented by Rudolf von Jhring and Sir Henry Maine. Hobbes's writing on law and government and Karl Marx's *Das Kapital* become significant influences on his scholarly production. By accepting a secularized concept of natural law and recognizing the importance of economic aspects of social life, Tönnies forms his own approach to the study of society and concludes that "what is social emanates from human willing, from the intention to relate to each other, a together-willing (*Zusammenwollen*), as it were; and I set myself the task of penetrating to the essence of this willing" (1971a, 4). At the same time, he accepts the basic ideas of historical materialism, although he proposes a sociological rather than an economic explanation of society. In his way of thinking economics could not be identified with the well-being of individuals or the community, that is, with essential will.

According to Tönnies, sociology must be divided into general and special sociology; the former describes the study of human relationships and coexistence with approaches through social biology or social psychology, whereas the latter is divided into pure, applied, and empirical sociology. Pure sociology deals with the basic concepts of *Gemeinschaft* and *Gesellschaft*, and theories of social entities, norms, values, and structures of institutions. Tönnies bases the subdivisions of pure sociology on the social entity as the underlying concept of the system. He explains social entity as "that which is not directly experienced; it must be seen and comprehended through the medium of the common thought and will of those individuals who are part of such an entity and who designate it" (1971b, 131). He insists that *Gemeinschaft* and *Gesellschaft* are fundamental concepts that help define types of human existence. Accordingly, their meaning "is that all relations among people, as well as the derived relations of social corporations with individuals and with each other, even the relations between men and their gods, which like social entities are products of their imagination—all these complexes of positive relations that constitute a bond among men (vinculum)—have a twofold origin: either man's essential will or his arbitrary will" (1971b, 132).

Tönnies understands *Gemeinschaft* as grounded in essential will with its roots in feelings, habits, and beliefs, and *Gesellschaft* as built on arbitrary will as an artificial, deliberate, or conscious act. With these descriptions, he not only tries to depict the full range of human existence but also attempts to offer a new way of understanding the origin and growth of Western society. The reasons for the division of sociology are to be found in methodological differences; for him, "pure sociology is constructive, applied sociology is deductive, and empirical sociology is inductive" (1971b, 131). In addition, he sees differences between pure and applied sociology also in the fact that the former "restricts itself to the study and description of a social entity as static, that is, in the state of rest, [whereas] applied sociology is concerned throughout with the dynamics or the state of motion, social entities" (Jacoby 1973, 92).

Differences between applied and empirical sociology hinge on the question of method; the latter suggests integrating an inductive empirical social research method with the need for concept formation and theory building. Tönnies considers describing and analyzing specific rather than general social phenomena to be the first task of empirical sociology. Thus he advocates a study of facts and their relationships based on true insights and knowledge of the subject matter. He proposes, for instance, that "for empirical sociological studies, our own country in which we were born and reared will always present itself intellectually as the nearest and most easily penetrable subject, not considering emotional attachment" (1971c, 237).

In this quest for understanding the social environment, Tönnies feels that empirical sociology must utilize a variety of analytical methods. And he insists that "a science cannot emerge from mere application of a particular method. If the description of social reality is the object of such a science, then every available means of analysis ought to be utilized" (1971c, 238), resulting in the use of both quantitative and qualitative methods in empirical sociology.

His studies of contemporary social problems (crime, suicide, strikes) serve as examples of how empirical sociology may be used for understanding social conditions and providing a firm basis for critical judgments and corrections of social ills. This work also reflects his continuing engagement as a concerned social scientist who brings his interests in the social and political circumstances of society to the task of improving social conditions in Germany. Tönnies joins the Social Democratic Party in the wake of Hitler's rise to power, demonstrating his commitment to change, political commitment, and opposition to the pending Nazi regime. His political leanings—which he had previously kept from the public to protect his scholarly work—now surface on many occasions.

For instance, in an open letter to a Kiel newspaper[1] he reveals the intensity of his reaction to the rise of Nazism in Germany when he writes,

> The NSDAP is a party that does not want to be a party, yet necessarily must be one. It is a party whose leader is a foreigner who does not know anything

> about our problems. He is a man distinguished by ambiguous enthusiastic thinking, based on his ignorance of reality, a feeble-minded man who imagines that he can solve some problems addressed for centuries—and many of them certainly during the last hundred years—by the best minds of the nation; it is a party whose final goal could be nothing but to cause an irreparable disruption of all social conditions. . . . The NSDAP is a party which promises everything to everyone which makes all promises unrealizable; it is a party which substitutes deliberate disregard of truth, massive errors, and blind emotions for rational thought. In brief, it is a party to which a thinking person, particularly a politically thinking person, cannot commit himself. (Cahnman 1973, 286–87)

In the course of his career, Tönnies comments repeatedly and extensively on the role and function of the press in society, but most extensively in *Gemeinschaft und Gesellschaft* and particularly in *Kritik der Öffentlichen Meinung*, a book that became a significant contribution to the theoretical literature on public opinion.

COMMUNICATION AND PUBLIC OPINION

Tönnies bases his contributions to a theory of communication and public opinion, in particular, on the notion that social phenomena are products of human thought and will. Thus, knowledge, whether scientific or common, rests on experience and recall, facilitated by language, which is a "fixation in memory." He confronts issues of communication, for instance, with his description of ideal and spiritual values—in which common language, together with "native customs and habits," becomes a particular social value that is expressed by a social sign. He distinguishes among signs standing for social values, purposive signs, and symbols, and he stresses that meaning and validity are their most valuable properties.

Belonging to signs standing for social values is "language as a system of signs for the ideal value of mutual understanding and the capability to communicate; further, writing, including printing, as a sign of signs. Finally, all the so-called value symbols are included here, the most important of which is money" (1971c, 139). Purposive signs stand "for the will that something should be done. They are differentiated according to the norms that indicate what ought to be. Consequently, we have signs of valid order, valid law, valid morality" (1971c, 139). Symbols, according to Tönnies, are "signs expressed in words, actions, or objects, denoting in a more specific sense relations, situations, or norms that are understood as existing, that is, having validity" (1971c, 140). He adds that those signs could be determined or conditioned by essential or arbitrary will.

Tönnies returns to the discussion of signs and symbols in his *Introduc-*

tion to Sociology (Cahnman 1973), in which he offers an elaborate and rather precise formulation of these concepts; he locates them firmly in his sociological perspective on society and conveys the idea of the importance and significance of social signs as a type of social value separate from individual signs, sense perceptions, and memories.

A sign, according to Tönnies, "is what is effective as a sign. One concludes from signs that something exists, or used to exist, or is going to exist" (Cahnman 1973, 177). Whether natural or artificial, signs must remain individual signs as long as they are not commonly shared. They can become social signs only "by serving several individuals, on the basis of a quality which is commonly known and serviceable to these several individuals, in such a way that it has the same effect on all participants, that it is understood and consequently correctly interpreted by all." In other words, only "a social will creates social signs" (Cahnman 1973, 178).

Consequently, language becomes the most important system of social signs for mutual understanding and the creation of community; it develops from individual signs "through imperceptible changes and through gradual growth" (Cahnman 1973, 179). Since language—as a way of participating in the community—rests on shared experiences and interpretation, its use leads to the creation and circulation of social norms. Tönnies suggests that "comparable to individual orders or commandments, social regulations may be made known not only through the general system of language but also by means of special signs, the meaning of which is mutually familiar" (Cahnman 1973, 180).

Signs can be defined as signals, documents, and symbols. Tönnies describes the use of artificial signs as examples of signals that are easily perceived acoustically or optically while remaining clear and distinct at the same time. He refers to international code books, for instance, which contain signals that are universally understood among seafarers, but he also includes examples of communication in ciphers or coded dispatches to safeguard information.

The assertion of authority and proof of its validity are connected to the use of distinct signs, or certain forms, such as "formulae are the signs for the validity of such decisions" (Cahnman 1973, 181). Documents, for instance, are testimonials, which—written or oral—serve as proof of facts, "especially of such facts that are chiefly facts of validity and therefore not provable by means of visible or other sensual evidence" (Cahnman 1973, 181).

Tönnies raises the question of communication in the context of social norms also when he addresses specific conditions regarding signs of domination and servitude, the promise of an oath, and the consequences of acts such as commandments and prohibitions. The latter involve communication (i.e., the use of language) for the purpose of prescribing what will or will not happen. They may also be seen as attempts to restrict human freedom, "to move or to induce someone to do or not to do something by words, spoken, written, or expressed in some other way. Words may be supported by actions, their influences strengthened, under certain circumstances, even substituted, by means of gestures" (Cahnman 1973, 187).

Since social norms are based on forms of will, public opinion as a societal form of will plays a major role in definitions of individual and common goals. Tönnies proposes that public opinion is, in fact, "a common will that exercises critical judgment for the sake of a common interest and thereby affects 'private' forms of conduct and action in either a restraining or furthering manner" (1971b, 139). The connections between language, signs as documents, and forms of will emerge as important processes for an understanding of social norms.

Addressing symbols as social signs, Tönnies notes that "these are visible signs represented by certain objects whose significance is to be understood in such a way that they indicate something that cannot be mentioned in words" (Cahnman 1973, 182). He suggests that symbols claim enhanced value, in particular, when communication with invisible or unreal beings is involved, like myth or religion. Thus "religious symbols cause a pious shudder in the heart" (Cahnman 1973, 182). But after tracing the Greek roots of the word "symbol," he concludes that even in the word's origin "is an element of something that secretly binds persons; hence it gained its significance that made it develop its particular religious connotation" (Cahnman 1973, 183). Tönnies adds that other symbols, without religious significance, are used for "decoration," often by an authority or the state, to encourage individuals or commend them for various activities. These social signs "always retain their significance in a centralized order, therefore chiefly in the army and similarly regulated large administrative bodies where order is definitely based on superordination and subordination, hierarchically descending from the chief to the private" (Cahnman 1973, 185).

His discussion of social signs suggests their importance for constructing and maintaining community and organizing the state. Founded on language and communication, society must be careful not to ignore the role of social signs. For instance, Tönnies warns of the danger for a democratic system that deemphasizes or abolishes these "decorations" because such decisions may increase the possibility of losing cooperation and control over individuals and groups in society.

Tönnies affirms the essential nature of public opinion and its close relationship with the press early in his discussion of forms of "Concerted Will, Commonwealth, and States," in the context of *Community and Society*. Specifically, he explains the significance of communication as a process through which public opinion will reach individuals; he stresses the effects of literature, in particular, when he suggests that "such encounter is mainly brought about through that kind of communication wherein all human relationship, faith and trust between speaker and teacher on one side and listener and disciple on the other, is, or at least can be effaced: the literary communication" (1963, 221).

Language and social communication are key elements in his construction of the social (as well as his specific) understanding of community and society. They remain basic concepts in his writings on public opinion, its role and function in society, and its evolution and interpretation as an expression of the collective will.

In his *Kritik der Öffentlichen Meinung*, Tönnies examines and explains the concept of public opinion; he explores the historical-political dimensions of the term and describes different states of public opinion throughout the rise of civilization.

His treatment of the concept suggests a need for separating studies of public opinion and analyses of popular feelings and beliefs, and it encourages discussion of the former underexpressions of the social will. Tönnies mentions, specifically, the close relationship between religion and public opinion; both are regarded as sources of strength that could unite society internally—exemplifying a binding will among members of society—often expressed in the form of moral indignation and intolerance toward those with different ideas (1922, vii).

Tönnies agrees with the general notion that public opinion remains a hard-to-define concept,[2] and he adds that "it is more convenient to determine what it appears to be, find what it is believed to be, rather than what it is." Public opinion is an apparent power in societal life; but the belief that public opinion is "strong and forceful" also suggests the possibility that this "belief has become part of public opinion itself" (Cahnman and Heberle 1971, 251).

He differentiates "clearly and sharply" between notions of public opinion and "the" Public Opinion and suggests that "the former is an external entity of multifarious, contradictory opinions, which are publicly voiced, and the latter a uniformly effective power." His insistence on a scientific explanation separates "unarticulated" public opinion and "articulated (real) Public Opinion," involving the general public or an "essential, politically united public," respectively (Hardt and Splichal 2000, 133–34). Tönnies distinguishes between public opinion, however, that is the sum total of all voices reflected in the press—as one kind of power—and public opinion that consists of a "unified harmony of many thoughts and opinions," constituting a "generalized opinion of a people or a public as a whole" (Cahnman and Heberle 1971, 258). It was his intention throughout *Kritik der Öffentlichen Meinung* to differentiate between those terms, one describing "a conglomerate of diverse and contradictory views, desires and intentions'' and the other standing for ''a unitary force, the expression of a common will'' (1922, vi).

Tönnies uses an analogy to describe these differences; an assembly, for instance, displays the features of public opinion (*öffentliche Meinung*) under conditions of deliberation, when it is divided and torn apart by argument; it resembles the Public Opinion (*Öffentliche Meinung*) under conditions of making decisions or rendering verdicts, when it stands behind these decisions or verdicts as ''a unified whole or moral person'' (Cahnman and Heberle 1971, 258).

He describes the latter also in terms of a ''unified public opinion'' and as an ''expression of social volition,'' which claims binding powers and strives for general acceptance. Tönnies adds that ''public opinion may be compared to a dominant faith, it is all the more intolerant the more sovereign its rule'' (Cahnman and Heberle 1971, 260).

He felt that public opinion, not unlike religion, is part of the ''spiritual-moral sphere of social life; they compete within this sphere to the point of conflict.'' In fact, he concludes that moral supremacy is the goal of both, religion and public opinion. Also, both ''are engaged in propaganda. Public opinion propaganda, especially political propaganda, is modeled on religious propaganda. As religious propaganda propagates faith, so political propaganda propagates opinion'' (Cahnman and Heberle 1971, 261).

Commenting on the lack of theoretical consideration by those who judge public opinion, Tönnies observes that decisions are made on the basis of ''certain signs by which public opinion can be recognized'' (Cahnman and Heberle 1971, 252). Typically, such an identification occurs by what is heard, seen, and read, according to a general belief. But he argues against this simplified and overconfident approach to describing public opinion and warns that what can be heard, seen, and read is frequently misleading and often results in wrong judgments.

In his discussion of the concept and theory of public opinion, Tönnies traces the idea of ''the'' Public Opinion from individual to collective expressions, differentiating, finally, among six forms of collective will under the aspects of community and society and noting varying degrees of complexity. He summarizes (1922, 219) the major points of his approach under the following categories:

A. Community	*B. Society*
(a) understanding, (b) tradition (c) faith	(d) contract, (e) norm, (f) doctrine
	(dd) convention
(aa) concord, (bb) custom	(ee) legislation
(cc) religion	(ff) Public Opinion

Tönnies stresses the interdependence and relationships of these forms of collective and social will, and he presents their existence in a description of the historical process (i.e., the shift from community to society) when forms of the collective will also change (i.e., convention takes the place of concord, customs are followed by legislation, and Public Opinion replaces religion). It is a historical process that marks the change from culture to civilization (1922, 80).

Tönnies makes further distinctions in his discussion of public opinion when he introduces three major states of aggregation that characterize individual and social opinions. Following examples from the natural sciences, he defines solid, fluid, and gaseous states of Public Opinion (1922, 257) and demonstrates differences among them by drawing on the social-economic, political-legal, and intellectual-moral realms of society, often in a comparative way.

Consequently, solid Public Opinion must be understood as a steadfast conviction of a public that represents a people or even a larger circle of civilized individuals. The ideas of personal and economic freedom, forms of government, and rationality *(Vernünftigkeit)* are examples of solidity that typify aspects of modern European societies. They also describe the prevailing foundation of the social, political, and economic order at the time.

The state of fluid Public Opinion, according to Tönnies, may be understood as short-lived public opinion, made for the day and therefore less stable, since it is also formed without the support of solid public opinion. Instead, this type of Public Opinion consists of partial opinions, formed, joined, and generalized often in opposition to solid public opinion. His examples are drawn from contemporary issues, such as attitudes toward work and women in the labor force, ideas about the rise of a constitutional monarchy, juvenile delinquency, and a loose morality regarding positions on prostitution or fraudulent politicians.

The gaseous (ephemeral) Public Opinion has several characteristics. According to Tönnies, it is highly unstable and appears or disappears because it frequently changes the objects of its attention. For example, it may be observed in cities such as Paris, an urban site where public attention is easily distracted and shifts from one subject to the next. This type of Public Opinion is fast moving and hastily established, aided by rapid and regular transportation and communication, which change countries into urban societies where news circulates quickly. It is also superficial, since it must rely on speed and lacks the thoroughness that comes with proper study and evaluation. Thus news must appear incorrect and unreliable, if not completely false, to readers. This type of Public Opinion must be seen as credulous and uncritical, filled with prejudice, often persistent, and always affected by the events of the day. And yet, not unlike Public Opinion in solid or fluid states, it may emerge to act in support of the generally accepted social and moral framework (1922, 245–50).

Tönnies's discussion of various states of Public Opinion provides a way for distinguishing between highly influential (solid) and minimally effective (gaseous) Public Opinions and the possibility of change from one state to another; it allows for categorizing a wide variety of social, political, and economic activities that are commonly grouped indiscriminately under the label of public opinion, although they may differ in strength and endurance.

Religion as a system of dogmas and cultural forms is an essential component of Tönnies's theory of public opinion. The idea of Public Opinion as a changing phenomenon—moving from gaseous through fluid to solid states of aggregation—approaches ideally the concept of religion when it appears as a firmly settled and widely accepted weltanschauung. Both religion and public opinion are expressions of the social will, binding for those who come under their influence and equally determined in their rejection of opposing ideas. Also, both may be described in terms of their states of aggregation; religion too embraces a number of conditions, describing various degrees of depth or firmness of religious belief (1922, 232). Religion, rooted in the tradition of a people and in common experiences, and based on belief in an absolute truth, represents an earlier stage of human development, according to Tönnies, whereas Public Opinion rose from an era of criticism and rational thought and belief in the age of science, which diminished and even negated the influence of theological or religious opinions. The Church and its priests were replaced as spiritual leaders when Public Opinion emerged under the leadership of scientists as teachers and "natural and real leaders of public opinion, directly, and even more so indirectly, insofar as their thoughts, research, and teaching covered or were related to questions of general significance" (1922, 207).

The future of religion, according to Tönnies, is tied to the future of Public Opinion, which he sees as developing into a universal weltanschauung that stresses a belief in humankind. Incorporating the ideals of religiosity, Public Opinion may move a step closer to a world religion. Tönnies cites the recognized need for improved economic conditions, for instance, as a way of lifting the spirit of people *(Volksgeist)*. Social reform is a necessary condition, and he observes in this connection that "public opinion does not yet risk accepting 'socialism,' but it does no longer dare reject it" (1922, 572).

In his examination of public opinion, Tönnies elaborates on a variety of essential elements in the communication process, recognizing the importance of not only signs but also audience characteristics, message construction, communication functions, and media roles (e.g., books and newspapers).

Specifically, Tönnies distinguishes between mute and audible signs, which express intellectual and emotional states and are capable of communicating thoughts and feeling to others. Audiences are defined as consisting of a number of individuals, sharing a particular space, and—although different in many ways—acting united in their specific, common interests in an event. Large audiences *(grosses Publikum)*, on the other hand, are described as individuals who think and judge alike but do not gather in a given place, although they may be heard. Tönnies thinks of the world of educated individuals and political publics that are united by their knowledge and information disseminated through the media, and messages (described by Tönnies as pictorial, oral, or written) from specific audiences that respond as a unit.

Turning to issues of the press and journalism, Tönnies begins by depicting writers and thinkers as communicators whose opinions create different kinds of followers. While creative writers and poets express ideas that often share an enduring quality regardless of the circumstances of their creation, philosophical and scientific works may be short-lived and characterized as expressions of particular places and times. But in all cases, books and newspapers are vehicles for these ideas and could become weapons in the hands of political forces. Tönnies specifically points to the power of the press in social and political affairs and suggests that the "tremendous power [of the press] may become fully transparent in this [the twentieth] century" (1922, 91).

In a section entitled "News and the Public," Tönnies discusses communication as a social phenomenon, using a dichotomous approach to explain its differences in the contexts of community and society. He suggests that opinions, dogmas, and beliefs are transmitted in community settings by those interested in the continuation of certain traditions (considered necessary for the survival of the group) in a spirit of cooperation and common ideals that not only embrace contemporaries but also unite generations within a community. Thus community may be defined in terms of a hierarchical communication structure through which information is passed to those "inferior" (e.g., younger or less experienced in life). His remarks are reminiscent of John Dewey's suggestion of the proximity of communication and community; both refer to the traditional ideal of shared experience and common interests in hierarchical structures (e.g., extended families).

In a modern societal context, on the other hand, communication is manipulated by the conditions of equality (e.g., equal rights and equal status). As a result, information, opinion, and knowledge are passed on by everyone. Tönnies suggests that authority is replaced by ideas of exchange and social intercourse as primary forces of advancing and preserving society. Consequently, books and newspapers are addressed to a large, anonymous public. Differences may be detected, however, in the "intent" of specific media; books, for instance, may have a tendency to address readers from a higher, more elitist position, whereas newspapers strive to remain on a level with their readers. They offer a service and need acceptance. Newspapers want to communicate from "stranger to stranger," regardless of the personal status of authors or writers, but under the cloak of anonymity, which tends to help underscore the idea of factual and objective presentation of information (1922, 94).

Since news is of particular importance in the context of societal communication, Tönnies focuses on two major yet related forms: political and business news. Political news consists of reporting domestic and foreign affairs, while business news is about "the position of markets, and also about the prospects for business" (1922, 95). Tönnies observes the interdependence of both types of news in the interplay between economic and financial powers and political leadership in its internal and external policy-making roles. Since both merchant and statesman need a variety of information, they obtain their news through a number of channels. For instance, newspapers may supplement privately obtained official or business news; but their major function lies in the distribution of those kinds of news that are intended for the public or have escaped from secrecy. He describes the newspaper as a "printed marketplace" (1922, 97).

The importance of information and the dissemination of news for the maintenance of society raise questions about the press as a carrier of true and false news items, its participation in cases of intentional or unintentional falsification of events, and, more generally, the manipulation of information. Tönnies offers wartime reporting as an example of specific propaganda efforts that colored the news and notes the impact of the general news coverage on business activities. He stresses this point because the presentation of news, plain or distorted, remains a crucial element in shaping opinions. More blatant, however, must be the effects of editorials or news analyses, which lend substance to a set of facts and provide "color." Their use establishes the press as a source of adopting ideas to help shape opinions more credibly than through outright falsification of news events.

Newspapers, in particular, are the center of constant observation; they are indispensable for the expression of opinions by any individual or group in society. At the same time, they are held accountable by their particular economic and political sources. Since the press as a capitalistic enterprise is organized to make profits for its owners, newspaper journalists must take into account the real interests of the newspaper: the likes or dislikes of (1) readers, (2) subscribers, and (3) advertisers (1922, 180). Tönnies describes effectively the dependence of journalists on the conditions of the workplace and echoes the concerns of Karl Knies, among others, regarding freedom of expression.

He knows, for instance, that newspapers as a business rely more heavily on advertisers than on subscribers; therefore, managers of the press must respect business interests and may have to yield to their pressures; the resulting activities may be confusing and misleading to readers. Tönnies cites the widespread practice (not limited to the German press) of disguising advertising messages in editorial sections of newspapers and not confining them to business pages (1922, 181–82). Also, general corruption—a sign of modern life—had already affected the press. Tönnies suggests the paradoxical situation that immediate transactions of the press serve the power of capital in the press—and through newspapers—public opinion, which is not the most effective power (1922, 183).

In this context, Tönnies devotes considerable attention to the press and propaganda and its formidable role as a social force, since the power of public opinion often seems to be equated with that of the press. The latter plays a crucial role in the propaganda campaigns of public opinion and involves activities of political parties and their backers. As a result, public opinion is often created. Tönnies observes "that a particular public opinion has been manufactured, as one manufactures any merchandise. One produces merchandise in order to sell, and one sells in order to make a profit. One produces opinion because one expects an advantage from it—if it should come to be shared by many—and this advantage differs little from profits sought by the merchant and entrepreneur." At the same time, he is aware of the wider, more far-reaching implications of controlling the production of public opinion in society. He suggests that "the powers of capital are intent not only on bringing about a favorable opinion regarding their own products and an unfavorable one about those of their competitors, but also on promoting a generalized public opinion, designed to serve their business interests, regarding, for instance, policies of protective tariffs or free trade, favoring a political movement or party and supporting or opposing an existing government" (Cahnman and Heberle 1971, 262).

He states, in effect, that governments, in their attempts to influence public opinion, seek to convert their own opinions into public opinion. Similar activities can be attributed to spiritual-moral powers in society. Religion, for instance, and the sciences also have a stake in shaping public opinion, not only regarding their own affairs but also with respect to political matters. Tönnies notes that "public opinion is easily accessible to these influences, because it is itself a spiritual force" (Cahnman and Heberle 1971, 262). And the use of words, printed and published by the press, in particular, becomes a most effective instrument. Indeed, he concedes that the power of the press "is more obvious than the power of public opinion" (Cahnman and Heberle 1971, 254).

In his attempt to identify sources and participants in the public opinion process, Tönnies differentiates between the activities of an educated elite and the masses, whose social mobility includes the potential for participation and thus influence. He explains that "the more the masses move upward and the more they participate in the advance of education and political consciousness, the more they will make their voices count in the formation of public opinion. But public opinion remains the judgment of an elite, that is, a minority, and frequently, to be sure, a representative minority, but at times a minority that is entirely out of contact with the masses" (Cahnman and Heberle 1971, 264). In fact, there are several powers in modern times, including political, economic, and intellectual forces, which constitute another kind of elite, standing behind the press and joined by "industrial capital," which had become a more powerful influence than landed aristocracy.

Tönnies argues that capital, specifically, regulates the power of the press for several reasons:

> (1) commerce, communication, banking, and industry are more intimately connected than is landed estate with the spirit of modernity and thereby with the press; (2) commerce, and capital generally, is closely related to the world of information and communication, which is served by the press, and thereby to the doings in national and international politics; (3) the newspaper itself is and becomes more and more a capitalist enterprise; the main business of a newspaper is advertising, which is a tool of commercial and industrial capital; (4) the press is in line with the great body of literature inasmuch as it is carried along by the progress of scientific thinking and stands in the service of a predominantly liberal and religiously as well as politically progressive consciousness; consequently the press, *ab initio*, has been an effective weapon of the cities—especially the large, commercially oriented cities—against feudal forces that are rooted in the dominion over the soil; the press addresses itself primarily and preferentially to an urban, especially a metropolitan, public because this is the public that is most eager to read, most accustomed to and capable of reading, and therefore most inclined to do battle by means of script and speech. (Cahnman and Heberle 1971, 255–56)

He describes the particular power of the press over access to the public or other constituencies and argues that in the competition of capitalistic ideas, a capitalistic press is at least theoretically in the position of rebuffing other capitalistic forces until they manage to gain control over the press. He cites examples of corruption in a capitalistic press system—caused by monopoly ownership and corporate control—and interprets these developments, particularly in the United States, as more general expressions of the corruption of public life. Although he acknowledges the work of press critics, he predicts that they will eventually disappear as independent voices or surrender to the dictates of conglomerates and monopolies instead of remaining an unconstrained reflection of public opinions.

Tönnies lists a number of American sources[3] to support his arguments, among them Edward A. Ross, who had stated in 1920 that the sellout of newspapers to business interests had never been so widespread (1920, 288), and Lester Ward, who had declared in *Pure Sociology* that newspapers were organs of deception: "Every prominent newspaper is the defender of some interest and everything it says is directly or indirectly (and most effective when indirect) in support of that interest. There is no such thing at the present time as a newspaper that defends a principle" (1922, 184–86).

Tönnies's description of the use of modern communication media by special interest groups, governments, and others, as well as their mode of operation, focuses on business practices and foreshadows media practices during the later part of the twentieth century. Information is prepackaged and offered to consumers, "judgments and opinion are wrapped up like grocers' goods and offered for consumption in their objective reality. It is prepared and offered to our generation in the most perfect manner by the newspapers, which make possible the quickest production, multiplication, and distribution of facts and thought, just as the hotel kitchen provides food and drink in every conceivable form and quantity." Accordingly, Tönnies finds that

> the press is the real instrument [organ] of public opinion, weapon and tool in the hands of those who know how to use it and have to use it; it possesses universal power as the dreaded critic of events and changes in social conditions. It is comparable and, in some respects, superior to the material power which the states possess through their armies, their treasuries, and their bureaucratic civil service. (1963, 221)

Tönnies recognizes the potential power of a modern press system—and he does not confine his observations to a particular country; on the contrary, he envisions a worldwide influence, a force capable of uniting others and establishing a world power. The press is an international phenomenon in "its tendencies and potentialities" and "thus comparable to the power of a permanent or temporary alliance of states." It is conceivable that the ultimate goal of a media system is "to abolish the multiplicity of states in exchange for a single world market, which would be ruled by thinkers, scholars, and writers and could dispense with other than psychological means of coercion." His writings anticipate the global power of a free market economy and the dominance of a few major producers of news (and creators of world visions) in the form of global television networks or news agencies. Although Tönnies is not sure about the realization of these ultimate goals at the time of his writing, he suggests that "their recognition serves to assist in an understanding of many phenomena of the real world and in a realization of the fact that the existence of natural states is but a temporary limitation of the boundaryless *Gesellschaft*." And he cites the United States as an example of a modern society that "can or will least of all claim a truly national character" (1963, 221).

Tönnies concludes that the press must be understood as an instrument of liberal thought and a force used to exert influence on more conservative elements in society; this assessment implies an allegiance with ideas of less "church-oriented religiosity" and "an agnostic worldview connected with the natural sciences." Consequently, he argues that "if and insofar as public opinion is subject to the same influences and developmental causations as the press, public opinion will be reflected in the press, so that the power of the press expresses the power of public opinion to the extent that the identification of the press and public opinion becomes understandable and within certain limits justified" (Cahnman and Heberle 1971, 256).

Tönnies discusses the overriding effects of liberalism as a "constitutive part of public opinion everywhere, except in areas of cultural transition." He concludes that given the development of the modern age, the press had become a protector and defender of liberal ideas. Consequently, "the power of a unanimous press reflects the power of a unanimous public opinion, and if both follow the same direction they are irresistible. The press, then, is the organ of the public opinion. It is the power of the 'spirit of the age' " (Cahnman and Heberle 1971, 257).

The future of public opinion, its rise—perhaps to a world religion—and its role as the social conscience of humankind must be accompanied by improvements in the communication system. Since the press would continue to play an important part in the dissemination of ideas, Tönnies envisions the establishment of an independent press. Although he mentions Karl Bücher's ideas to reform the German press as yet another example of a possible direction of change, his suggestions are based on the writings of an American journalist (1922, 574–75) who had advocated the creation of a completely independent press system with newspapers that could rely on an independent news service and were financially independent, supported by a large circulation rather than advertising.[4]

For Tönnies, the press is a central force in a society in which public opinion has become its guiding spirit. His publications about the press and his leading role in the German Sociological Association brought him into contact with members of German institutes for the study of the press (*Zeitungswissenschaft*), who had jealously protected their exclusionary claims regarding systematic, scholarly investigations of the press. Tönnies, however, refuses to believe in a separation of media studies and repeatedly expresses his views in public.

The 1930 convention of the German Sociological Association includes a debate about the press and public opinion, with Tönnies presiding and raising a number of relevant issues. For instance, he expresses disappointment over the fact that none of the speakers attempted a systematic treatment of the press as a capitalistic enterprise that developed into a powerful social force with the production and sale of news. He comments on the dangers of interference by advertisers in the process of social communication and the threats to freedom of expression for journalists. But he also wonders about journalists who are generating opinions and expressing value judgments in their publications, and he asks how free these opinions really are, how they are related to other opinions, and how close they come to other "verified" opinions present in other areas of social life. He specifically refers to opinions of educated individuals, whose contributions to social policy and reform are needed, but whose ideas are either distorted or rarely published. For instance, the writings of national economists—among them Lujo Brentano (1844–1931), Gustav von Schmoller (1838–1917), Adolph Wagner (1835–1917), and Georg Knapp (1842–1926)—are suspect in the eyes of the bourgeois and, in particular, the Catholic press, because they seem to be grounded in socialism. Tönnies concludes, almost despairingly and as a result of his own lifelong experience, that "when men and women of this caliber are dead, they may receive rather gracious obituaries; as long as they live, they will find themselves pushed to the wall and rarely listened to" (1931a, 74).

He also rejects the accusation by members of newspaper institutes, in particular, that he dislikes a science of the press (*Zeitungswissenschaft*) as an area of special inquiry. In a response to Emil Dovifat, a leading representative of this field, Tönnies states[5] that there is really no need to establish a new science for every new area of scholarly investigation; he thought that the advocates of *Zeitungswissenschaft* could make rather valuable contributions to a critical history of the press, especially under philosophical and sociological aspects. And he expresses the hope—with a reference to a lack of critical press studies by the representatives of *Zeitungswissenschaft*—that the annual sociological convention might contribute toward a liberation from the influence of the press, in general, and from party affiliations and dependence on respective newspapers, in particular (1931a, 72–74).

Tönnies elaborates his position vis-à-vis *Zeitungswissenschaft* again in a letter published early in 1931, in which he denies the charge of wanting to define the study of the press as an exclusive part of sociology. Nevertheless, he feels that press analyses constitute an important area of sociography, that is, empirical sociology. He suggests that the literature of society—which includes newspapers—must be treated as a significant aspect of the social life of a people and blames the failure of sociology to address the study of press systems on its fairly recent introduction as a discipline in Germany (1931b, 1–2).

CAPITALISM, PUBLIC OPINION, AND DEMOCRACY

Tönnies provides an extensive discussion of communication phenomena, including public opinion and the press, as part of his efforts to develop a broad sociological framework, beginning with *Gemeinschaft und Gesellschaft*. In this context, he contributes a detailed historical analysis of the concept of public opinion and offers a definition that is based on the dynamic nature of his own conceptual understanding of social development. He seems particularly concerned about the rise of public opinion in connection with the growth of capitalism and comments on the dangers inherent in the capitalistic nature of the press in modern society. In this context, he problematizes the democratic nature of public opinion and the role of the press, since both remain open to corrupting influences and manipulation by commercial or political powers that also own the press.

Like his predecessors, Schäffle, Knies, and Bücher, Tönnies articulates a critique of the modern press that focuses on economic and commercial aspects of journalism and raises questions concerning the incompatibility of public service and private business interests, which threatens the credibility of the press and the integrity of journalists. But unlike them, he develops a systematic approach to communication in society that privileges the notion of public opinion and is contained by the social and cultural boundaries of specific notions of community and society, which become the intellectual markers of his inquiry. He demonstrates effectively the necessary relationship between a theory of society (or community) and communication.

Despite his interest in the political events of his time, and his understanding of Marxism, Tönnies does not focus on the relationship of politics and the press, or the role of the state in the protection of a free flow of information; however, he develops an appreciation of propaganda and the role of the press—guided by governments—in the dissemination of propagandistic messages, based on his experience of World War I and the use of propaganda techniques in the struggle over public opinion.

His ideas regarding the rise of public opinion to a universal social conscience vis-à-vis religion, as well as the role and function of the press in this evolutionary scheme, suggest a novel approach to popular culture phenomena. Tönnies does not believe in a utopian future of modern society with the aid of communication, participation, and the rise of public opinion. On the contrary, the notion of public opinion as the spirit of modernity may contain the potential for a democratic way of life; but more likely it offers troubling possibilities for social and political control—especially with the arrival of sophisticated technologies of communication (e.g., broadcasting). Tönnies realizes these dangers, and his demands for analyzing commercial influences on the press—media generally and public opinion specifically—remain a challenge for contemporary communication research and media studies to remain critical and be responsive to the need for solving social problems.

7

The Conscience of Society: Max Weber on Journalism and Responsibility

JOURNALISM AND POLITICS

The scholarship of Max Weber (1864–1920) crosses a number of disciplinary boundaries from economics and history to law, religion, and sociology. Much of his work seems to reflect his lifelong interest in the problems of leadership in society. Although numerous books[1] have focused on his contribution to the social sciences, this chapter concentrates on his interests in journalism and the role of the press as public authority and vehicle for the dissemination of social and political thoughts.

Specifically, Weber's own concerns about the press may be an indication of the importance he attached to the role and function of journalists as disseminators of ideas and the press as a source of information about social and political issues of the day. Furthermore, if (as Talcott Parsons once suggested [1965, 174]) conditions of successful control provide an appropriate focus of sociology for Weber, then the study of the press and its agents as components of social and political decision making in modern society becomes a major task of sociological research. And finally, Weber's own position as a scholar-publicist may contribute to an understanding of this theory of political leadership in light of his own experience with political journalism in early twentieth-century Germany.

Weber's social and political writings represent a substantial intellectual effort; they reflect not only his intimate knowledge of political problems but also his continued participation in public life through journalistic activities. They also reveal his fascination with the idea of leadership; as a political journalist, he writes with charismatic authority, but as a social theorist, he recognizes the dangers of charismatic leadership to individual freedom and liberty.

Underlying much of Weber's analysis of Germany's political and economic problems during the latter part of the nineteenth century is his awareness of social change, specifically, the rise of labor, the failure of the bourgeoisie to provide responsible leadership, and the advances of big business and industry toward a new form of feudalism. In his early effort to seek solutions to Germany's internal problems, Weber is attracted to Martin Rade's *Chronik der Christlichen Welt*,[2] with its interest in labor-related issues and the development of social policies. He joins the publication in 1890 as a contributor and only one year later assumes editorial duties for *Evangelisch-soziale Zeitfragen*, a publication founded by his cousin, Otto Baumgarten, whose activities in the Christian-Social movement bring Weber into contact with a number of liberal theologians (Mommsen 1974, 21). Among them was Friedrich Naumann, who represented the left-wing interests of the organization. Naumann succeeds in 1894 with the publication of *Die Hilfe*,[3] and he asks Weber to become a contributor. The journal embarked on a major editorial campaign in support of a social democratic movement and against powerful industrial interests that attempted to suppress liberal sentiments; consequently, it becomes recognized and establishes itself firmly among journals with an appeal to liberal intellectuals rather than to workers and artisans, whose broad support had been envisioned earlier (Taubert 1973, 260). At the same time, Weber publishes an attack on Germany's industrialists in the *Neue Preussische (Kreuz-)Zeitung*.[4] Basically interested in strengthening the idea of collaboration in German society for the purpose of retaining its status of a powerful state, Weber joins the condemnation of a growing intolerance against Social Democrats and other liberal groups and individuals. The article appeared only after considerable editorial changes, however (Baumgarten 1964, 692).

In the meantime, Weber's friendship with Naumann leads to more intense participation in the political life of the 1890s, culminating in the establishment of the Nationalsozialer Verein in 1896. Weber remains critical of Naumann's program, but he joins his effort to launch a daily newspaper and establish a platform for the new party. The result was the founding of *Die Zeit*, a daily newspaper that survived for about a year,[5] when a lack of popular support for the party and dwindling funds contributed to its early demise (Weber 1926, 233–36).

A few years later, however, Weber finally discovers his own public forum when he begins writing for the *Frankfurter Zeitung*, one of Germany's leading newspapers at the time, on topics ranging from the democratization of Germany to problems of academic freedom.[6] Not unlike readers of *Die Hilfe*, readers of the *Frankfurter Zeitung* belonged to the social and intellectual elites of the nation, and Weber could expect an unusually high degree of knowledge and understanding of most subject matters and, as Lachmann suggests, "a degree of sophistication which would permit them to discount some of the rhetorical excrescenses of his polemic style, and nevertheless realize the very serious nature of the issues at stake" (1971, 95–96).

On one occasion, after a series of articles on parliamentary rule in Germany that attacked the kaiser as a political dilettante, the *Frankfurter Zeitung* experienced official pressures when military censors confiscated one issue and stepped up their censorship of the newspaper. This confrontation became a political issue and led to a question about the nature of preventive censorship before the Reichstag (Baumgarten 1964, 710). Furthermore—and as an example of his intense feelings about political issues—Weber insists among acquaintances that he would continue his attacks on Wilhelm II after the war to bring about a legal confrontation in hopes of seeing men like Bernhard Fürst von Bülow, Alfred von Tirpitz, Theobald von Bethmann, Jagow, Faldenhayn, Paul von Hindenburg, and Erich Ludendorff reveal under oath their sins committed against the German people. Theodor Heuss, who recalled the episode, suggests that Weber saw himself in the role of a direct opponent of Wilhelm II (Winckelmann 1958, xvi).

Although destined to play a major part in the political development of postwar Germany, Weber decides to continue his scholarly work. He also returns to his editorial duties as a contributor to the *Frankfurter Zeitung* and participates in discussing events leading to the establishment of the Weimar Republic. Intent on persuading members of the editorial staff to share his views (on revolution, for instance), he is disappointed in his results, noting, "I am writing one article after another. . . . but it is impossible to influence the editorial staff, it cannot be done by an outsider, they rebel internally" (Baumgarten 1964, 501).

There were other outlets for his journalistic writings as well, such as the *Berliner Tageblatt*, another of Germany's major liberal newspapers, and the *Berliner Börsenzeitung*. In addition, he writes for the *Münchner Neueste Nachrichten*, a major newspaper in southern Germany which, at that time, was also a liberal newspaper.[7]

Many of Weber's major political contributions to these and other publications are included in his collected political essays, *Gesammelte Politische Schriften*.[8] Together they show Weber's intimate knowledge of political events before and during World War I and the missionary zeal with which he engages his sharp analytical mind to reveal and report on the social and political conditions of the day. For instance, Dronberger concludes—

summarizing Weber's merits as a journalist analyzing the events of World War I—that he succeeded "with a profoundly exhaustive analysis of German political institutions of his time—all by the means of an account of historical events and the role played by the Kaiser, the chancellor, other influential public figures, the military, the bureaucracy, groups with vested interests, and political parties" (1971, 6).

His work as a political journalist, or publicist, reflects his concerns with problems of power and responsibility among political leaders. He, too, had assumed leadership among contemporary journalists, whose political *Weltanschauungen* were widely disseminated by influential newspapers. It was, after all, his journalism that contributed to his rising popularity and made him a potential candidate for a political career.

However, Weber also liked his involvement with the press for personal reasons: he appreciated being around decent and intelligent journalists who knew their business. Heuss (1958, xxiv) suggests that the *Frankfurter Zeitung* provided not only a platform for his political views but also an opportunity for close contacts with professional journalists for whom he had gained much respect over the years. The attractions of journalism as a professional career and an engagement in the role of the press are appropriate contexts for Weber's own intellectual activities. Heuss (1958, xxiv) says that Weber was extremely taken by the role of educated and responsible journalists, that he appreciated their participation in the formulation of public opinion, and that he sought and needed the exchange of ideas with them. To be sure, Weber also must have valued the freedom he experienced as a publicist in the choice of topics and the manner of their presentation in the *Frankfurter Zeitung*, whose editorial staff consisted of carefully selected, well-educated individuals with collective decision-making powers concerning editorial matters of content or political direction. It was a unique experience for Weber, whose close association with journalist colleagues was as rare as his working conditions, given general relations between editorial staffs and newspaper management in Germany.

JOURNALISTS, THE PRESS, AND DEMOCRATIC SOCIETY

Weber's most extensive statement regarding the role of political journalists is contained in his lecture on politics as a vocation (1966, 83; also Gerth and Mills 1946, 77–128), in which he discusses the ethical consequences of a career in public life. Characterizing the political journalist as the most important representative of the "demagogic species," Weber describes the fate of journalists who lack a "fixed social classification with lawyers and artists" but belong to "a sort of pariah caste, which is always estimated by 'society' in terms of its ethically lowest representative" (Gerth and Mills 1946, 96).

Coming to the defense of the responsible journalist, Weber suggests that "the strangest notions about journalists and their work are abroad. Not everybody realizes that a really good journalistic accomplishment requires at least as much 'genius' *(Geist)* as any scholarly accomplishment, especially because of the necessity of producing at once and 'on order,' and because of necessity of being effective, to be sure, under quite different conditions of production." He comments on the fact that the responsibility of journalists is rarely acknowledged, although it is "on the average, not a bit lower than that of the scholar, but rather, as the war has shown, higher. This is because, in the very nature of the case, irresponsible journalistic accomplishments and their often terrible effects are remembered" (1966, 96).

Weber speaks with the experience of a veteran journalist and the insights of a highly respected scholar, who knows about the agony of journalistic decision making and the consequences of scholarly discoveries in the face of negative public sentiment, misjudgments, or misunderstandings. He observes,

> Nobody believes that the discretion of any able journalist ranks above the average of other people, and yet that is the case. The quite incomparably graver temptations, and the other conditions that accompany journalistic work at the present time, produce those results which have conditioned the public to regard the press with a mixture of disdain and pitiful cowardice. (1966, 96–97)

But Weber is interested in more than the professional integrity of journalists or the quality of news work. He wants to raise "the question of the occupational destiny of the political journalist and of his chance to attain a position of political leadership."

Therefore, any political writing for mass consumption is more than an ordinary editorial assignment but may well constitute the foundation of a political career. Journalism, in this sense, becomes a training ground, a vocational education for political activists. The press is an ideal institution because newspapers are not only an appropriate medium for political communication, but also—by their very nature—potential leaders of the masses. Differently expressed, political journalists are in a position of power, since they control—at least theoretically—the dissemination of information and opinion while rising simultaneously to positions of political prominence.

In reality, however, there was little evidence of these conditions in Germany, and Weber ponders the failure of political journalists to succeed in political careers. He notes that only the Social Democratic party had provided a chance for journalists to obtain official positions, although "editorial positions have not been the basis for positions of leadership." The situation was worse in bourgeois parties, however, where "the chances for ascent to political power along this avenue have rather become worse, as compared with those of the previous generation" (1966, 97–98).

Politicians, on the other hand, need the press, including influence over it, and yet "that party leaders would emerge from the ranks of the press has been an absolute exception and one should not have expected it." Weber feels that the "reason for this lies in the strongly increased 'indispensability' of the journalist, above all, of the propertyless and hence professionally bound journalist, an indispensability that is determined by the tremendously heightened intensity and tempo of journalistic operations." He sees that the need to perform regularly with a stream of articles affects aspiring political leaders and harms their careers. Weber notes, "I know of cases in which natural leaders have been permanently paralyzed in their ascent to power, externally and above all internally, by this compulsion." He criticizes conditions in Germany, specifically, and remarks that although elsewhere circumstances are different, "there also, and for all modern states, apparently the journalist worker gains less and less as the capitalist lord of the press, of the sort of 'Lord' Northcliffe, for instance, gains more and more political influence" (1966, 97–98).

Weber blames the larger capitalistic press organizations for breeding political indifference and advertising for its potential as an economic determinant of political influence. His remarks are directed at the development of a mass circulation press with commercial overtones and ideological constraints that have their roots in capitalism as the driving force in modern society.

He regrets the lack of political engagement, in particular, when he observes that "our great capitalist newspaper concerns, which attained control, especially over the 'chain newspapers,' with 'want ads,' have been regularly and typically the breeders of political indifference. For no profits could be made in an independent policy; especially no profitable benevolence of the politically dominant powers could be obtained" (1966, 97–98).

Weber singles out attempts to influence the press politically through its dependence on advertising (especially during World War I) and expresses his fears that the pressures from advertising as a business will continue. He observes that although "one may expect the great papers to escape this pressure, the situation of the small ones will be far more difficult" and concludes that for the time being journalism as a "normal avenue for the ascent of political leaders, whatever attraction journalism may otherwise have and whatever measure of influence, range of activity, and especially political responsibility it may yield" is not available. "One has to wait and see. Perhaps journalism does not have this function any longer, or perhaps journalism does not yet have it" (1966, 97–98).

Weber addresses the inevitable question of sensationalism, which occurs with the commercialization of news work and increasing competition for readers, vis-à-vis the future of responsible journalism and political leadership, in particular. He differentiates between profit motives and promotional needs in the production and dissemination of sensational news and notes that the

> publishers as well as the journalists of sensationalism have gained fortunes but certainly not honor. Nothing is here being said against the principle of promoting sales; the question is indeed an intricate one, and the phenomenon of irresponsible sensationalism does not hold in general. But thus far, sensationalism has not been the road to genuine leadership or the responsible management of politics. How conditions will further develop remains to be seen. (1966, 98)

Nevertheless, Weber still regards the activities of responsible political journalists as avenues to political careers, at least for individuals strong enough to gamble; in fact, "the journalist's life is an absolute gamble in every respect and under conditions that test one's inner demands that are directed precisely at the successful journalist are especially difficult." He comments on the abilities of journalists to function in social situations of inequality, disproportionate power, and prejudice, "knowing all the time that having hardly closed the door the host has perhaps to justify before his guest his association with the 'scavengers from the press.' " In addition, journalists must be able to respond swiftly to reader demands and without losing pride or dignity in their attempts to balance public and commercial interests. Weber realizes that "it is no small matter that one must express oneself promptly and convincingly about this and that, on all conceivable problems of life—whatever the 'market' happens to demand—and this without becoming absolutely shallow and above all without losing one's dignity by baring oneself, a thing which has merciless results." Given the demands of the workplace and the conditions of reporting, in particular, Weber contemplates the fate of his colleagues, observing that "it is not astonishing that there are many journalists who have become human failures and worthless men. Rather, it is astonishing that, despite all this, this very stratum includes such a great number of valuable and quite genuine men, a fact that outsiders would not so easily guess" (1966, 99).

According to Weber, individual, ethical conduct is guided by one of two maxims: an ethic of ultimate ends or personal responsibility. Without specifically referring to journalists and their activities, however, he proposes that a political calling necessitates a union of both maxims of human conduct, and he suggests that it "is immensely moving when a mature man—no matter whether old or young in years—is aware of a responsibility for the consequences of his conduct and really feels such responsibility with heart and soul." The result is the pursuit of an ethic of personal responsibility to a point where the individual utters,

> "Here I stand; I can do no other." That is something genuinely human and moving. And every one of us who is not spiritually dead must realize the possibility of finding himself at some time in that position. Insofar as this is true, an ethic of ultimate ends and an ethic of responsibility are not absolute contrasts but rather supplements, which only in unison constitute a genuine man—a man who can have the "calling for politics." (1966, 127)

Weber's view of political journalists and their role in modern society may also be relevant in the context of legitimizing charismatic domination by journalists as types of political leaders. This is especially true because Weber acknowledges the power of the press and grants political journalists the freedom to use their abilities for political causes. He speaks as an insider whose acquaintance with journalists adds to his own experiences, including his desire to exercise political power. Raymond Aron points out that Weber "dreamed of being a statesman rather than a party leader—the head of state being, at least in the imagination of outsiders, a man who accedes to the mobility of politics without accepting its servitude. Max Weber was neither a politician nor a statesman, but an advisor to the prince" (1967, 282).

Having chosen an academic career, however, Weber's desire for political engagement finds an outlet in his journalistic writings; thus he is able to combine the life of what he calls "a responsible journalist" with an academic interest in the social sciences. He reaches a compromise between *Gefühl* and *Verstand*, that is, between emphasizing action as an expression of political power and knowledge as a goal of scientific inquiry. As a result, he participates in both worlds, respected as diagnostician of society and leader among social theorists. When Otto Groth (1960, 119)—who had followed up on Weber's later suggestions to engage in empirical studies of the press—suggests that journalists are not unlike missionaries, applying Weber's own terminology, he introduces a fitting description of Weber as a publicist working for the cause of a strong German state.

Weber had long recognized the central role of the press in the political milieu of a democratic society, but he also sees it as an important instrument of social and political change and a necessary tool for the success of political activities. Although he acknowledges the close relationship between political status and access to the press, he also warns that the creation of new parties along with their press organizations may result in financial burdens that often make it quite impractical to consider political moves against an already established press empire (Winckelmann 1958, 389–90). And yet the press remains a primary tool of persuasive communication in the machinery of political propaganda and an indispensable tool in the political arena.

Implicit in Weber's articulation of the utility of newspapers as sources of information and opinions is his strong belief in the effectiveness of the press as a public medium. For instance, in the context of discussing national unity and cultural heritage, he concludes that "newspapers, which certainly do not collect the most sublime examples of literary culture, however, cement the masses together quite effectively" (Baumgarten 1964, 422). Consequently, it becomes important to organize a well-functioning system of communication to support political campaigns at all levels of political life, including "party correspondences and ready print services for the party press as well as for advertisements of all kinds." But also other forms, such as the creation and domination of local media, are important. Weber notes that the "experiments to create a local press that depends completely on the ruling bureaucracy have not ceased" (Winckelmann 1958, 83).

Underlying these concerns about availability and control of communication for the purposes of serving a political movement, however, is the struggle for authority. It is a struggle in which the masses participate according to the wishes of their political leaders. Thus Weber observes that "so-called 'public opinion' under the conditions of mass-democracy is a communal activity born of irrational 'feelings' and normally stage-directed by party leaders and press" (Jaehrich 1971, 235). In other words, Weber places the press in the hands of the few, typically members of a political elite, who are responsible for manipulating the masses. Under these circumstances, politics turns into a vocation, and the idea of democracy—including the notion of a free press—serves to maintain and reinforce charismatic leadership. In this context, Weber's statement regarding political journalists takes on the character of an imperative: with the rise of a plebiscitary democracy, journalists must reach for the realm of politics. Their ethics of responsibility dictate a devotion to action.

Given Weber's personal involvement in journalism and his political concerns regarding the press in a democratic society, it must come as no surprise that he invents and insists on a systematic, scientific treatment of the press from a social scientific perspective to replace mere political curiosity and speculation with scholarly earnestness and scientific hypotheses. Although he realizes the difficulties of a social scientific study of the press, he also anticipates that such a study—if completed successfully—would yield valuable insights into the relationship between the practice of newspapers and the conduct of society.

Weber had been a cofounder of the German Sociological Association in 1909 as an outgrowth of his interests in the theory and practice of the social sciences. His fascination with concrete empirical research is reflected in his address to the first Sociological Congress a year later in Frankfurt, where he introduces three empirical research projects, among them a study of the German press. The latter project reflects his own assessment of the press as a significant and powerful institution in modern society and reinforces his earlier statements and observations.

According to Lazarsfeld and Oberschall (1965, 92), the proposed press study was Weber's sixth and final empirical effort. Although Weber was innovative and introduced a new sociological topic, he was not alone with his acknowledgment of the press as an important social institution and useful source for sociological inquiry. His proposal helped reinforce already existing ideas in Germany that public considerations of the press must receive appropriate attention from a social scientific community (Hardt 1974).

Weber's address to his colleagues during the 1910 meeting of German sociologists is, in effect, the second attempt to provide an empirical foundation for the interpretation of the press as a societal institution.[9] He envisions a project that would involve the cooperation of practicing journalists as well as theorists such as Emil Löbl, whose *Kultur und Presse* (1903) had been an attempt to develop a scientific system of the periodical press and a pioneering effort to conceive of *Zeitungswissenschaft* systematically.[10] Löbl's work had also caught the attention of Ferdinand Tönnies—another founding member of the German Sociological Society—and receives some attention in his study of public opinion.

Based on the premise that quantification of relevant data is the first step toward formulating qualitative statements about the role and function of the press, Weber introduces the framework for his investigation in broad terms. "We must examine the press to this end: What does it contribute to the making of modern man? Second, how are the objective, supraindividual cultural values influenced, what shifts occur, what is destroyed and newly created of the beliefs and hopes of the masses: of the *Lebensgefühle* (as they say today), what is forever destroyed and newly created of the potential point of view" (1924, 434)?

Karl Weber reports on Max Weber's remarks to the Congress, which are based on an earlier, undated, six-page plan for a press survey entitled "Preliminary Report of a Suggested Survey of the Sociology of Newspapers." The latter attempts an outline of the project in this report and proposes a number of specific issues that address the general goals of a press survey. "In the last analysis, a survey of the newspaper system must be aimed at addressing significant, contemporary cultural problems: (1) The way in which this instrument—which influences minds and is continuously in the service of modern society to adapt and conform the individual—is organized: the press as one of the means of forging the subjective character of modern man; and (2) the conditions created by public opinion—whose most important determinant today is the newspaper—for the formation, maintenance, destruction, and change of artistic, scientific, ethical, religious, political, social, and economic aspects of culture: the press as a component of the objective character of modern culture" (1937, 421–22).

The investigation of the press was to be organized under two distinct categories: "newspaper business" and "newspaper opinion." The former contained a number of preliminary questions concerning quantitative measures of formal, business aspects of the newspaper industry, while the latter concentrated on questions about qualitative tendencies of the press.

Weber intended to deal with the business aspect of the press in a number of ways. He proposes to look at a series of specific elements, ranging from ownership, the need and turnover of capital, and running costs of production, to the procurement of materials. Under the latter heading Weber envisions inquiries into news services (telegraphic agencies), the production of features and special sections, party and political news, and official and semiofficial materials, as well as origin, costs, and the special nature of business news. He suggests that commerce and industry exert a particular influence on the press, and their presence must be addressed in a specific way. Consequently, the "influence of business conditions on the objective content of the newspaper should be divided into subproblems that are connected with the aforementioned, such as internal service and ways of distributing materials" (Weber 1937, 423). He includes in this category also the role of editorials, as well as the possibility of multiple daily editions of large newspapers, the rise of "Americanism" in the press, and ways of distributing materials among employees. Also connected are advertising and advertising sales. Other elements in the analysis of the business aspects of the press include issues of income, competition, and monopoly; newspapers and journalism; and other newspaper employees.

The problems of newspaper opinions were to be dealt with in three major categories: production of opinion, external influences on newspaper opinions, and production of public opinion. Regarding the production of opinion, Weber enumerates and lists several issues:

> Collectivism and individualism in the creation of newspaper content. Anonymity in the newspaper; its reasons: business (e.g., differences between subscription and single sales press), political (e.g., greater or smaller degree of elasticity of the party organization), social (e.g., efforts to maintain tradi-

> tion and prestige of the newspaper as such and preservation of a balance of power between newspaper capital and journalism), cultural (e.g., greater or smaller authority of the printed word—particularly the anonymously printed word—which appears as a collective product before the reader according to the degree of his or her political education, etc.). Its effects on the journalist, the advancement or impediment of the development of public opinion, and the political and cultural significance of the newspaper as such. (Weber 1937, 423)

Weber is equally interested in the external influences or pressures on the views of the press. His notes concentrate on the binding force of tradition and mention the potential role of owners, stockholders, and readers, as well as other official influences on the position of the press.

The third topic area concerns the production of public opinion by the press. Weber pays considerable attention to the effects of reading (and particularly newspaper reading) on individual thought and expression. He also wonders about the role of the press in the creation of celebrities and wants to know about the demand readers make on press content. Finally, he asks about the relationship between the necessary conditions of publicity and public morality (Weber 1937, 424).

Weber realizes that these sets of questions may be relatively easy to answer in an essay, but they require rather laborious social scientific responses. His remarks, together with his explanations (which make up part of his speech to the Sociological Congress), reflect not only Weber's understanding of the relationship between press and society but—more interestingly and challenging—also describe the path communication research will take through most of the twentieth century. Weber succeeds in defining crucial areas for social scientific inquiry; his interdisciplinary expertise directs him to considerations of economic and political components of media practices, cultural issues, as well as psychological and sociological explanations concerning the effects of the press on individuals and society.

For instance, Weber's insight into the economic problems of the press leads to questions about an "Americanization" of the German press (Weber 1937, 422), that is, tendencies of monopoly ownership of newspapers (initially experienced through newspaper chains in the United States) and its effects on the independent and party press in Germany. "Americanization" was a hotly debated issue at the time in Germany—summarized by Walter Hammer, who predicts that in the "Americanized press everything will be up for sale, from the editorial to the local news item" (Koszyk 1966, 274).

But Weber is equally concerned about the psychological impact of the press and is aware of a mounting literature on the effects of newspapers on individuals. For instance, in his formal presentation to his colleagues in 1910, he refers to the contradictory nature of many findings and suggests that while exposure to newspapers and other reading material may have an effect on individuals, it is difficult, if not impossible, to separate the impact of the press from other influences, which rather complicates a precise definition of the problem.

Weber proposes two basic areas for sociological study—the press and formal organizations in German society—and develops a full account of his plan for a systematic study of German newspapers and the beginnings of a sociology of the press.[11]

He argues for a study of the press involving academics and professionals that will make use of expert knowledge and draw on historical explanations as well as contemporary collections of facts concerning newspapers and journalism. While confirming the central role of the modern press in society, Weber is well aware of cultural and political differences across nations. He effectively promotes comparative studies with his frequent references to conditions elsewhere. He wants to make sure that differences in French and English journalism, for instance, find their explanations in the respective cultural conceptualizations of the press. At the same time, global developments (e.g., the role of capital and the rise of commercial interests in the press) are significant and noteworthy phenomena that also affect the investigations of the German media situation.

In addition, however, Weber moves beyond purely institutional concerns or global economic explanations to focus on the professional and intellectual conditions of news workers. He wants to raise questions about the specific effects of a modern, commercial culture on journalists before he turns his attention to the social, political, and cultural impact of the press on society.

The latter effects range from the impact of its mere presence or availability (e.g., on reading habits) to the consequences of exposure to content matter, which, taken together, constitute new and different ways of seeing or knowing the world. Undoubtedly, Weber considers the modern press a change agent, with society being under the spell of a powerful medium. Likewise, Weber is aware of the effects of a mediated reality (to use a late-twentieth-century expression) and wants to begin his study with content analyses that reveal the inventory of news and opinions and expose the workings of "mass" communication in an effort to offer some preliminary explanations concerning the outcomes of media (re)presentations.

A project of this magnitude, however, needs the cooperation of not only newspaper practitioners, including publishers, but also colleagues, particularly those with an interest in studying the press. Weber's proposal is highly ambitious with clearly marked goals; it is, in a sense, typical of his approach to theoretical problems. He needs evidence to construct a theory of the press, and he wants to confirm the place of the social sciences in the search for practical explanations of significant social, political, and economic issues in contemporary society. Indeed, Oberschall remarks (1965, 142) that Weber's press study reflects, more than any other research proposal, his plan to establish social scientific research permanently in Germany.

Unfortunately, Weber's ambitious plan for a comprehensive study of the press did not succeed. He becomes involved in a lawsuit against a newspaper (for an anonymous attack on his wife and her role in the women's emancipation movement) and feels obligated to resign as chief investigator. With little or no interest among other members of the sociological association to provide relief and share these duties, the project loses momentum. Weber gives an account of these developments during the 1912 meeting of the German Sociological Association and expresses confidence in the future of the study; he also reports about attempts to support some of the current work, including a variety of studies, ranging from the meaning of classified advertising in the German press, the press in Württemberg, the local press of West Prussia, to the development of the newspaper feature article. He also confirms his availability for consultation. But according to Marianne Weber, none of the "great ones" was willing to save the project and lead the collective investigations. Thus the organization of the press survey remains in Weber's hands; he tries for months to start the work but is left to seek help among beginners. Although a few valuable investigations are finally produced, because of the difficult nature of the subject matter they provide only a partial answer, and Weber realizes after many months that "he is merely wasting his energies" (Weber 1926, 429).

The beginning of World War I may have contributed to his decision to permanently delay the work. His ideas, however, continued to survive in a number of dissertations that address Weber's original plan, among them Otto Groth's (1915) quantitative content analysis of ten newspapers in Württemberg over a one-year period. Groth also became a major contributor to the scholarly literature on the German press between the world wars.

CONCLUSION

Weber's understanding of journalism and the press must be viewed as a response to the political situation in Germany; it is also a confirmation of his academic commitment to a search for practical knowledge. His academic education and professional attachment to the world of rigorous scholarship equipped him with the necessary conceptual framework to ask penetrating questions about his political and social environment; but as a social theorist he also benefited from his practical experiences as a journalist. In fact, his intellectual interests in politics and social science merge in his political journalism. Unlike Marx, whose political commitment informed his journalism and merged with his theoretical interests, Weber's political ambitions are restrained, less passionate, and more rational, perhaps, to serve his role as a liberal political journalist.

Although Weber acknowledges the separation of politics and science in his writings, practicing journalism and theorizing about the role and function of the press provide the best example of his pragmatic approach to life. He draws freely on all of his experiences while understanding that each profession has its own rules and ways of defining responsibility.

Weber's assessment of the role and function of the modern press occurs amid observations of an increasing bureaucratization of society. Since newspapers are major instruments of social and political change that shape ideas, journalists occupy key positions in the struggle for authority to determine all facets of public opinion and organize political, social, and economic aspects of culture.

Like Tönnies, he recognizes the influence of economic pressures on the press, in particular, and sees a need for a detailed, scientific study of newspapers for a precise, contemporary assessment of the press. Although unsuccessful, his ideas (as outlined in notes and speeches) nevertheless form a comprehensive agenda for communication research; he anticipates major social and political issues related to questions of consumption and effects, dissemination, and material conditions of communication, which surface decades later in an era of late capitalism and in the specific historical context of accelerated technological expansion and the rise of an information society—particularly in the United States.

Weber's approach to the press represents the culmination of late-nineteenth-century considerations of the press and its role in an emerging, industrialized German society in which democratic sentiments began to influence public life. Like his predecessors, in this account of an academic tradition that focuses on the press, public opinion, and the public, Weber combines theoretical insights with a need to serve practical, if not political, goals. He understands the need for information concerning the practice of journalism and insists on a social scientific study of newspapers before engaging in theoretical assessments of the press and its social, cultural, economic, and political role in modern society. And he anticipates, on the verge of World War I, the importance of the press in a democratic setting that emerges with the political renewal of Germany during the Weimar Republic.

8

The "American Science" of Society: Albion Small, Edward Ross, and William Sumner on Communication and the Press

SOCIOLOGY AND SOCIAL CHANGE

The history of the social sciences in the United States is a modest chapter in the history of Western ideas. However, it includes a fascinating story of intellectual movements that are based on the transfer of knowledge and the adaptation of social thought in a nineteenth-century transatlantic migration of ideas. The adaptation of recent Western European social thought—ranging from post–World War II Marxism to structuralism and the advent of postmodernism—may serve as a reminder of the latest enhancement of knowledge and conquest of interests that began about a century earlier with rising demands for intellectual insights from an ambitious academic and professional class in the United States that was inspired by a cultural if not physical proximity to European ideas. At that time, American students flocked to universities abroad, including Germany, for encounters with world-class scholarship at universities like Leipzig, Berlin, and Heidelberg.

Indeed, thousands of American students engaged in graduate work in Germany throughout the latter part of the nineteenth century, among them future intellectual and academic leaders in their respective fields of sociology, economics, or political sciences.[1] Jürgen Herbst describes their experiences and the influence of German thought on the development of American scholarship. Recognizing the complexity of tracing any direct effects or a "transfer of culture" in specific instances, Herbst (1965, 232) concludes that "the Americans who went to German universities to acquire the tools of scholarship brought home not only tools but ideas as well. When the ideas proved difficult to assimilate to American conditions, the scholars sought to modify or discard them, only to realize that their scholarly equipment, torn from its ideological setting, would no longer serve until a new context of ideas could be developed."

This context was provided by a focus on public life, a recognition of process and change as elements in a working definition of modern society, and a perceived need for social reform. Consequently, an emerging social science tradition approaches issues of societal needs as relevant and becomes a useful source of suggestions for changing and improving social conditions. Although German scholars from Karl Marx to Max Weber were also engaged in discussing social reforms, this approach was a uniquely American way of combining academic pursuits and commonsense social action.

This chapter concentrates on the rise of an "American science" of society, which emerges from acquired knowledge about German scholarship and social concerns and becomes an important source for understanding the language of the social sciences that came to dominate the discourse of American "mass communication research" in the twentieth century.

It has been suggested that American sociology, in particular, develops in response to urbanization and industrialization through the work of a number of individuals and institutions; together they represent an intellectual commitment to improve social conditions and to operate through evolving university-level courses that stress social problems and help identify social issues. Hinkle and Hinkle conclude (1954, 2) that the discipline "emerged in a social context in which the city and the factory were principal monuments of change. Few of the early sociologists would have seriously questioned the prosperity of defining as progress the accumulating artifacts of living and the increasing mastery over nature wrought by the application of science to technology in the nascent urban-industrial society." Describing potential problem areas, such as differences between urban and rural interests, power of economic and political control, and the effects of technology on working conditions, Hinkle and Hinkle single out sociologists "among those who hoped to employ science in the amelioration of social evils" (1954, 2).

The contributions of early Americans sociologists are based on the theories of Comte and Spencer, in particular, and show the impact of other European scholars, notably Schäffle, while reflecting the particular social, economic, and political conditions of the time. Thus Albion Small—one among several founders of American sociology whose work influenced the direction of the field for several generations—met widespread agreement among his colleagues when he formulated four basic assumptions which, according to his observations, provide the framework for sociological thought in the United States.

He describes specific reactions to these propositions by sociologists in 1906, writing that

> (1) They accepted the task of searching for scientific laws of human behavior, which resemble invariant natural laws governing physical and organic phenomena. (2) They identified social changes as social evolution and interpreted it as progress toward a better society. (3) They regarded such upward human development as subject to acceleration by direct human melioristic intervention, using knowledge of sociological laws. (4) Finally, they conceived of social behavior and society as constituted of individual behavior and particularly emphasized the motivations of individuals in association. (Hinkle and Hinkle 1954, 8–9)

In the context of German social thought concerning the press, public opinion, and the importance of communication, in general, and the rise of an American sociology with a similar understanding of communication, in particular, this chapter will focus on ideas about communication and media, as reflected in the works of Albion Small, Edward A. Ross, and William Summer, which are rooted in the writings of Albert Schäffle, Karl Knies, and Karl Bücher. Later contributions to the study of communication in society show intellectual links to the works of Karl Marx, Max Weber, and Ferdinand Tönnies.

The first group of American sociologists represents a generation of intellectuals that witnessed decisive economic and social changes during the latter part of the nineteenth century. For instance, the rise of industrialization, coupled with the growth of American capitalism, particularly, provides a major target for criticism of the economic system and elicits suggestions for social reform. Among the many protests and pleas are the calls of social scientists and journalists—many later identified as the muckrakers of their time—who attacked corruption in the cities, the plight of workers, and the power of big business. Among them were E. L. Godkin, founder of the *Nation* magazine, with his attacks on plutocracy in America, and Henry Demarest, whose *Wealth against Commonwealth* (1984), a "reporter's book of facts," anticipates the muckraking crusades of a few years later. With the aid of S. S. McClure, a number of individuals launch attacks on the social and economic conditions of the United States in his magazine and reach a fast-growing number of readers. For instance, in a January 1903 promotional advertising *McClure's* concludes that

> capitalists, workingmen, politicians, citizens—all breaking the laws, or letting it be broken, Who is left to uphold it? The lawyers? Some of the best lawyers in this country are hired, not to go into court to defend cases, but to advise corporations and business firms how they can get around the law without too great a risk of punishment. The judges? Too many of them so respect the laws that for some "error" or quibble they restore to office and liberty men convicted on evidence over-whelming convincing to common sense. The churches? We know of one, an ancient and wealthy establishment, which had to be compelled by a Tammany hold-over health officer to put its tenements in sanitary condition. The colleges? They do not understand. There is no one left: none but all of us. (1903, 336)

Problems of big business and the effects of technology and industrialization are reflected in the writings of individuals such as Ida Tarbell, Ray Stannard Baker, and Lincoln Steffens, who, together with Josiah Flint *(The World of Graft)* and James Howard Bridge *(The Inside History of the Carnegie Steel Company)*, set the pace for others whose work was to appear in such magazines as Edward Bok's *Ladies' Home Journal*, as well as *Everybody's*, *Leslie's*, *Hampton's*, *Cosmopolitan*, and *American Magazine*, which had been taken over by Steffens, Tarbell, Baker, Peter Finley Dunne, and William Allen White. These writers and editors, together with others, represent what has been described by Louis Filler as "a new moral, radical type of writing by men and women who yesterday had been entirely unknown or had written less disturbingly" (1976, 9). Filler adds, "These writers savagely exposed grafting politicians, criminal police, tenement eyesores. They openly attacked the church. They defended labor in disputes which in no way concerned them personally, decried child exploitation, wrote pro-suffragist articles, and described great businesses as soulless and anti-social."

But the press also came under attack after decades of advancing into the ranks of big business interests in the United States, when managers and owners of the press defined independence in terms of economic stability after realizing that profitability rests on advertising revenue and their abilities to attract large numbers of readers. Thriving on its visibility, the press was admired and condemned at the same time by those who recognized its powers as friend or foe of society. Thus an admirer such as Mabel Dodge, who called her time the "age of communication," surrounded herself with representatives of power and influence, among them "heads of newspapers" (Luhan 1936, 80–84), while others, such as Upton Sinclair, whose *The Brass Check: A Study of American Journalism* appeared in 1919, left little doubt about his negative experiences with American journalism.

Concerns about the proper role of the press are also reflected in contributions to scientific and literary journals. Articles appeared in the *Ameri-*

can Journal of Sociology, for instance, that deal with the press and public opinion, journalism education, effects of newspaper coverage, and press ethics. They are sometimes accompanied by references to the fact that sociologists, in particular, had an obligation to deal with the role and function of the press in society and should address such problems in their work.[2] It is in the context of such a widespread discussion of economic and social problems of the press and journalism among literary, philosophical, and journalistic circles that social scientists add their own ideas and provide yet another perspective to the social reform movement that emerges at the time.

The slow but steady development of a diverse and critical literature of press responsibilities, including the rights and obligations of journalists in the United States, however, not only reflects intellectual-political or scholarly concerns but also signals a perceived need for a regular and systematic treatment of media problems in modern society. These writings, particularly by social scientists, are reminders of the vitality of critical thought at the start of media studies in the United States; they also reflect the universal problems that accompany the commercialization of social communication in modern societies and their complexity, despite significant efforts throughout the latter part of the twentieth century to understand the relations of media and society.

This chapter focuses on a small group of early American sociologists whose ideas on communication and media offer some insights into the cross-cultural nature of their scholarly concerns. Not unlike their German teachers, these sociologists were widely educated and applied their expertise to concrete and timely issues of the day. For instance, after practical experiences, Ross began his career in economics, while Sumner and Small added theology and history to their studies in economics. Although Small and Ross focused on academic careers, they often participated in contemporary public events; Sumner, a clergyman, also did work for a religious newspaper. Their intellectual interests bridge academic knowledge and public concerns, not unlike the work of their German teachers and colleagues, who combined practical professional experience and scholarly pursuits. Thus Sumner represents a conservative position with his belief in the good of the individualistic enterprise, while Small favors a broad interpretation of democratic ideals and Ross champions political and economic equality.

Their work, in particular, parallels the work of Thorstein Veblen, an influential and contemporary evolutionary social philosopher, and foreshadows or accompanies the contributions of John Dewey, George Herbert Mead, Charles Horton Cooley, or Robert Park, in particular, whose own work reinforces the place of communication and media in considerations of American society.

SMALL AND THE LEGACY OF ALBERT SCHÄFFLE

Albion Woodbury Small (1854–1926) was a keen observer of German sociology after his initial contact with German scholarship and the work of Albert Schäffle early in his academic career. Small discusses some of his own experiences (1915–1916, 773) in his review of American sociology, and he admits that for several years, his "lectures were an elaboration of Schaeffle, with one eye constantly on Spencer and Ward. This is a deliberate confession that during those years these writers about social phenomena got between me and the reality itself." Small had reviewed Schäffle's *Bau und Leben des Sozialen Körpers* for the *American Journal of Sociology* (1896–1897, 310–15), and he describes his own approach to general sociology several times throughout his discussion of the "Scope of Sociology," which appeared in the same journal a few years later (1899–1900, 1924–1925).

Acknowledging the contributions of a functional theory of society, Small notes (1900–1901, 522–23) that this trend in sociology "gives to Schaeffle's work its permanent value despite the limitation. . . . Structural and functional analysis of activities within the state, or within society as a whole is prerequisite to classification of the associations that make up the state of society."

Small continues to outline Schäffle's contribution to a detailed analysis of society. Thus he "showed in great detail how different parts of the associational process interpenetrate each other and together maintain the entire individual and social life-process. He was far ahead of his time in prevision of the scientific and practical demand for this analysis." At the same time, Small is aware of the mounting critique of Schäffle's work, which he dismisses as uninformed. "It has been the rule, ever since the first edition of his work appeared, to abuse and misrepresent it and its author in a fashion which indicates more plainly than anything else that people had not read the volume" (1900–1901, 522–23).

Small sees, instead, a rising appreciation of Schäffle's contribution, particularly by Gustav von Schmoller, which "shows that people who have less ability to make up sane opinions on the merits of evidence, but who are not above echoing secondhand judgments, will soon be obligated to acquire a new set of estimates of *Bau und Leben*." Small considers Schäffle's analysis "only an incident in progress toward teleological analysis and classification of associations within states" (1900–1901, 523).

A few years later in his elaboration of a general sociology, Small concludes that Schäffle and Spencer must be given credit for a new interpretation of society. Outlining the process of intellectual labor in an emerging field of European sociological studies, he notes, "Almost at the same moment with the publication of Roscher's book, Schäffle was writing the preface of *Bau und Leben des socialen Körpers* (1875), and Spencer was delivering the first installment of *Principles of Sociology* (1874–1877)" (1912–1913, 205–6).

It was the rediscovery of society by Schäffle and Spencer, characterized by Wilhelm Roscher, according to Small, as "certainly one of the foremost economists of our time" and "a cosmic philosopher who was doing more than any contemporary to advise the world of the significance of Charles Darwin's generalizations." Despite ridicule and abuse by their opponents, Small lauds their "achievement in objective apprehension of human reality," admitting at the same time that although "both overworked biological analogies as vehicles for exposition of the interconnections between human facts . . . all their crudities of method were outweighed by their service in visualizing literal relations between different human activities." More specifically, Small concludes that "Schäffle and Spencer had outgrown the obsessions which credited 'state' and 'society' with 'spheres' set off in mystical ways from persons. They had advanced to the perception that human experience, from earliest to latest, is a function of innumerable group relationships." In fact, Small characterizes the "Schäffle-Spencer stage of society interpretation" as "assured of the continuity of human relationships" and interconnections. He says, "The clue which their analyses followed was that society is a plexus of personal reactions mediated through institutions or groups. One among these reaction-exchanges was the state; but the state was no longer presumed to be in the last analysis of a radically different origin, office or essence from any other group in the system. It simply had to pass muster with the other groups, on the merits or the demerits of its performance" (1912–1913, 205–6).

Small's identification with Schäffle's study of society also occurs in his definition of sociology, which moves from a direct adoption of Schäffle's formulation to a more elaborate discussion of human associations which, many years later, still shows signs of Schäffle's influence. For instance, in his 1890 syllabus, "Introduction to the Science of Sociology," Small argues that sociology is "the science which has for its subject-matter the phenomena of human society, viz., the varieties of groups in which individuals are associated, with the organization, relations, functions and tendencies of the various associations. In other words, sociology is the science which combines and correlates all the special social sciences" (1924–1925, 329).

Small elaborates (1905, 619–20) on the essence of sociology and summarizes his ideas of an "associational process" with specific acknowledgments of Spencer, Schäffle, and Ratzenhofer. He emphasizes human interests and desires that result in efforts to satisfy wants and thus create contact, if not clashes, which forge opposing groups and associations. He adds that "incidental to this pursuit of purposes, and to the process of adjustment between persons, individuals enter into certain more or less persistent structural relationships with each other, known in general as 'institutions,' and into certain more or less permanent directions of effort, which we may call the social functions." Small explains that these "social structures and functions are, in the first instance, results of the previous associational process; but they no sooner pass out of the fluid state, into a relatively stable condition, than they become in turn causes of subsequent stages of the associational process, or at least conditions affecting details of the process." Furthermore, individuals relate to their immediate surroundings; they "think of their family, their clan, their tribe, their nation, as having interests of its own, instead of confining themselves to impulsive action stimulated merely by their individual interests. . . . That is, the groups, as such, entertain purposes, and combine their efforts with some degree of reference to them." Small concludes that

> interpretation of specific stages or areas of human experience is consequently a matter of qualitative and quantitative analysis of the experience in terms of these primary factors. History, or our own current experience, records its meaning in the degree in which it discloses the forms, the quality, the force, and the proportions with which these various powers of the different elements and conditions of association participate in the given action. (1905, 620)

These reflections indicate Small's commitment to an organismic view of society, while demonstrating his knowledge of theoretical discussions in Europe and the controversies that surround Schäffle's work, in particular. He is aware of differences between categories of "organism," however, as they appeared before and after the 1850s and suggests that the "technical difference" was "that in the former period it was used in the most obvious popular sense, while in the latter it was elaborated and criticized and deliberately employed for what it was worth as a tool of analysis" (1912–1913, 450).

Given his theoretical orientation, Small follows Schäffle's emphasis on communication as a necessary condition for the development of society and privileges language as a medium for passing on traditions. He describes the need for "a free, rapid and accurate communication of physical impulses throughout the organism" and focuses on the family as a pivotal element in the process of social communication. He suggests that "ideas do not enter the family circle, however, through only one parent or both, but are introduced by every member and communicated to all who are mature enough to comprehend" (Small and Vincent 1894, 246).

In fact, communication relies on language, the "most flexible means of capitalizing human experience and of making it at the same time a circulating medium.'' Small characterizes language further by pointing out that it ''stores up previous experiences in forms available for present application . . . makes past discoveries instantly available . . . [and] is a master-key to choice between processes that will and will not serve present purposes.'' He adds that it is also ''a deposit of valuations which are like lighthouses for the sailor'' that ''make navigation a matter of comparative safety and certainty, whereas without these guides it would be extra-hazardous'' (1914–1915, 640).

In their 1894 *Introduction to the Study of Society*, Small and Vincent develop a communication model that appears based on the biological analogy of Schäffle's theory of communication. Accordingly, communication as part of a regulatory system in society penetrates the social organism and operates ''as the nerve fibers to the coordinating and controlling centers in the animal organism'' (1894, 215). Communication in society consists of a combination of psychical and physical changes that bring about the successful transmission of messages. Small and Vincent argue that ''every social communication is effected between individuals, and every individual is a part of many different channels in the social nervous system'' (1894, 216). Their model implies that individuals are not only mediating but also ''terminal'' cells in the communication process; they are ''structurally a center from which radiate a greater or less number of psycho-physical channels. If we regard any two of these converging channels as continuous, the individual is a connecting cell. On the other hand, from the standpoint of the individual, he is a terminal cell, or end organ, of all the lines of communication which radiate from him into society'' (1894, 217–18).

Individuals communicate ideas through a variety of symbols that preserve and render them transmissible. Small and Vincent (1894, 219) list among those symbols ''oral, written, and printed language, vocal and instrumental music, gestures, drawing, photographs, paintings, status, theatrical and operatic representations,'' following Schäffle's elaboration on symbols and communication, which render the basis for discussing the dissemination and transmission of knowledge and information throughout society. The preservation of ideas through writing, printing, sculptures, or pictorial presentation, as well as the coordination of communication efforts through postal services or telegraph companies, suggests a structure that could provide technical devices to accommodate the presentation of symbols over space and time.

In their discussion of the arrangement and coordination of communication channels, Small and Vincent note that social communication systems are based on the existence of communication channels in social groups and on coordination with a source of authority. Thus they identify a general communication system in society as consisting of a number of clearly distinguishable parts: "(1) the press, (2) the commercial system, (3) public address, (4) the educational system, (5) the ecclesiastical system, (6) the government system." These parts are inseparably interwoven with other parts of the system; for instance, they add that the press "is incorporated in nearly every division of the psycho-physical communication apparatus, and is almost as general in its scope as the post office itself" (1894, 223). The authors emphasize the significance of these specific communication systems in society by selecting several examples, such as the communication process in economic organizations, "by which production, transportation, and exchange of wealth are coordinated"; the public speaker as a center of "as many different psycho-physical channels as he has hearers," the functions of schools to increase and communicate knowledge; the church, which presents "peculiar psychical impulses" from a religious standpoint; and finally organized government, which is described as "the clearest and most complete example of a social communicating structure" (1894, 227–32).

Most significant, however, is their description of the press, which represents "all the arrangements of communication channels for the collection of ideas, the embodiment of them in printed symbols, and the distribution of the latter throughout social groups of greater or less magnitude." More specifically, Small and Vincent see the organization of the press as a "convergence of psycho-physical channels towards a center, where there are devices for making symbols, which are distributed by various means of transportation among larger or smaller numbers of individuals" (1894, 224).

They comment on the existence of general interest newspapers catering to the needs of larger segments of society and "group" newspapers designed to satisfy special interest groups or organizations. The communication network also consists of news agencies on national and international levels, press syndicates, and plate makers, all of which help disseminate identical messages throughout the societal system with the aid of special agents, such as wholesalers, retailers, and carriers, who are responsible for transporting printed materials.

To illustrate the communication of news items, Small and Vincent use the working conditions of a telegraph editor, who is "the connecting link between the paper and the outside world." They note the process of selection throughout the organization and trace the movement of news, concluding that "the report of an anarchist outrage in Seville finds a ready channel via Madrid, Paris, London, and New York or Chicago to any American city or large town" (1894, 226).

But the authors also emphasize the effects of social and economic developments on the spread of knowledge; with the division of labor, for instance, demands for information increase among individuals. "Other important means of education in the form of books and newspapers now enter the community in considerably larger numbers, relatively to the population—an increase due both to greater regularity of transportation, and to the new demand which, as we have seen, is created by the modified conditions of village life" (1894, 133).

Industrialization and the expansion of urban life result in the rise of opinion leaders and increase the power of newspapers as social institutions beyond their immediate environments. Small and Vincent describe the growing impact of those whose expertise in one field leads to their acceptance as opinion leaders over a wide range of topic areas, giving "direction to social knowledge, feeling, and volition" (1894, 325).

Their views of the press in its relation to leaders and their publics recall Schäffle's discussion of newspaper practice in the context of political and social advancements of society. The press becomes the most important instrument for the communication of ideas between authorities and their followers, since personal contacts and public meetings present severe limitations to exerting direct and constant influence. Small and Vincent enumerate the sources of expertise and their uses of public communication. They observe that

> scholars present the results of their researches in books and journals; theological leaders have papers of their own, and also gain admission to the general press; statesmen and politicians often control personal newspapers; which parties, factions, syndicates, and other groups either manage their own organs or exert influence upon other journals. The authorities of fashion communicate impulses by means of special newspapers, as well as through the general press. (1894, 326)

In addition, Small and Vincent comment on the social and cultural role of the press and note the rise of opinion leaders; their daily experience with newspapers demonstrates widespread use among those who seek to impress and lead their fellow citizens in matters of public interest. They are confident that advanced studies of society will yield more evidence to show the "immense influence of the press" and add that the impulses of the press "give stimulus and direction to social activities of every kind. The fact that large numbers of individuals are not reached directly by the newspaper does not materially weaken this statement. The press influences all, at least, who are capable of exercising leadership, and through them makes itself felt to the very limits of the psychical organism" (1894, 326). At the same time, the authors understand that the press may used by different interests for purposes of manipulation and effect or may be managed and controlled by other means. They suggest that coercion of authority, for instance, can be accomplished by the use of letters to the editor and "personal communications to officials, mass meetings, etc., [which] are among the means employed by the public to influence authority" (1894, 329).

Small and Vincent include a critical assessment of press performance in their discussion of newspapers because they seem convinced that the press wields formidable influence. Thus they advocate a close examination of press enterprises and their services, including a review of press practices and detailed comments on the duties and responsibilities of newspapers.

For instance, they conclude that the press does not provide adequate services in reporting facts, giving direction to public opinion, and respecting the form and content of their information. Despite its highly organized character, the press remains careless and inefficient in its news coverage; the "average newspaper as a reporter of reality is the old-time gossip in print" (1894, 295). Sensationalism combined with self-interest, and sometimes corruption, leads to distortions of facts, which makes it almost impossible to glean from newspapers knowledge of social activities and a proper sense of ethical behavior.

In fact, Small and Vincent comment on the negative effects of publishing questionable materials, reflecting a later preoccupation of "mass communication research" with the impact of violence, sex, and obscenity on society. But they remain sensitive to the interdependent character of the press as a societal institution and modify their conclusions with specific references to the larger social conditions of industrial society. For instance, they complain that "suggestive pictures and plays are a constant menace to society, as a source of psychical changes in individuals, which, finding outward expression in ill health and vice, affect the whole organism from the family to the state" (1894, 295). But they refrain from condemning the press as being solely responsible for causing antisocial behavior. For them, the press is part of the social fabric, and its expressions have to be seen as reflecting societal developments. Most importantly perhaps, they observe that newspapers "exhibit all the phenomena of interdependence that characterize other organs" (1894, 329).

This approach includes considerations—and a critique—of the economic dependence of the press; not unlike their German colleagues, they conclude that subscriptions and advertising are major economic determinants of the commercial well-being of newspapers, otherwise "an organ which fails to secure adequate sustenance, must perish. Hence the first question with any newspaper is, in the nature of things, economic." Also, newspapers must cater to the interests of their readership to remain attractive to sufficiently large numbers of individuals. Thus content reflects the products of authorities as well as the results of public reaction and must "adapt itself, in a measure, to that public's opinion, tastes, and prejudices" (1894, 329).

Nevertheless, newspapers as representations of social and political authority and cultural power must not be held accountable for the general problems of society. Small and Vincent understand the complexity of social processes and favor a much broader approach to issues of effects, for instance. They strongly suggest that although the press may exhibit pathological phenomena, "the responsibility must be distributed throughout the whole organism, not fixed upon the newspaper as the ultimate source of the evils" (1894, 330). Their position suggests not only the inclusive nature of public communication but also a strong sense of public participation and, therefore, a shared public responsibility for the behavior of the press.

Since Small's work, in particular, reflects the strong and lasting influence of notably Schäffle's social theories, his writings on society privilege the notion of communication as a social process at the center of sociological inquiries. Beyond recognizing the importance of symbols and language as means of social communication, he insists on the interdependence of various communication channels and emphasizes the systemic character of communication. Since the press, as part of a system of public communication, occupies a central role as collector and disseminator of information, it warrants close scrutiny. For instance, when Small addresses the gatekeeping function of editors and describes the two-step flow of communication, he identifies future activities of "mass communication research."

His assessment of the press as a powerful and effective instrument of social communication implies that suggestions for improvements of society must begin with a critical investigation of the existing media system, involving all facets of society; after all, a sound and well-functioning system of public communication is a burden shared equally by all participants in the process of social communication.

ROSS AND THE PUBLIC ROLE OF SCHOLARSHIP

Edward A. Ross (1866–1951) combines scholarship with an intense public engagement in social issues of the day; his orientation toward social action makes him unique among early American sociologists, notably Lester Ward, Charles Cooley, Franklin Giddings, Albion Small, and William Sumner. He is a keen observer and reporter of his social and economic environment, and his wide-ranging interests at home, as well as his travels abroad, are amply reflected in a large number of publications. Since his contributions also appeared in a variety of popular magazines and books, Ross may be considered a serious contributor to the investigative journalism of the day.

Indeed, problems of communication and media remain part of his theoretical and practical concerns in many of his writings. Theoretically, Ross considers communication one of the most important examples of the social process, which plays a central role in his earlier scholarly work, while public opinion and the processes of publicity are problematized as external agencies of social control. In practice, he considers the growing commercialization of the press, the impact of radio, and the effects of film on the minds of young individuals to be manifestations and consequence of improved social communication in the modern age.

Ross not only defines communication in terms of symbols but also includes the means of dissemination. Thus the notion of communication embraces both and "takes in facial expression, attitudes and gestures, tones of the voice, speech, writing, printing, the newspaper, telegraphs, telephones, radios, railways, automobiles, airplanes, and whatever else facilitates mental contacts." He sees the development of transportation and communication as ways of improving human interaction and constituting the rise of "congenial association" beyond the physical limitations of small towns or neighborhoods and the intellectual confines of small groups. "But with the aid of modern facilities for communication you may discover distant spirits who are more congenial and stimulating to you than your near relatives or next-door neighbors" (1938, 140).

Earlier, Ross had suggested that the patterns of economic life demand changes in the system of communication. Thus the "growth of potential exchange, in consequence of the greater local surpluses to be disposed of and the greater local deficits to be supplied from outside sources, makes it worth while to create avenues of communication, and these, in turn, promote the territorial division of labor" (1904–1905, 84). But the subsequent advancements of communication technologies had a number of consequences for individuals, who were not only able to travel farther and exchange ideas faster but also capable of receiving a variety of social stimuli and belong to a number of different publics, because of various media at their disposal. Ross notes that "by taking a number of newspapers one can belong to several publics with, perhaps, different planes of vibration" (1903–1904, 362). In fact, he defines the public as a "dispersed crowd, a body of heterogeneous persons, who, although separated, keep so closely in touch with one another that they not only respond to a given stimulus at almost the same moment, but are aware of each other's response" (1903–1904, 361).

Ross also describes the differences between face-to-face and mediated communication (by newspapers, for instance) and comments on their respective effects as a result of one or the other form of exposure. Media create delayed responses, for instance, and in each other's presence "the means of expressing feeling are much more copious and direct than the facilities for expressing thought. In a dispersed group feeling enjoys no such advantage. Both are confined to the same vehicle—the printed word—and so ideas and opinions run as rapidly through the public as emotions; perhaps more rapidly, for is it not easier for a writer to be clear than to be forceful" (1903–1904, 362).

When reading replaces face-to-face communication as a source of ideas, however, especially with the spread of new communication technologies, problems of isolation, if not alienation, must be recognized and addressed. Ross feels that it would "be bad for the bulk of people never to get beyond so unstimulating a way of gaining ideas." And he welcomes a new or modern pedagogy that "encourages the pupil to self-activity and trains him to debate and the oral interchange of ideas! Even more promising is the spread of 'social centers,' where neighbors in their common hall consider community problems of which they have first-hand knowledge" (1916–1917, 318).

Since Ross observes an antitraditional bias of new media, he wants to make sure that readers understand the consequences of a media system that privileges the present and uses an ahistorical approach to social or political explanations of their existence. He understands that literacy makes for progress but concludes that today "at least, the power to read opens a door to the newspaper, which is the natural enemy of tradition, because it is bound to emphasize the new and to exaggerate the momentousness of the present" (1918, 231).

Ross remains critical of the lack of tradition or historical consciousness even twenty years later (and after the introduction of radio and film), when he argues that with "its emphasis on the present the newspaper weakens the grasp of traditions which hold groups apart." Reading the same newspaper produces the same orientation and common interests; newspapers homogenize and simplify. Thus it happens that "the American 'yellow' newspaper, which by means of scare-heads, color pictures, comic strips, and gong effects gains the attention of foreign-born, has been a potent agent of Americanization" (1938, 337).

Although newspapers are organs of public opinion, their self-serving interests often destroy their value as a reflector of societal interests or demands. Ideally, organs of public opinion not only express existing views but also help shape judgments. Newspapers therefore are potentially dangerous instruments of manipulation in the hands of individuals or groups who are determined to enhance their own causes by creating a favorable climate of public opinion. Ross admits that newspapers have a "great and growing power over the public mind owing to its fixing the perspective in which current events are seen by the reader," and he elaborates on various strategies of deception. He feels, for instance, that by

> controlling the distribution of emphasis in the telling of facts, by stressing day by day one sort of facts and keeping the opposite sort in the background, by giving the news which he wants noticed the front page and bold type, while giving the news he wants overlooked an inside page and nonpareil, the newspaper-owner manufactures the impressions that breed opinion and, if he controls a chain of important newspapers, he may virtually make public opinion without the public knowing it. (1917–1918, 629–30)

These remarks project the problems of chain ownership, one-newspaper towns, and local monopolies of information, which would become major targets of media criticism a generation later.

Ross traces these activities to the competitive nature of the newspaper business, which relies on advertising revenues and circulation figures to survive and prosper. In addition, to enhance its economic condition, the press must exploit unique and bizarre aspects of life, resulting in the growth of sensationalism. The result is a press that succeeds not only in "distorting the significance of the moment" but in generating superficiality, particularly in the sensational press. Ross suggests that "the constant flitting from topic to topic brings upon the confirmed newspaper reader what we may call paragraphesis, i.e., inability to hold the mind on a subject for any length of time. Reading so inimical to poise, self-control, and mental concentration as the sensational newspaper should be cut down to a minimum" (1918, 86).

His comments reveal a remarkable understanding of significant changes in the production and reception of information that have come about with the arrival of new communication technologies; headline news services, or the world in a minute, but also intercutting and editing of visual material (film and television), have become part of the daily media fare that confronts the public with a new and increasingly fractured public discourse.

Ross is convinced that newspaper publishers are rarely aware of the press as an instrument of social reform but relate to their enterprises as businesses with concerns about investments and profit margins. Consequently, "the capital factor gains constantly on the service factor; less and less is the editor-owner able to hire the capital he needs, while more and more the owner is a capitalist who hires the editors he needs" (1938, 563).

His modern, if not contemporary, critique of the press acknowledges the peculiar position of the media, which performs public and commercial services in the form of news, opinion, and advertising. But it is the commercial service—because of the economic strength of advertisers—

rather than the political interest that exerts influence and translates into censorship of editorial matters. In fact, the controlling influence of the commercial mind is due in part to the poor, if not irresponsible, behavior of the press. He charges that the "clandestine prostitution of the great bulk of the newspapers to advertisers is the secret of the astounding domination the business classes have gradually gained over us, a domination which arrests the attention of every philosophic foreigner on his first visit to the United States" (1928, 564). And he warns that complete control by business interests over the American mind could be resisted by teachers and some members of the clergy only as long as attacks on them do not succeed in undermining their spirit.

His comments on the rise of the press—as a major weapon in the hands of commercial interests and its insistence on a special status in society—are reminiscent of a tradition of media criticism that has taken on more urgency in recent years with the increasing identification of media with business interests. His suggestions for reform sound like earlier comments by German scholars such as Bücher, Knies, or even Tönnies.

Ross observes that "the pretensions of the commercialized press to a priestly status have come to be so ridiculous that increasingly the public is indifferent to the so-called 'invasion' of the traditional 'freedom of the press' by government officials and to the newspapers' clamor to be carried in the mails for a pittance" (1938, 566). He asks why ordinary taxpayers should carry the burden by meeting "postal deficits caused by hauling to readers for almost nothing thousands of tons of advertising circulars containing only a little tainted reading matter?" And he suggests that perhaps "the classic privileges should be withheld from newspapers which derive more than a third of their income from advertising. The 'daily paper' would cost more to be sure, but then it might tell more truth!"

His passion as a social critic and his interests in contemporary developments of society are best reflected perhaps in his *Changing America*, a collection of articles dedicated to "my irenic and catholic-minded co-laborer Albion W. Small" and the chapter entitled "The Suppression of Important News," in particular. Ross analyzes the problems of the daily press and its desire to give the public what it wants, which must result in sensationalism, since a press that tries to cater to millions cannot be expected to remain dignified: "To interest errand-boy and factory girl and raw immigrant, it had to become spicy, amusing, emotional, and chromatic. For these, blame, then, the American people" (1912, 109). The real problem of daily newspapers, however, is their failure to present the news, despite a number of significant factors of modern life, such as the utilization of new technologies in the pursuit of information, the increase of more educated men and women in journalism, the near disappearance of personal journalism, and the establishment of schools of journalism—"with high hopes."

But Ross, like most of his predecessors, returns to the political economy of the media for a detailed explanation and lists three economic factors that contribute, in particular, to the failure of the daily press.

First, the American press is a capitalistic enterprise. Large sums of money are necessary to establish and maintain newspapers, especially with rising costs for printing plants, staffs, and news agencies. Editors, because they do not have the capital, are no longer owners of newspapers. Instead, businessmen have taken over and find it difficult to understand why they should run their properties "on different lines from the hotel proprietor, the vaudeville manager, or the owner of an amusement park. The editors are hired men, and they may put into the paper no more of their conscience and ideals than comports with getting the biggest return from the investment." In other words, Ross charges that "the paper is likelier to be run as a money-maker pure and simple—a factory where ink and brains are so applied to white paper as to turn out the largest possible marketable product. The capitalist-owner means no harm, but he is not bothered by the standards that hamper the editor-owner" (1912, 112).

Second, the growth of advertising is a significant factor in assessing newspaper services. Ross succinctly characterizes the two major functions of the press—providing news and selling advertising space. "One calls for good faith, the other does not. The one is the corner-stone of liberty and democracy, the other a convenience of commerce" (1912, 113). Since advertising contributes substantially more to the income of the press (and thus to its stability), concerns for subscribers remain less urgent; the results threaten the independence of news and editorial matter. Ross fears that "when news columns and editorial page are a mere incident in the profitable sale of mercantile publicity, it is strictly 'business-like' to let the big advertisers censor both" (1912, 114). He acknowledges, however, the existence of critical judgment and good sense in society and does not anticipate a complete suppression of news and information as a result of advertising pressures. Instead, he suggests that the "intelligence and the alertness of the reading public" help regulate newspaper content, although he warns that the "immunity enjoyed by the big advertisers becomes more serious as more kinds of business resort to advertising" (1912, 115).

Third, the merger of newspapers with greater business interests and the acquisition of press properties by big business suggest the danger of information control by larger corporations. His observations confirm the beginning of an inevitable process of consolidation and concentration of power over information (and entertainment). Consequently, Ross is afraid that the press could easily become the mouthpiece of special interests that would reinvent the nature of the press by subverting traditional notions of journalism to influence public opinion. Thus the "magnate-owner may find it to his advantage not to run it as a newspaper pure and simple, but to make it—on the sly—an instrument for coloring certain kinds of news, diffusing certain misinformation, or fostering certain impressions or prejudices in its clientele. In a word, he may shape its policy by non-journalistic considerations" (1912, 116).

Ross cites a number of cases to illustrate the power of economic interests over newspaper coverage and editorial decision making. He talks about "kept newspapers" or "killing important news" and the existence of "sacred cows," while demonstrating the ways in which content matter is manipulated by owners and editors. He sees metropolitan daily newspapers, by and large, "as allies of those whom—as Editor Dana reverently put it—"God has endowed with a genius for saving, for getting rich, for bringing wealth together, for accumulating and concentrating money" (1912, 128–29).

Even newspapers that had been engaged in successful crusades against misconduct and corruption would cease to be effective. They would become valuable properties, remain guarded, and protect their commercial investments to resemble newspapers with purely commercial histories.

Instead of "arraigning and preaching," Ross wants to seize opportunities for social communication in various ways. He cites examples that range from muckraking magazines as "vehicles for suppressed news" to the emergence of socialist papers, "less to spread their ideas than to print what the capitalistic dailies would stifle." In addition, he identifies other specialized publications, even oral presentations; he maintains, for instance, that the "demand for lecturers and speakers is insatiable, and the platform bids fair to recover its old prestige. . . . Congressional speeches give vent to boycotted truth, and circulating widely under the franking privilege. City clubs and Saturday lunch clubs are formed to listen to facts and ideas tabooed by the daily press" (1912, 130).

His own solution to the corruption of the press, however, is the establishment of endowed newspapers. Since the public is unable to recognize and pay for the truth, much may be gained from the idea of preserving democracy by turning from the inadequate services of commercial media to the potential of publicly owned newspapers. Therefore, "endowment is necessary, and, since we are not yet wise enough to run a public owned daily newspaper, the funds must come from private sources" (1912, 133). However, to prevent control of public newspapers by individuals who may advocate a conservative (i.e., safe) approach to the printing of news and opinions, Ross suggests governing boards of public newspapers to be selected from among members of civic and professional groups so that "the endowment would rest ultimately on the chief apexes of moral and intellectual worth in the city" (1912, 134).

According to Ross, endowed newspapers would not play up crime, sensational events, or trivial occurrences but would concentrate on presenting interesting, serious news. They constitute an elitist project that would not even attempt to reach millions of readers but would typically focus on opinion leaders, such as teachers, preachers, and other public figures. Endowed newspapers would become a social or cultural corrective and help keep the commercial press honest. Consequently, "the endowed newspaper in a given city might print only a twentieth of the daily press output and yet exercise over the other nineteen-twentieths an influence great and salutary" (1912, 136).

The idea of change through introducing corrective influences appears also in connection with his discussion of manipulating news and information. At the time Ross suggests that a more positive influence on the individual could be achieved through exposure to other life experiences. Instead of "curbing newspapers," Ross advocates the "strengthening of corrective influences." He identifies many of them and argues that the "pulpit addresses itself to the deeper parts of human nature rather than to the more easily awakened instincts. The teacher relies on organized information rather than on organized emotion to bring about the reforms he desires. The writer of a book more often addresses the reader's intelligence than the newspaper writer, so that the use of public libraries has a steadying effect" (1917–1918, 630).

A few years later, with the rise of a cinematic society in the United States, Ross turns to increasing media exposure and the effects of motion pictures on children. In an address to the National Motion Picture Conference in Chicago, he attacks the failure to recognize the needs of adolescents and the effects of unregulated access on the minds of children and juveniles. In particular, he concludes that city children "are [more] sex-wise, sex-excited, and sex-absorbed than any generation of which we have knowledge. Thanks to their premature exposure to stimulating films, their sex instincts were stirred into life sooner than used to be the case with boys and girls from good homes, and as a result in many the 'love chase' has come to be the master interest in life" (1928, 179). He is convinced that more exposure to certain types of films will result in even greater harm to society and advocates guidelines and censorship for children's movies and the right of communities to bar films unsuitable for children.

These concerns are also reflected in his consideration of propaganda and the "wholesale manufacture of misconception." Ross suggests that propaganda and censorship are the new methods of manipulating people and winning political support. He observes, "To be obnoxious propaganda need not resort to falsehood and misrepresentation; it may employ nothing but the truth, yet be anathema to the decent because under its fine professions it hides or suppresses the counter-balancing truth" (1940, 483). He cites the use of newspapers as carriers of one-sided information for the benefit of large corporations, utilities, or politicians, and he sees opportunities for radio to provide a counterforce in attempts to propagandize the public. He advocates the widespread use of broadcasting to deflate unscrupulous propaganda, since radio has certain advantages in combating propaganda. "The spoken word can be more inflammatory than the written, and the human voice can stir emotion quicker than the printed page." Furthermore, he notes the economic advantages of radio and suggests that "a broadcasting station requires little capital, its chief asset is the 'cleared channel of the air' which has been granted it for a brief term on the ground of 'public interest, convenience and necessity' " (1940, 487–88).

Not unlike Small, Ross explains communication as a necessary condition for the growth of society and discusses economic and technological determinants of public communication systems. But, because of the rapid rise of broadcasting and film, he concentrates much of his commentary on the societal effects of modern media. He warns that newspapers, with their exclusive treatment of contemporary events, may contribute to a loss of tradition and sense of history.

The danger posed by the modern press—and its ultimate failure—must be sought in capitalism, which uses newspapers as carriers of commercial messages or controls them through mergers with business interests. Ross, not unlike Bücher, describes the peculiar double nature of the press as public servant in its dissemination of news and opinion and salesperson in its marketing of products. He urges the establishment of publicly owned or endowed newspapers to liberate the press from economic pressures. His discussion of communication effects—including the exposure of children and young adults to motion pictures—anticipates later American "mass communication research" agendas and policy decisions regarding self-regulation of the motion picture industry (or television, for that matter). He advocates censorship based on community standards (of decency) and addresses issues of public communication that have yet to be decided in the spirit of a crusade for access to truthful information and fairness, and in support of freedom of expression, to help strengthen ideas of a democratic system of media and communication in society.

SUMNER AND PROBLEMS OF MASS COMMUNICATION

William Graham Sumner (1840–1910) showed great interest in economics and social problems from the beginning of his academic career, when his work centered on ideas of individualism and laissez-faire, as well as on the role of the "forgotten man" in society. His writings suggest the influence of Herbert Spencer, Ludwig Gumplowicz, Gustav Ratzenhofer, and Julius Lippert, in particular, whose *Kulturgeschichte der Menschheit in ihrem organischen Aufbau* (1866–1867) is reflected forty years later in Sumner's most famous treatise, *Folkways*, published in 1906. The book expresses Sumner's evolutionary view of social life, which denies the possibility of human intervention and social change. "The great stream of time and earthly things will sweep on just the same in spite of us. . . . It will swallow up both us and our experiments. . . . That is why it is the greatest folly of which man can be capable, to sit down with a slate and pencil to plan out a new social world" (1911, 210). Instead, he is convinced that social progress must come gradually and be based on the rather unconscious operations of social, economic, and intellectual forces.

Sumner, too, considers language the most important instrument of communication among individuals and a necessary condition for social and cultural mobility. The "first and prime instrumentality for the exchange of anything between human beings is language. It might be called a tool without stretching that term out of all recognition; it is, at any rate, no organic product, but a societal one" (1934, 160). The gradual development of language is an evolutionary process that involves all members of society. Thus the invention of writing becomes a major accomplishment in the individual's search to overcome time and space. Sumner speaks of "writing as a means for the preservation and transmission of ideas and culture across time and space," and he privileges literature, which "discharges an important function in acquainting peoples with one another's characteristics; the novel has been highly effective in that way."

Intercommunication, according to Sumner, is seen in terms of the transmission of materials and ideas and becomes an important function in the development of human civilization. Indeed, "language is a product of the need of cooperative understanding in all the work, and in connection with all the interests, of life. It is a societal phenomenon" (1906, 134). With the rise of technology, communication improved and brought about the dissemination of ideas over large areas of the world; at the same time, progress also led to different forms of information retrieval and resulted in overcoming space and time while drawing individuals together. Older forms of associations are replaced as "correspondence, travel, newspapers, circulars, and telegrams bring employers and capitalists the information which they need for the defense of their interests" (1974, 76). Consequently, information supports primarily the activities of commercial forces rather than the interests of labor, because of its lack of capital and influence. But Sumner allows that the press, for instance, could begin reporting about the labor market and not necessarily solely in the interest of employers.

As a matter of fact, Sumner sees in the advancements in transportation and communication a rising need for reorganizing industrial efforts on a worldwide scale. He anticipates the social consequences of industrial or technological development and argues that the direction of industrial growth forces inevitable changes on society that cannot be ignored, including the loss of freedom for the small, independent individual, which is "as inevitable as the introduction of machinery and the consequences of machinery" (1932–1933, 736).

The communication of intelligence becomes a dominant cause and reason for reorganizing control, since the rise of communication provides the capability of "close, direct, and intimate action and reaction between the central control and the distributing agents," and he adds that "the highest degree of organization which is possible is the one which offers the maximum of profit; in it the economic advantage is the greatest" (1914, 85–86). Such a view includes the organization of media and foresees the inevitable reorganization, centralization, and increasing profitability of media organizations in the United States. Thus Sumner predicts the social and economic conditions of media practices that would occupy the work of Small and Ross about twenty years later.

The modern press is a creation of the nineteenth century and develops along with industrialization and the revision of economic patterns in American society. Torn between its public responsibilities in a democracy and its potential in a commercial world, the press "is, on the one side, an institution of indispensable social utility, and on the other side a foul nuisance. It exerts a tyranny which no one dare brave." Sumner notes that

> one of the most remarkable facts, however, about the newspaper at this turn of the century is that a great newspaper becomes an entity independent of the opinion or will of its managers. It gets headway and drags them along with it. It has a reputation and policy and becomes subject to the law of consistency. Its managers are hampered by considerations, and obligations, and if they try to do justice to them all, they dare utter only colorless platitudes." On the other hand, getting a chance "to 'pitch into' something or somebody who has no power of defense, they seize the opportunity to manifest freedom and independence.

Sumner concludes that "what priestcraft was to the fourteenth century, presscraft is to the twentieth" (1934, 233–34).

Sumner's notions of the effectiveness of the press are tied to his understanding of class relations, like those between common individuals and societal institutions, including newspapers. The former represent the shallow, prejudiced, and narrow-minded segment of the masses. Sumner suggests that for them, "thinking and understanding are too hard work," and the masses often live "by routine, set formulae, current phrases, caught up from magazines and newspapers of the better class." They also react to the press in ways that reinforce their prejudices, while the press—recognizing the needs of common individuals—caters to their interests. Thus,

> the yellow newspapers thrive and displace all others because he [the common individual] likes them. The trashy novels pay well because his wife and daughters like them. The advertisements in the popular magazines are addressed to him. They show what he wants. The 'funny items' are adjusted to his sense of humor. Hence all these things are symptoms. They show what he 'believes in,' and they strengthen his prejudices. (1906, 48–51)

The common individual is the result of the evolution of democracy during the nineteenth century, although his day of glory would come in the twentieth century, when he would speak as a symbol for "the people" and when "newspapers bow down to him, flatter him, and treat him as the specimen type of 'the people' " (1932–1933, 744). Sumner remains convinced, however, that the press, together with other societal institutions (e.g., universities and churches), had embraced the ideas of the common man for the worse of society. He laments, "The newspapers have taken their cue from him, and our destiny has been settled without any reason or sense, without regard to history or political philosophy." And he muses, "That the press . . . and magazines could have so given up their functions and prostrated themselves before this organ of folly, for fear of falling out of sympathy with the man-on-the-curbstone, would have been incredible if we had not lived through it" (1932–1933, 745).

Indeed, the press prospers with the creation and dissemination of shallow, sensational news, and there is no reason to believe that a quality press would become more successful. Sumner concludes that "it is idle to deny that the worst papers are the most popular and make the most money" (1934, 233–34).

Consequently, he expresses doubts about the usefulness of public discussions and newspaper presentations of extremely complicated issues, as long as numbers of individuals make the difference. He asks, "What is the use of education, learning, training, discipline, if the numbers can solve the questions? or if numbers hold the ultimate test by which to revisit and verify results?" And he warns that newspapers are in no position to participate in reflection and debate because they "are forced to catch everything as it flies. They have no time for quiet and sober reflection. They never finish anything. They never go deeply into anything and never go back to correct mistakes" (1932–1933, 748).

Still, common individuals generate public opinion as the life force of a democratic society, and Sumner agrees that public opinion is "the basic force which underlies all [forms of societal self-regulation]" and defines it as "a matter of feeling rather than of intellect; and the feeling is developed in connection with a more or less localized interest" (1927, 727–28). Thus, based on sentiment and interest rather than on knowledge and intellectual analysis, public opinion seeks outlets not only in modern political processes but also in those media which reflect these interests and sentiments.

Together with formal schooling, newspapers contribute to helping create the type of individual who represents the educational efforts of a democracy. That is to say, Sumner comments on the dangers of public schooling and public communication in their efforts to achieve "big results on a pattern." He observes, "An orthodoxy is produced in regard to all the great doctrines of life. It consists of the most worn and commonplace opinions which are current in the masses. It may be found in newspapers and popular literature. It is intensively provincial and philistine. . . . The popular opinions always contain broad fallacies, half-truths, and glib generalizations of fifty years before" (1906, 631).

Sumner sees the power of language, communication, and public opinion as elementary forces in society; they are major concepts for an evolutionary social process—the preservation and transmission of culture, and political and economic decisions—without being addressed directly in their function as change agents. He is not a social reformer like Small or Ross, who could be identified with the social movements of their times in the United States; however, in his assessment of the American press he sounds very much like other authors, including many contemporary press critics. His assessment of the common individual predates Walter Lippmann's consideration of the masses, and his appraisal of communication as a social process comes close to the definitions of writers like Small and Ross, or those of his German contemporaries. Where he differs, however, is in his belief that inequality is an inevitable sign of freedom and that social reform movements are based mostly on the confusion and ignorance of their proponents. He continues to preach his doctrines in the face of a changing nation, in which social reforms shape political and economic agendas of the day, thus demonstrating that the power of symbols and the success of communication do bring about changes in the minds of people and ultimately changes in the political and economic structure of society.

These writings of Small, Ross, and Sumner are vivid examples of earlier considerations of communication (and the press) that have their roots in German scholarship but also meet the specific historical conditions of their own time and place. They scrutinize the practical, everyday activities of public media, for instance, and ponder the social (and political) consequences of capitalism for communication in society. As such, they offer a range of ideologically informed responses to the rise and legitimation of modern media as major social and cultural institutions in the United States. But they also describe the scope and direction of twentieth-century developments in the media, including topics of ''mass communication research'' and media criticism, in general.

9

Communication and Social Thought: Decentering the Discourse of Mass Communication Research

MIGRATION OF IDEAS

The migration of ideas about communication preceded and overcame world conflicts and ideological differences during the twentieth century and continues to carry alternative visions across cultural borders to confront the dominance of domestic social thought. Collectively, the German and American scholarship described in previous chapters documents the presence of theoretical and practical concerns regarding communication and the role of the press in society across cultures, beginning in the middle of the nineteenth century. It also anticipates content and direction of "mass communication research" agendas ranging from issues of mediation, effects, manipulation, and control to concrete suggestions involving the press and its role in the making of a democratic society. The privileging of communication in these writings only confirms their significance as nineteenth- and early-twentieth-century sources of an intellectual history of "mass communication research" as a discursive formation.

The realization of the role of communication (and the press) in the modern age—as proclaimed in the theoretical discourse of the time—occurs in the context of specific social conditions and technological-economic developments that shaped the symbolic uses of culture and politics, resulting in the emergence of historically specific definitions of the press and the public, the public sphere, and public opinion as constitutive elements of a democratic form of communicative practice.

These authors—and particularly German political economists during the nineteenth century—expect an acceleration of social, economic, and political progress; they also see a need for the rapid and efficient spread of knowledge through new means of communication (ranging from the telegraph to radio) and the concomitant problems of supply and demand of information and production and consumption of news and opinion, as well as control over dissemination in a concrete political-economic context of media organizations. Their articulation of these problems provides further evidence of the centrality of communication in their theories of society.

In addition, the scholarly discourse strongly suggests that a critique of society must begin with a critique of public communication and the institutional construction of realities that involve media practices, including the work of journalists, and public expectations of the role of the media. It demonstrates not only the connectedness of communication and society—enhanced by an evolving critique of the press—but, in turn, points the way to later and more intensified analyses, particularly by American social scientists such as Charles H. Cooley, Robert Park, George Herbert Mead, and John Dewey, whose work expands on the pivotal place of communication in modern thought and sociological inquiry, in general. Similar German efforts at the time involve more philosophical deliberations, beginning perhaps with Fritz Mauthner's *Sprachkritik* (1901–1903) and his suggestion that "philosophy is theory of knowledge. Theory of knowledge is critique of language. Critique of language, however, is labor on behalf of the liberating thought that men can never succeed in getting beyond a metaphorical description of the world utilizing either everyday language or philosophical language" (1910, xi). They also surface in the later work of Ernst Cassirer, Martin Heidegger, and the social-psychological inquiries of Karl Jaspers, as well as Walter Benjamin and his contemporaries during the days of the Weimar Republic, such as Siegfried Kracauer or Bertolt Brecht.

At the same time, European social thought, in general, continued to be open to divergent influences, accepted the idea of change, and reflected the persisting search for different political and social solutions, particularly in the aftermath of World War I; U.S. social thought, on the other hand, was preoccupied with notions of social control and the improvement (and reinforcement) of already existing, ideologically fitting social formations. Thus in contrast to the abundant production and dissemination of material goods in the United States (and the reinforcement of free market ideas) represented in the language of democratic ideals, there had been an insufficient supply of alternative political and, in the widest sense, philosophical ideas. The encounters with communism and the rise of scientific socialism remain mostly European experiences, as Marxism confronted liberal democratic positions and seriously challenged capitalism and establishment politics. In the United States there has been a steadfast reliance on the powerful influence of a democratic perspective of capitalism and its potential for self-correction, which helped determine the boundaries of critical assessments, including the role and function of societal institutions—among them the press and its leading role in the production of social and political realities—until well after World War II.

Thus the early writings of Small, Ross, and Sumner, for instance, and their critiques of the press or public communication in the United States must be appreciated in the context of an emerging social reform movement, which was accompanied by the rise of the social sciences as a science of society during the 1920s and 1930s. Consequently, their work remains within the limits of what could be described politically as a bourgeois-democratic bias of an economic interpretation of media practices. Any acknowledgments of socialism or expressed concern for the welfare of the common individual are mere signs of recognition, not new directions for social criticism with concrete political consequences.

Knowledge of these specific historical conditions, which shaped the analysis of the press and social communication, is not only important for understanding the history of "mass communication research" and media studies, but also meaningful for conceiving contemporary efforts to construct theories of culture and society that take into account the political and ideological realities of communication under the conditions of late capitalism.

Specifically, these American authors and their German predecessors realized that ownership of the means of communication not only reflects economic power or political status but may also determine definitions of education, democracy, and freedom of expression, while affecting the ability of people to think critically about their political environment and to act responsibly in the conduct of public and private affairs. For instance, as education serves to support a political and economic system that encourages consumerism and stresses the value of material well-being, media help reinforce these activities in their advertising and editorial functions. In fact, as advertising replaces education as an institution of lifelong learning for the common individual, the lack of communicative competencies and the rise of public opinion polling turn democracy into an illusion of participation in political decision-making processes of society. Finally, when freedom of expression is limited by the economic determinants of media practices, including the conditions of news work and public access to a relevant forum for public discussion, communication in society becomes a privilege accorded to those empowered by class positions.

Thus the roots of the traditional production of "mass communication research" as a specific social subject are found in the work of previous generations of American social scientists and secured by the legitimation of communication and media as central social scientific concerns. Its rise as a subject of scholarly inquiry occurred within the discourse of the social sciences, with its particular understanding of communication and the location of media in society, and produced the formation of "mass communication research" as a specific social scientific practice of producing and circulating knowledge about "mass communication."

A contemporary theory of communication, conscious of these earlier considerations of German and American scholarship, must consider the economic-political determinants of social communication and develop alternative perspectives, particularly in light of the challenges of neo-Marxist theories of culture and communication that go beyond appeals for the creation of publicly owned or endowed media—a recurrent theme throughout much of the writing. It is based on liberal assumptions regarding social, cultural, and economic equality, educational opportunities, and political commitment.

A more current and comprehensive approach would have to contemplate theorizing the notion of participation and introducing basic changes in the preparation of individuals to partake fully in their own affairs. Postulating and helping create conditions more favorable to their own progress than currently possible, as well as promoting communicative competencies across gender, race, class, and ethnicity, for instance, are key aspects of reconstructing the idea of participation. The emergence of alternative paradigms of communication and media studies has challenged traditional models of "mass communication research" and raises new questions about the process of theorizing itself.

MARXISM, CULTURE, AND COMMUNICATION

The migration of ideas—which had originated in Germany shortly before the turn of the twentieth century—was barely interrupted by the developments of World War II. Emigration and subsequent participation in U.S. intellectual life provided German academics in positions of intellectual leadership within university environments—inspired by the logical positivism of the Vienna Circle or the Western Marxism of the Frankfurt School—with ample opportunities for publicly sharing their thoughts about language, communication, and society.

At that time, "mass communication research" in the United States had gained an independent status as a field of empirical inquiry into the conditions of media and communication in society—separate from the disciplinary concerns of political economy or sociology, for instance, which had already assimilated communication as a social process and theorized media as sources of institutional narratives and societal expansion since the beginning of the twentieth century.

The introduction of Marxist analyses of society into the United States—from the writings of C. Wright Mills to the specific work on media and communication by Dallas Smythe and Herbert Schiller, for instance—received additional support from a critique of capitalism by the émigré scholarship of Max Horkheimer, Theodor Adorno, Herbert Marcuse, and Erich Fromm, whose critical analyses included the role of media in the process of alienation and subordination. Their writings, beginning in the 1940s, have enriched and reinforced progressive thought in communication and media studies since the 1960s.

The importance of their perspectives on communication and culture was underscored by the arrival of British cultural studies and the work of Raymond Williams and Stuart Hall, in particular, who deepened the impact of critical theory with their own theoretical preoccupation, which incorporated and popularized continental social thought (e.g., Georg Lukács, Lucien Goldman, Michel Foucault, Louis Althusser, and Antonio Gramsci) among American academics. The emerging emphasis on ideology, hegemony, and the notion of power provided additional incentives for innovative practitioners of traditional "mass communication research" to engage in alternative analyses of media in society.

The migration of ideas from Europe (and lately from Latin America with the work of Martin Barbero and Garcia Canclini, in particular) was accompanied by another movement from and among academic disciplines: a realignment of disciplinary boundaries with a rising uncertainty about the source and location of knowledge and the process of interrogation. By extending the search for explanations of an increasingly interdisciplinary field of inquiry into the realm of ethnography and literature, for instance, and privileging qualitative research methods, questions of authority, agency, and participation inspired a new vision of culture and communication and redefined the limits of understanding media in a politicized construction of reality (Hardt 1992).

The work of Jürgen Habermas, specifically, invigorated discussions of participation and democratic communication and encouraged the development of alternative models of public communication by focusing on the importance of a "public sphere" in the life of democratic societies, not only in light of an apparently bankrupt political model of participation, but also because of the apparent inability of traditional "mass communication research" to provide viable alternatives. The mounting predicament of communication in late capitalism as a reflection of social, political, and economic problems of society required nonconformist explications, which were typically found in (and identified with) "foreign" contributions to theories of culture, communication, and society in late-twentieth-century America.

The new accessibility of ideas is a vivid reminder of a process that began with the contributions of German—and European—scholarship earlier in the nineteenth and twentieth centuries and continued with conceptualizations and practices that streamed in the opposite direction by the end of World War II. At that time, educational exchanges, remigration, and the free flow of scientific knowledge helped (West) Germany's social science establishment—and *Publizistikwissenschaft*, in particular—acquire social scientific theories (and methodologies) of media and communication. They were adopted—without a significant or lasting critique—as the reigning paradigm of "mass communication research," which was part of an ideologically charged missionary project of democratization that included the collaboration of the U.S. social science establishment to provide theories and methodologies for a postwar European society.

The consequences of an intellectual migration continue to affect American social thought, and considerations of communication and media in particular, beginning with the educational experiences of scholarly elites during the nineteenth and early twentieth centuries in Europe (and in Germany, specifically) and ending with the global spread of ideas; the latter is facilitated by the mobility of intellectuals and the sagaciousness of commercial interests, which resulted in the worldwide dissemination of intellectual products, including music, film, fiction, and social thought.

The contemporary English-language literature of communication and media studies in the United States is filled with references to European, Latin American, and Asian contributors to notions of culture and definitions of communication; they compete for scholarly attention, thus affirming the potential of intellectual work and challenging dominant social thought. Consequently, domestic communication research and media studies in the United States have been uprooted, pushed out of their "splendid isolation," and confronted with alternative explanations in an expanding atmosphere of internationalizing cultural, political, and economic considerations of communication and media. This global expansion of scholarly discourse has been augmented by an increasingly interdisciplinary approach to issues of "mass" communication beyond traditional ties to sociology, social psychology, or even political economy. The resulting formidable intellectual force bears down on the established ideas of the field and creates new possibilities for extrication and liberation.

As a result, the traditional academic pursuit of communication as an essential social practice with its cultural, political, and economic consequences regarding the nature and quality of participation in society has been destabilized by significant theoretical shifts, accompanied by persuasive interdisciplinary claims on the centrality of media and communication for the study of culture and society in a new, politicized scholarly discourse. Scholarly attention has shifted from society to culture as the newly discovered perspective on communication and media, while ethnography and literature have replaced sociology and political science as the nexus of communication and media studies. For instance, in his most recent work John Durham Peters engages a formidable historical/philosophical literature in reflections on the idea of communication which affirm that "communication will always remain a problem of power, ethics, and art" (1999, 268), and therefore will remain a political issue with a specific social, if not communal, relevance. By writing in the tradition of Martin Buber rather than Wilbur Schramm, Peters responds to the need to embrace communication as an imperfect human condition and suggests that to surrender to its frailty and incompleteness becomes a liberating first step toward an authentic existence.

CHALLENGING U.S. MASS COMMUNICATION RESEARCH

The decentering of "mass communication research" as a traditional social scientific enterprise advances alternative visions of "mass communication" that arise from changing ideological perspectives and the emergence of a socially conscious consideration of communication and media in society. The latter is a response to the need for self-reflection and for considering the creative potential of change. It involves a return to the idea of "communication" as the result of a shifting discourse that produces alternate forms and subjects of knowledge about the nature of communication and media.

The study of "mass communication" as the object of an evolving discursive formation (to use Michel Foucault's conceptualization), particularly after World War II, remains identified with the surge of social scientific research practices that characterize the period and dominate attempts to understand media and their effects. Based on work in sociology, social psychology, and psychology, in particular (and therefore associated with a traditional institutional, social scientific apparatus and its disciplinary practices), "mass communication research" is characterized by a strong bias toward quantitative methods and shares the guiding principles of positivism or postpositivism.

Such guiding principles determine thought about how communication "really" works as they construct their reality of "mass" communication and ultimately confirm a social scientific process that promises detached, value-free, and objective observations. The result is a search for a scientifically knowable world—the lived conditions of a media environment—which is the only world that matters as a legitimate terrain of scientific exploration. Whether such a reality is perfectly (positivism) or imperfectly (postpositivism) captured, however, according to the reigning theories of the past decades, remains part of a struggle, particularly after the 1970s, over the preservation of a dominant discursive practice that defines the reality of media and communication in terms of invasive technologies and their institutional and collective purposes (or functions). The latter typically cater to specific social, political, and economic interests and provide the context for the rise of "mass communication research" as the source of (social) knowledge and (political) power.

For instance, these interests have been institutionalized by a decisive turn from "communication" to "information" that coincided with the emergence of cybernetics and a scientific or technical explanation of its significance for society. The notion of an information society, in particular, epitomized already existing social scientific canons of context-free generalization and cause-and-effect explanation and celebrated the potential of prediction and control, Better yet, the conceptualization of an information society as a logical consequence of technological development also removed the uncertainty or ambiguity of the older concept (communication)—problematized and applied during an earlier period of progressive thought by members of the Chicago school—and allowed for a scientific construction of social and cultural uses of media technologies. Such an understanding of communication as information arose and was reinforced through the research practices of the field (of journalism and mass communication) and provided the grounding for a instrumentalist perspective on modern communication processes that became part of the reigning ideology of "mass communication research." The increasing need for identification, definition, and explanation of information phenomena contributed to its success and legitimated its claims as a field of inquiry; it also fostered the success of the "mass communication" expert with professional ties to commercial and political interests and therefore links to the production of knowledge and the exercise of power, as issues of communication became socially and politically relevant in the context of rising social problems in American society that ranged from illiteracy to violence.

In fact, the presence of "mass communication research" reflected an era of certainty that appeared with the development of a sophisticated social scientific apparatus. It was the outcome of an accelerated postwar development in science and technology and complements the political-military success of the United States in world affairs. Its reliance on the reign of facts revealed an irresistible bias toward the production of tangible social and political information. The emergence of public opinion polling, with its confidence in methodology and faith in prediction, reflected the endless possibilities of an applied science that serves the goals of commercial and political interests. It also legitimized the ahistorical and decontextualized nature of such practices, which focus on information rather than knowledge, in seeking solutions in immediate response rather than delayed explanation. Such activities were reproduced prominently in the journalism and advertising of the day as manifestations of social or political events. They perpetuated a theory of society whose notions of truth and reality—with the aid of a community of "mass communication" researchers—were imminently discoverable versions of the dominant ideology.

Consequently, "mass communication" as a social phenomenon became a prominent research topic with references to social, cultural, political, and economic practices that embraced the idea of communication as information. At issue typically were questions of compliance with the pronouncements of the reigning social, economic, and political practices—and therefore control of information and information flows couched in terms of media effects—rather than issues of absence or resistance (e.g., who or what is not represented and why not, or who does not own the media and why not?). To paraphrase Antonio Gramsci, the hegemonic struggle involves captivating, not capturing, the masses with a media environment that distracts from the real conditions of society. Thus accessibility of media technologies and standardization of content—or what Theodor Adorno and Max Horkheimer call the industrialization of culture—are the foundations of an information society that exists with the expenditure of a minimum of communicative efforts or competencies. Their combined effects—important for military and economic purposes during periods of external and internal competition and conflicts—constituted the tangible evidence of production and consumption practices. They provided a measure of "mass communication" in society that speaks to the distribution of power and influence.

Under these conditions, progress in "mass communication research" was the accumulation of knowledge based on perfecting prediction and control of media and information phenomena; it typically occurred under the label of administrative research—to use Paul Lazarsfeld's frequently cited conclusion about contemporary research practices—and preoccupied the "mass communication research" community while providing academic status, including calls for its legitimation as a discipline, and supporting the reproduction of an ideology of "mass communication research" through university-level teaching and research.

Even today, the attempt to understand the notion of media effects and their consequences through experimentation and manipulation (of variables), in particular, reflects a central concern of the field as it continues to relate to social, commercial, and political issues of society. It also constitutes a major preoccupation with methodological issues at the expense of theorizing communication or developing alternative models of media applications. The lingering popularity of "mass communication research" as a legitimate social scientific enterprise has helped strengthen institutional claims by the media industry on leadership and control in society and successfully addresses the problem of source credibility while raising the expert status of the "mass communication" researcher.

By the end of the 1970s the field of "mass communication research" should have been considered a success in the context of competing forces, particularly among traditional university disciplines. However, the social scientific gaze of the observer enforced a regime of decontextualization or randomization that raises questions about the relevance of inquiries whose exclusionary nature provoked the possibility of new paradigms and encouraged critical voices from within the field. Thus, as the result of a theoretical position that produces knowledge by accretion, relies on verification of a priori hypotheses, and seeks a generalizability of its findings, "mass communication research" joined the ranks of a social science tradition whose basic belief structure had come under close scrutiny and outright critique by a growing number of alternative perspectives. After all, social scientific constructs, and the idea of "mass communication" specifically, are still cultural inventions and therefore subject to revision and change.

The social and political conditions of communication in the world, beyond the parochialism of American "mass communication research," have produced a creative and potentially useful atmosphere of critical introspection, encouraged by emancipatory movements and supported by historically conscious reconsiderations of knowledge about communication. As a discursive shift produces a new understanding of communication, it exposes a contemporary generation of "mass communication" researchers to alternative perspectives on the field by introducing them to a number of useful options to rethink the notion of communication as information. Thus it is no accident that during the latter part of the 1980s, in particular, refocusing on the "critical" in communication becomes widespread as the field is looking for new ways of understanding its own history and meeting the challenges to its traditional paradigm.

Accessibility to the more recent cultural discourse in Europe—including a sustained critique of capitalism—also introduces alternative ways of thinking about communication. Its reception by a growing number of theoretically impoverished and politically disillusioned individuals whose academic experience had been confined to working within a "mass communication research" tradition provides the historical context for the adoption of Marxism and particularly British cultural studies. These new perspectives are particularly effective because they address directly the traditional concerns of American "mass communication research" related to the role and function of media in society. Their different theoretical possibilities, however, contain the potential for a major paradigm shift in the history of the field.

Thus the previous notion of information society undergoes an ideological critique when communication is reintroduced as a viable, if complex, concept of human practice. In fact, the idea of communication is related again to agency and the emancipatory struggle of the individual, and the political considerations of communication and media encourage practical responses to concrete problems. The result is a discursive shift that provides opportunities for alternative ways of conceptualizing society, the public sphere, and the nature of democratic practice itself, based on an understanding of a historically grounded reality of institutions and practices that can be grasped, interrogated, and reconstructed through a dialectical process. It reflects a materialist-realist position and suggests the importance of material differences in terms of the conditions of communication or the place of the media at a given historical moment.

Furthermore, Marxism and Cultural Studies introduce an ideological dimension to the study of communication; they recognize the importance of power and confirm the significance of human agency for communicative practices. Both insist that the goals of their respective inquiries are the critique and transformation of specific social, political, or economic conditions for the purposes of social and political change, specifically, and emancipation, generally. Thus they insist on the role of advocacy and are apt to embrace (social or political) activism grounded in the changing nature of historical knowledge and its potential for different explanations of a contemporary way of life.

Communication inquiry is never value-free; in fact, values help shape outcomes and constitute part of a critical theory of media and communication. Under these conditions, the acquisition of knowledge and the emancipatory goals of critical communication studies are defined by the prospects of change and reconstruction as ideas become obsolete and are overruled by new insights and practices. In fact, a critical communication theory renews itself as it confronts different conditions and is propelled into different historical situations.

As a result of these developments, "mass communication research" has been challenged to abandon the secure ideological location of unattached observation and become part of the inquiry by joining an agenda that reflects the activist (and often confrontational) stance of critical communication inquiry. Such a position suggests that facts cannot be separated from the domain of values, that the relationship of meaning and language to culture is central to constituting reality, that the interpretive nature of culture and communication precludes a fixed or final truth, that the relations between representation and reality are political, that thought is mediated by historically grounded power relations, and that privilege and oppression in society are reproduced, although perhaps unwittingly, by traditional research practices.

When "mass communication research" comes up against an alternative critical discourse (produced by a convergence of writings identified with the critical theory of Max Horkheimer, Theodor Adorno, Herbert Marcuse, and Erich Fromm, the later work of Jürgen Habermas, the contributions to cultural studies by Raymond Williams and Stuart Hall, and specific references to the works of Louis Althusser, Antonio Gramsci, and Michel Foucault, in particular), it faces a formidable challenge to its traditional position. Together, these writings produce a new and different type of knowledge that focuses on notions of culture, empowers the individual, and addresses the consequences of an "industrialization of the mind" to expose relations of power in the process of communication and provide a forceful critique of cultural practices—to use Hans-Magnus Enzensberger's phrase.

Critical communication studies reproduce such theoretical considerations and construct research agendas that reflect the need for alternative readings of communication and media. When postmodernism arrives in the United States amid such an ongoing critique of "mass communication research" and culture in general, it is met with ambivalence or suspicion, although its arguments help deconstruct the received notion of "mass communication." For example, the work of Jean Baudrillard, whose understanding of media and audiences (which is based on the collapse of the subject into the social and the real into simulacra) results in a radically different understanding of "mass" communication, approximates the totalizing vision of Adorno's and Horkheimer's cultural critique. Similar possibilities fascinate and preoccupy cultural studies, where postmodernist debates are revisited to acknowledge their substantive critical potential without surrendering control over its own transformative qualities.

Thus a Marxian tradition open to the critical currents of postmodern social theories promises a postmodernized practice that extends the critique of culture and communication beyond deconstructing the dominant discourse of "mass communication research." Its responsibility in the context of a shifting discourse of communication and media studies is twofold: to identify contradictions and negations located in the objective narratives of empirical "mass communication research" while exposing its ideological nature, and to connect theoretical considerations of communication and media with the specifics of everyday experiences.

The first task involves the review and analysis of the discursive practices of "mass communication research" in its institutional manifestations, including the decontextualized construction of "mass communication" as a social process and the adoption of its definitions across social and political formations. Such a review reveals the discursive practices of "mass communication research" over a considerable period and suggests its limitations as a socially and politically responsive approach to an emancipatory social strategy involving communication and media.

The second task addresses a systematic, historically grounded, and politically informed examination of the nature of contemporary social communication, ranging from issues of access to the means of communication involving all groups in society to questions of domination by specific media interests—including their economic foundations—and notions of alternative systems of communication.

Most significantly, perhaps, both tasks require active participation and suggest social and political commitment to concrete involvement in emancipatory causes that lead to transformations in communication and media with the disclosure of contemporary practices, discourses, and representations of culture. Participation as advocacy of change always occurs in a specific historical and structural framework that helps shape the emerging discourse of critical communication studies.

Paradigm shifts in the context of academic work are the result of complex social, political, and cultural developments that enable ideas to rise and take hold of the imagination of individuals in their own struggle against a dominant professional ideology. The decentering of "mass communication research" occurred under such circumstances, aided by the influence of modernist and postmodernist European ideas related to notions of culture, ideology, and power and the increasing relevance of language (and the production of meaning) in the study of social formations—in addition to a rapidly shifting terrain of communication studies away from narrow conceptualizations of media and toward the inclusive category of culture. Other disciplines, such as ethnography or literary studies, also have helped push considerations of communication and media beyond the traditional boundaries of "mass communication research" with creative and innovative analyses that apply a qualitative approach. The resulting practice of theory and research reflects the workings of a critical consciousness on issues related to the privileged and authoritative knowledge of "mass communication research" and contributes to a blending of the humanities and social sciences as a major intellectual project of recent years. Contemporary writings about communication and culture explore these extensions of the field and offer evidence of "mass communication research" as a blurred genre among signs of a more radical break with tradition.

It would be foolish to suggest, however, that decentering "mass communication research" has resulted in terminating universal or general claims to authoritative knowledge of communication and media, and that "mass communication research" in its institutional guise of journalism and mass communication has joined in a sustained critique of media practices or embraced a critical pedagogy for the benefit of future intellectual work. Instead, in a general atmosphere of collaboration between business and education, commercial interests in the production of facts about communication and media in the marketplace increase the political capital of "mass communication research" in the academy and elsewhere.

It is equally clear, however, that "mass communication research" has been challenged by intellectually and ideologically formidable alternatives, and that the process of demystification proceeds with the help of a socially and politically conscious examination of communicative practices and the articulation of emancipatory ideas through an expanding literature that engages the field in a critique of culture and commodification in a democratic society.

More specifically, these opportunities create a space for reshaping the research agenda of a media-centered approach to the study of culture and constructing an emancipatory learning environment for intellectual workers, including journalists, with the goal of strengthening their own professional autonomy in the context of the market-driven practices of intellectual labor.

For instance, a recovery of the history of news work constitutes a first step in the process of recognizing news workers as reified objects in the discourse of commerce and industry and identifying the workplace as a site of economic interests focused on issues of production and profitability rather than public service or social significance. Understanding their position in a system of discourses that constructs the meaning of journalism and describes the boundaries of their own work, news workers discover the limits of their participation in the surveillance of society and their loss of control over news and the flow of information.

There is some hope for reconstructing a more responsive—and responsible—history of news workers, with a more general recognition of the changing nature of journalism and its effects on news workers. For instance, James Carey, an early critic of American journalism history (1974), more recently calls for a "usable history of journalism" (based on the fact that "journalists are constituted in practice"), not to be confused with "technology or media or communication" but "usefully understood as another name for democracy" within the public realm (1997, 331–32). Grounding practice (or work) historically and recognizing individual efforts to retain a discernible professional identity vis-à-vis the shifting character of journalism from news work to entertainment reinforce professional self-consciousness among journalists as alienated intellectual workers and ultimately compel them to raise questions about the nature of democracy.

Indeed, critical communication studies as an institutional framework may help promote the importance of self-reflection as a first step in a process of reconstructing relations of domination by offering theoretical insights, providing interpretive, qualitative research strategies, and encouraging resistance with the goal of implementing a democratic vision of communication and media. Such a task can only succeed as a socially conscious practice, however, after critical communication studies expose the relations of power in the production of knowledge and the dissemination of information. Challenging the instrumental rationality of an administrative or a corporate discourse reconfirms its own role as a historical agent of change.

An intellectual history of "mass communication research" with its roots in the social scientific traditions of the nineteenth century documents the migration of ideas and the production of a literature of social thought that champions the role of communication in the making of community and society. It also legitimates the field of "mass communication research" among other disciplines and reinforces its reign as a dominant discursive formation.

The creative, if not speculative, writings of German political economists and sociologists on issues of language, communication, and the press, as well as the work of their American colleagues, mark the beginning of a modern history of nonconformity concerning explanations of an earlier scientific discourse, with challenges that ranged from exposing ideological differences (feudalism, liberalism, socialism, capitalism) to privileging specific perspectives (economics, culture, politics) or focusing on a codeterminate explanation of civil society. Their challenges have been met over the last century in historically specific circumstances (e.g., the industrialization and increasing commercialization of public life under changing technological conditions) with a series of critical narratives that respond to the impact of the dominant ideology (capitalism) on social scientific thought and "mass communication research," in particular, with alternative explanations of communication in society.

Notes and References

CHAPTER 1: MASS COMMUNICATION RESEARCH AND SOCIETY

Notes

1. This is a point at which historical and sociological interests meet to form an alliance of shared research questions. The debate concerning the relationship between history and sociology continued for some years. See, for instance, Hughes (1960), Eisenstadt (1963), and Woodward (1968).

2. Their contributions may be found in the works of the following: Dröge (1972), Holzer (1971), Enzensberger (1962), Knilli (1970), and Prokop (1971).

References

Bohrmann, Hans, and Rolf Sülzer. 1973. "Massenkommunikationsforschung in der BRD: Deutschsprachige Veröffentlichungen nach 1960: Kommentar und Bibliographie." In Jörg Aufermann, Hans Bohrmann, and Rolf Sülzer, eds., *Gesellschaftliche Kommunikation und Information*, vol. 1. Frankfurt: Atheneum.

Bottomore, Tom B. 1968. *Critics of Society: Radical Thought in North America.* New York: Pantheon.

Chafee, Steven H., and Everett M. Rogers. 1997. *The Beginnings of Communication Study in America: A Personal Memoir by Wilbur Schramm.* Thousand Oaks, Calif.: Sage.

Dahrendorf, Ralph. 1967. *Pfade aus Utopia: Arbeiten zur Theorie und Methode der Soziologie.* Munich: Piper.

Dennis, Everette E., and Ellen Wartella, eds. 1996. *American Communication Research: The Remembered History.* Mahwah, N.J.: Erlbaum.

Dewey, John. 1927. *The Public and Its Problems.* Chicago: Swallow.

Dröge, Franz. 1972. *Wissen ohne Bewusstein: Materialien zur Medienanalyse.* Frankfurt: Atheneum.

Dröge, Franz W., and Winfried B. Lerg. 1965. *Kritik der Kommunikationswissenschaft.* Bremen: B. C. Heye. Reprinted from *Publizistik* 10, no. 3 (1965): 251–84.

Eisenstadt, A. S. 1963. "American History and Social Science." *Centennial Review* 7: 255–72.

Enzensberger, Hans Magnus. 1962. *Einzelheiten l: Bewusstseins Industrie.* Frankfurt: Suhrkamp.

Frankfurt Institute for Social Research. 1972. *Aspects of Sociology.* Boston: Beacon.

Fromm, Erich. 1961. *Marx's Concept of Man.* New York: Frederick Ungar.

Gouldner, Alvin. 1970. *The Coming Crisis of Western Sociology.* New York: Basic.

Hardt, Hanno. 1992. *Critical Communication Studies: History and Theory of Communication in America*. London: Routledge.
Hawthorn, Geoffrey. 1976. *Enlightenment and Despair: A History of Sociology*. Cambridge: Cambridge University Press.
Holzer, Horst. 1971. *Gescheiterte Aufklärung? Politik, Ökonomie, und Kommunikation in der Bundesrepublik Deutschland*. Munich: Piper.
Hughes, H. Stuart. 1960. "The Historian and the Social Scientist." *American Historical Review* 66: 20–46.
Jay, Martin. 1973. *The Dialectical Imagination: A History of the Frankfurt School and the Institute of Social Research, 1932–50*. Boston: Little, Brown.
Knilli, Friedrich. 1970. *Deutsche Lautsprecher: Versuch zu einer Semiotik des Radios*. Stuttgart: Metzler.
Kutsch, Arnulf, ed. 1984. *Zeitungswissenschaftler im Dritten Reich: Sieben Biographische Studien*. Cologne: Studienverlag Hayit.
Lazarsfeld, Paul. 1972a. "Mass Media of Communication in Modern Society." In *Qualitative Analysis: Historical and Critical Essays*, 106–22. Boston: Allyn & Bacon.
———. 1972b. "The Role of Criticism in the Management of Mass Media." In *Qualitative Analysis: Historical and Critical Essays*, 123–38. Boston: Allyn & Bacon.
———. 1972c. "Administrative and Critical Communication Research." In *Qualitative Analysis: Historical and Critical Essays*, 155–67. Boston: Allyn & Bacon.
Leigh, Robert D., ed. 1974. *A Free and Responsible Press: A General Report on Mass Communication: Newspapers, Radio, Motion Pictures, Magazines, and Books by the Commission on Freedom of the Press*. Chicago: University of Chicago Press, Midway Reprints, 1974.
Luxemburg, Rosa. 1976. "The Problem of Dictatorship." In Irving Howe, ed., *Essential Works of Socialism*, 254–57. New Haven: Yale University Press.
Marx, Karl, and Friedrich Engels. 1970. *The German Ideology*. Edited by C. J. Arthur. New York: International.
Mills, C. Wright. 1970. *The Sociological Imagination*. Harmondsworth, U.K.: Penguin.
Pietilä, Veikko. 1977. *On the Scientific Status and Position of Communication Research*. Monograph no. 35. Tampere: Institute of Journalism and Mass Communication.
Prokop, Dieter. 1971. *Materialien zur Theorie des Films*. Munich: Hanser.
Rogers, Everett M. 1994. *A History of Communication Study*. New York: Free Press.
Schiller, Dan. 1996. *Theorizing Communication: A History*. New York: Oxford University Press.
Woodward, C. Vann. 1968. "History and the Third Culture." *Journal of Contemporary History* 3, no. 2: 23–35.
Wright, Charles R. 1975. *Mass Communication: A Sociological Perspective*. New York: Random House.

CHAPTER 2: COMMUNICATION AND CHANGE

Notes

1. The following translations are by the author; they are based on the original German text provided in Iring Fetscher's (1969) compilation of articles from the *Rheinische Zeitung für Politik, Handel, und Gewerbe* (1.1.1842 to 31.3.1843) and *Neue Rheinische Zeitung: Organ der Demokratie* (1.6.1848 to 19.5.1849), Karl Marx und Friedrich Engels (1967/68), and other documents related to the writings of Marx

and Engels on issues of press freedom. The citations also indicate the original source, e.g., *RZ* or *NRZ* (*Rheinische Zeitung* or *Neue Rheinische Zeitung*), number and date, and its location in Fetscher's book.

References

Althusser, Louis. 1965. *For Marx*. New York: Vintage.

Althusser, Louis, and Etienne Balibar. 1963. *Reading Capital*. London: New Left.

Baudrillard, Jean. 1973. *The Mirror of Production*. St. Louis: Telos.

Berner Zeitung. 1961. "Ankündigung." In Ulrich Groball, ed., *Dokumente der Deutschen Arbeiterbewegung zur Journalistik*, 1:29–30. Leipzig: Fakultät für Journalistik, Karl–Marx Universität.

Bittel, Karl. 1953. *Karl Marx als Journalist*. Berlin: Aufbau Verlag.

Christman, Henry M., ed. 1966. *The American Journalism of Marx and Engels*. New York: New American Library.

De la Haye, Yves, ed. 1980. *Marx and Engels on the Means of Communication: The Movement of Commodities, People, Information, and Capital*. New York: International General.

Engels, Friedrich. 1869. *Die Zukunft* 185 (August 11); Marx–Engels Archives, 2000.

———. 1961. "Brief an Karl Marx." In Ulrich Groball, ed., *Dokumente der Deutschen Arbeiterbewegung zur Journalistik*, no. 34. Leipzig: Fakultät für Journalistik, Karl-Marx Universität.

———. 1967/1968a. "Revolution und Kounterevolution in Deutschland." In Karl Marx und Friedrich Engels, *Über Kunst und Literatur*, 2:17. Berlin: Dietz.

———. 1967/1968b. "An Friedrich Graeber in Berlin." In Karl Marx und Friedrich Engels, *Über Kunst und Literatur*, 2:420–23. Berlin: Dietz.

———. 1967/1968c. "An Eduard Bernstein in Zürich." In Karl Marx und Friedrich Engels, *Über Kunst und Literatur*, 2:144. Berlin: Dietz.

———. 1967/1968d. "Deutsche Zustände." In Karl Marx und Friedrich Engels, *Über Kunst und Literatur*, 2:55–62. Berlin: Dietz.

———. 1967/1968e. "Grundsätze des Kommunismus." In Karl Marx und Friedrich Engels, *Über Kunst und Literatur*, 2:13–14. Berlin: Dietz.

———. 1969. "Marx und die Neue Rheinische Zeitung, 1848–1849." In Iring Fetscher, ed., *Karl Marx–Friedrich Engels: Pressefreiheit und Zensur*, 144–52. Frankfurt: Europäische Verlagsanstalt.

Fetscher, Iring, ed. 1969. *Karl Marx–Friedrich Engels: Pressefreiheit und Zensur*. Frankfurt: Europäische Verlagsanstalt.

Hutt, Allen. 1966. "Karl Marx as a Journalist." *Marxism Today* 10, no. 5: 144–54.

Koszyk, Kurt. 1966. *Deutsche Presse im 19. Jahrhundert*. Berlin: Colloquium.

Mann, Golo. 1968. *The History of Germany since 1789*. New York: Praeger.

Marx, Karl. 1967/68. "An Ferdinand Freiligrath." In Karl Marx und Friedrich Engels, *Über Kunst und Literatur*, 2:248. Berlin: Dietz.

Marx, Karl, and Friedrich Engels. 1967/68. *Über Kunst und Literatur*. 2 vols. Berlin: Dietz.

Marx–Engels Archives. 2000. marxists.firetrail.com/archive/bio/marx/eng-1869.htm.

McLellan, David. 1970. "Marx the Journalist." In *Marx before Marxism*. New York: Harper & Row.

Sorge, Friedrich Albert. 1961. "Zum 14. März." In Ulrich Groball, ed., *Dokumente der Deutschen Arbeiterbewegung zur Journalistik*, 1:20–21. Leipzig: Fakultät für Journalistik, Karl-Marx Universität.

CHAPTER 3: THE NERVES OF SOCIETY

References

Schäffle, Albert E. F. 1873. "Über die volkswirthschaftliche Natur der Güter der Darstellung und der Mittheilung." *Zeitschrift für die gesammte Staatswissenschaft* 1: 1–70.
———. 1881. *Bau und Leben des Sozialen Körpers*. Vols. 1–4. Tübingen: H. Laupp.
———. 1905. *Aus Meinem Leben*. Vol. 1. Berlin: Ernst Hofmann.
Small, Albion W. 1924. *Origins of Sociology*. Chicago: University of Chicago Press.

CHAPTER 4: THE NEWS OF SOCIETY

References

Knies, Karl. 1857. *Der Telegraph als Verkehrsmittel: Mit Erörterungen über den Nachrichtenverkehr Überhaupt*. Tübingen: H. Laupp.
———. 1883. *Die Politische Oekonomie vom Geschichtlichen Standpunkte*. Braunschweig: C. A. Schwetschke.
———. 1885. *Das Geld Darlegung der Grundlehren von dem Gelde, insbesondere der wirtschaftlichen und der rechtgiltigen Functionen des Geldes, mit einer Erörterung über das Kapital und die Übertragung der Nutzungen*. Berlin: Weidmann.
Scott, William A. 1933. *The Development of Economics*. New York: Century.

CHAPTER 5: THE LINKAGES OF SOCIETY

Notes

1. The bill, as drafted by Bücher, is reprinted in his *Gesammelte Aufsätze* (1926), 416–18, and reads as follows:

In each county with a population of 2,500, the county government must issue a county newspaper, to be disseminated without delay and free of charge to all households.

The county newspaper appears in counties with populations between 2,500 and 5,000 at least twice weekly, between 5,000 and 10,000 at least four times a week, over 10,000 daily.

The county newspaper has the exclusive right to publish state and communal announcements as well as all private advertising. Newspapers that are published privately are forbidden to engage in the printing of any advertisement.

The rate for advertisements is to be determined by local customs, and it must not exceed the linage rate of newspapers published previously in the town.

Besides advertisements, each county newspaper contains an editorial section, which must be confined to the reproduction of the latest news and instructional and entertaining articles. Any contributions aimed at spreading political influence are categorically excluded. It is permitted, however, to accept local news.

The content of the editorial section as well as state announcements are delivered to the counties on time for printing the newspaper and in the form of boilerplate and ready-print materials.

Contributions regarding county affairs must be accepted any time and, inasmuch as they do not contain punishable material, be printed in the next edition.

Advertisements of local significance are offers and demands for goods and labor as well as family advertisements, announcements of all kinds of presentations and meetings in town.

All official newspapers published by private persons cease publication on . . .

Persons who are not county residents may receive the county newspaper through the mail and after payment of a subscription fee that must reflect the production costs. Also, several small communities may combine the publication of a community newspaper with permission of the regional government.

The reprinting of official announcements and news that appear in the county newspaper by other newspapers is allowed only with the permission of the county governments and after payment of a reasonable fee.

Those who act against the regulations of this law will be fined up to . . . marks and, in the case of repeated violations, will face a jail sentence of not less than one month.

2. In this note I sketch the details of the journalism curriculum at Leipzig and Bücher's thoughts on journalism education. Courses as specified in the catalogue consist of

history (ancient, medieval, modern with special consideration given to contemporary events, cultural, social constitutional, economic)
political economy (general and special as well as economic policy), finance, history of political economy, social legislation, particularly labor questions, colonialism
statistics (history, technique, and organization, population statistics, demographics, economic, moral and cultural statistics)
geography (especially political and economic geography)
administration
politics and government
jurisprudence (international law, constitutional administrative, press law). In addition students were advised to select electives in philosophy, literature, and anthropology, depending on special interests (Jaeger 1926, 103).

Requirements for other sequences are equally comprehensive and demanding, and students are encouraged to complete a Ph.D. degree in one of the disciplines of the philosophical faculty. There were no particular exit examinations at the institute. Courses directed by practitioners are described as

an introduction to the work of political editors
style and technique of the feuilleton
business journalism
local and provincial editorial offices
production and accounting
press law, copyright, business law as it relates to publishing houses (Jaeger 1926, 106)

Although Bücher is convinced that the appropriate education of journalists within a university setting necessitates special courses, he remains unwilling to follow the example of American schools of journalism, for instance, which he considered undesirable examples for German conditions. In this context, he refers to editing courses in which students learn the art of writing headlines: "One can easily imagine how often truth and honesty are the losers" (1915a, 49).

Bücher hopes, on the other hand, that the establishment of university courses would aid students in finding journalism early enough, while discouraging those "unsuited elements" who could recognize their mistake of selecting a course of studies for which they were not talented enough (1915a, 70).

According to the curriculum, the University of Leipzig demonstrated that the education of journalists is as important as the education of other professionals, among them theologians, lawyers, and doctors. It provides solid guidelines for students to avoid prolonged studies, loss of time, and pitfalls in their selection of appropriate coursework. According to Bücher, the University of Leipzig intends to provide "the means for the education of professional journalists, who will be able to stand up to the important tasks of the contemporary daily press in terms of scientific, technical, and moral preparation" (Jaeger 1926, 106).

In another context Bücher refers to the need for educated journalists who could help bring about peace and understanding among nations. He envisions international cooperation among the press during the years following the war. In particular, he mentions the dangers of monopolistic press services, such as Reuters and Havas, which he considers official agencies and therefore biased sources of information and holds partly responsible for war propaganda activities. Bücher wants an international cooperative, fashioned after the Associated Press in the United States, to prevent the dissemination of government information. He also criticizes British ownership of transatlantic cables and suggests international regulations to neutralize this important transmission technology. And finally, formal education for journalists could lead to their recognition as serious and independent judges. He feels strongly that the "daily press must act as an incorruptible judge opposite individual parties and nations; otherwise it will lose its right to exist" (1915a, 63).

Implicit in these considerations of journalism education and the role of journalists is Bücher's continuing concern about the future of Germany's press system and therefore the future of society.

References

Bücher, Karl. 1901. *Industrial Evolution*. New York: Holt. This translation by Morley S. Wickett is based on Bücher's third edition of *Die Entstehung der Volkswirtschaft* (Tübingen: H. Laupp, 1898).

———. 1908. "Zeitungsstatistik für das Deutsche Reich im Jahre 1885 und 1906." *Bulletin d l'Institut International de Statisique*, 17.

———. 1909. *Arbeit und Rythmus*. Leipzig: B. G. Teubner.

———. 1912. "Das Zeitungswesen." In Paul Hinneberg, ed., *Die Kultur der Gegenwart, ihre Entwicklung, und ihre Ziele*. Berlin: B. G. Teubner.

———. 1915a. *Unsere Sache und die Tagespresse*. Tübingen: J. C. B. Mohr, Paul Siebeck.

———. 1915b. *Die deutsche Tagespresse und die Kritik*. Tübingen: J. C. B. Mohr, Paul Siebeck.

———. 1919. *Lebenserinnerungen*. Tübingen: H. Laupp.

———. 1922. *Zur Frage der Pressreform*. Tübingen: J. C. B. Mohr, Paul Siebeck.

———. 1926. *Gesammelte Aufsätze zur Zeitungskunde*. Tübingen: H. Laupp.

Bücher, Karl, E. Heimann, E. von Philippovich, and J. Schumpeter. 1924. "Volkswirtschaftliche Entwicklungsstufen." In Karl Bücher, ed., *Grundriss der Sozialökonomik*, sec. 1, pt. 1. Tübingen: J. C. B. Mohr, Paul Siebeck.

Groth, Otto. 1930. *Die Zeitung*. 4 vols. Mannheim: J. Bensheimer.

———. 1948. *Die Geschichte der deutschen Zeitungswissenschaft: Probleme und Methoden*. Munich: Konrad Weinmayer.
Jaeger, Karl. 1926. *Von der Zeitungskunde zur publizistischen Wissenschaft*. Jena: Gustav Fischer.
Lasalle, Ferdinand. 1930. "Die Feste, die Presse, und der Frankfurter Abgeordnetentag." In Otto Groth, ed., *Die Zeitung*, 3:335. Mannheim: J. Bensheimer.
Lippmann, Walter. 1920. *Liberty and the News*. New York: Macmillan.
———. 1922. *Public Opinion*. New York: Macmillan.
———. 1925. *The Phantom Public*. New York: Harcourt, Brace.
Muser, Gerhard. 1918. *Statistische Untersuchung über die Zeitungen Deutschlands, 1885–1914*. Leipzig: Emmanuel Reinicke. This was the first volume of a series edited by Karl Bücher under the title *Abhandlungen an dem Institut für Zeitungskunde an der Universität Leipzig*.

CHAPTER 6: THE MIRRORS OF SOCIETY

Notes

1. The article appeared in the social democratic newspaper, *Schleswig-Holsteinische Volkszeitung* (Kiel), 29 July 1932.
2. A discussion of his major points is available in an essay by Gillian Lindt Gollin and Albert E. Gollin, "Tönnies on Public Opinion" (1971); also, Hanno Hardt and Slavko Splichal, eds., *Ferdinand Tönnies on Public Opinion* (2000).
3. Tönnies is aware of the contemporary sociological literature in the United States and cites from relevant works. Here he refers to an article by Edward A. Ross (1920) and quotes from Lester Ward (1919).
4. Tönnies reports on the activities of Ferdinand Hansen and his suggestion that the American people establish a $1 billion fund for operating independent newspapers, among other projects.
5. The open letter is a response to a letter by Hans A. Münster, a member of the Deutsches Institut für Zeitungskunde in Berlin, who had raised the issue of studying newspapers as a science.

References

Cahnman, Werner, ed. 1973. *Ferdinand Tönnies: A New Evaluation*. Leiden: Brill.
Cahnman, Werner, and Rudolf Heberle, eds. 1971. *Ferdinand Tönnies, On Sociology: Pure, Applied, and Empirical*. Chicago: University of Chicago Press.
Gollin, Gillian Lindt, and Albert E. Gollin. 1971. "Tönnies on Public Opinion." In Werner Cahnman and Rudolf Heberle, eds., *Ferdinand Tönnies, On Sociology: Pure, Applied, and Empirical*. Chicago: University of Chicago Press.
Hardt, Hanno, and Slavko Splichal, eds. 2000. *Ferdinand Tönnies on Public Opinion: Selections and Analyses*. Boulder: Rowman & Littlefield.
Jacoby, E. G. 1973. "Three Aspects of the Sociology of Tönnies." In Werner Cahnman, ed., *Ferdinand Tönnies: A New Evaluation*. Leiden: Brill. The original appeared in Ferdinand Tönnies: *Einführung in die Soziologie* (Stuttgart: Ferdinand Enke, 1931).
Ross, Edward A. 1920. "Commercialization: Increasing or Decreasing?" *International Journal of Ethics* 30, 3 (April): 284–95.
Tönnies, Ferdinand. 1922. *Kritik der Öffentlichen Meinung*. Berlin: Julius Springer.
———. 1931a. "Remarks." In *Verhandlungen des Siebenten Deutchen Soziologentages, 28 September bis 1. Oktober 1930 in Berlin*. Tübingen: J. C. B. Mohr, Paul Siebeck.

———. 1931b. "Offene Antwort." *Zeitungswissenschaft* 6, no. 1: 1–2.
———. 1963. *Community and Society (Gemeinschaft und Gesellschaft)*. Edited and translated by Charles P. Loomis. New York: Harper Torchbooks.
———. 1971a. "Mein Verhältnis zur Soziologie." In Werner Cahnman and Rudolf Heberle, eds., *Ferdinand Tönnies, On Sociology: Pure, Applied, and Empirical*. Chicago: University of Chicago Press. The original appeared in Richard Thurnwald, ed., *Soziologie von Heute* (Leipzig: Hirschfeld, 1932), 103–22.
———. 1971b. "Einteilung der Soziologie." In Werner Cahnman and Rudolf Heberle, eds., *Ferdinand Tönnies, On Sociology: Pure, Applied, and Empirical*. Chicago: University of Chicago Press. The original appeared in *Zeitschrift für die gesamte Staatswissenschaft* 79: 1 (1925).
———. 1971c. "Statistik und Soziographie." In Werner Cahnman and Rudolf Heberle, eds., *Ferdinand Tönnies, On Sociology: Pure, Applied, and Empirical*. Chicago: University of Chicago Press. The original appeared in *Allgemeines Statistisches Archiv* 18 (1929): 546–58.
———. 1971d. "Macht und Wert der Oeffentlichen Meinung." *Jahrbuch für Geisteswissenschaften* 2 (1923): 72–99; Werner Cahnman and Rudolf Heberle, eds., *Ferdinand Tönnies, On Sociology: Pure, Applied, and Empirical*. Chicago: University of Chicago Press.
Ward, Lester. 1919. *Pure Sociology: A Treatise on the Origin and Spontaneous Development of Society*. New York: Macmillan.

CHAPTER 7: THE CONSCIENCE OF SOCIETY

Notes

1. Among the books are Reinhard Bendix (1962); Otto Stammer (1965); Ilse Dronberger (1971); Paul Honingsheim (1968); Julien Freund (1969); Arthur Mitzman (1970); Reinhard Bendix and Guenther Roth (1972); Walter G. Runciman (1972); and Donald MacRae (1974).

2. *Chronik der Christlichen Welt*, a weekly publication, appeared in newspaper format beginning in 1891. Details may be found in Joachim Kirchner 1962, 2:276.

3. *Die Hilfe* was founded for the dissemination of Christian ideas and focused on human welfare and social justice. Weber was among the financial guarantors of the publication, which reached a circulation of about 12,000 after one year. See Kirchner 1962, 288.

4. *Neue Preussische (Kreuz-)Zeitung*, a conservative newspaper, was published in Berlin, beginning in 1848. Details about the position of this newspaper in German politics are available in Koszyk 1966.

5. It was published in Berlin and edited by Heinrich Oberwinder and Hellmut von Gerlach beginning in October 1896; from 1887 until 1903 it was published as a weekly journal. See Koszyk 1966, 139, 158–59.

6. The politically liberal and prestigious *Frankfurter Zeitung* was published beginning in 1856 by Leopold Sonnemann. For details, see Paupit 1973, 241–56.

7. A chronology of Weber's journalistic writings is available in Weber 1926 and lists twenty entries; another useful source is the collection of materials in Baumgarten 1964.

8. The items were collected and issued by Johannes Winckelmann (1958) and cover Weber's talks and his writings about the political situation in Germany.

9. Weber's original remarks are published in Weber 1924, 433–41.

10. Emil Löbl (1861–1935) was an Austrian writer and journalist who worked for the *Wiener Zeitung* and became managing editor of the *Neue Wiener Tageblatt* in 1917.

11. The following extract is a translation from Weber's speech to the German Sociological Association at its first meeting in Frankfurt in 1910. In it he outlines two basic areas for sociological study: the press and formal organizations. This selection focuses on the press analysis (see Weber 1924, 434–41):

> Gentlemen, the first subject deemed suitable by the society for a purely scientific treatment is a sociology of the press. Admittedly, this is an enormously comprehensive topic, which not only demands an extremely large amount of material support for preliminary work but also—regarding the objectivity of this matter—requires the trust and goodwill of those leading circles interested in the press. Should we encounter suspicion among representatives of newspaper publishers, or on the part of journalists, that the society pursues—for whatever purposes—a course of moral criticism of the existing conditions, it will be impossible to reach our goal. I say this because we cannot succeed if we are not supplied more than adequately with material by just that side. A committee will be formed soon that will attempt to gain the cooperation of press experts, numerous theoreticians of the press—as you know, we have already some brilliant theoretical publications in this field (let me remind you of Löbl's book because it deserves to be known better than it is)—and press practitioners. [Weber refers here to Emil Löbl, *Kultur und Presse* (Leipzig: Duncker & Humbolt, 1903).] There is some hope, after preliminary talks, that we will be met with understanding when we turn, as expected, to large press organizations and newspaper publishers' and editors' associations. If this should not happen, the society would rather withhold publication than arrange for what will surely be an inferior effort.
>
> Gentlemen, it is useless to speak here of the overall importance of the press. I would be suspected immediately of flattering press representatives, the more, since what has been said already about the press by respected sources cannot be surpassed. The press was compared to commanding generals (this has been said of the foreign press only), nevertheless, everyone knows: there exists nothing worthier on earth, and it would be necessary to reach into regions of the supernatural to find any comparisons. I simply remind you: erase the press from your memories and think what modern life would be without the kind of publicity created by the press.
>
> Life in antiquity, gentlemen, also had its publicity. With horror did Jakob Burckhardt face the publicness of Hellenistic life, which includes the existence of the Athenian citizen in the most intimate details. [The mention of Jakob Burckhardt should be understood in the context of Burckhardt's work as a historian of ancient cultures. See his four-volume work, *Griechische Kulturgeschichte* (1898).] This kind of publicity does not exist today, and it is interesting, indeed, to ask, What does contemporary publicity look like, and what will it look like in the future: what is publicized by the newspaper and what is not?
>
> When the British Parliament 150 years ago forced journalists on their knees to apologize for a breach of privilege after they had reported about its sessions, and when the contemporary press forces Parliament to its knees with a mere threat not to publish the speeches of its representatives, then the idea of parliamentarians and the position of the press apparently has changed. At the same time, there must be local differences, when, for instance, American

stock market exchanges until recently used frosted glass windows to prevent the communication of market fluctuations to the outside, while, on the other side, almost all relevant aspects of making a newspaper are at least partly influenced by the need to account for stock market announcements. We do not ask what should be made public. Opinions differ widely, as everyone knows. It is, of course, interesting to discover today's opinions and those that existed earlier, and who held them. This too is part of our task, but it does not exceed this factual observation. Everyone knows, for instance, that on this issue, opinions in England differ from ours; when an English lord marries an American, one can read a detailed account of the physical and psychological attributes of the American woman and her dowry, of course, in the American press, while—according to our prevailing ideas at least—a self-respecting German newspaper would reject this approach. Where does this difference originate? When we must declare—in the case of Germany today—that strong representatives of the newspaper business seriously attempt to exclude purely private affairs from newspaper publicity—for what reasons and with what results?—we must also consider Anton Menger's opinion as a socialist publicist. [Anton Menger (1841–1906), lawyer, professor. A social democrat whose books reflected his political leanings.] According to him, in a future society the press will have the task of serving as a forum for events that cannot be placed under the authority of a court of law, and assume the role of the ancient censor. It is worthwhile to note which ultimate worldviews are the basis of one or the other tendency. Without an opinion being expressed, this will be our task.

It will be our task to examine the balance of power that is created by specific newspaper publicity. It is different and of decisively lesser importance for scientific accomplishments, for instance, than for short-lived ones, such as accomplishments of a performer or conductor, and it is especially important for everything reviewed in the feature section. In certain respects, the theatrical and also the literary critic is the individual on the newspaper staff who can most easily create and destroy careers. For every part of the newspaper, beginning with the political section, however, the balance of power varies most significantly. The relations of the newspaper to political parties here and elsewhere, its relations to the business world, to numerous groups and interests who influence and are influenced by the public, suggest an enormous area of sociological work, currently in an early state of construction. But let us return to the actual beginning of the examination.

A sociological treatment of the press requires an understanding that today's press is necessarily a capitalistic, private enterprise, but that the press also occupies a completely unique position in contrast to any other business; it has two totally different types of "customers," one consisting of newspaper buyers who, in turn, are either overwhelmingly subscribers or single-copy buyers, a difference that results in decisively different characteristics of the press in advanced societies. The other consists of advertisers. Between these groups of customers exist the most peculiar interrelations. For instance, for a newspaper to have many advertisers, it is certainly important to have many subscribers, and, to some extent, vice versa. But not only is the role of the advertiser in the press budget much more important than that of the subscriber, as we know. It actually can be stated that a newspaper can never have too many advertisers, however—and this is in contrast to any other seller of goods—but it can have too many buyers, namely, when it is unable to raise advertising rates to cover the cost of a constantly expanding circulation. This is quite a serious problem for some types of newspapers and generally means that, starting with a certain circulation figure, expansionary interests of newspapers cease—at least this could happen when an increase in advertising rates meets with difficulties. This is a characteristic of the press alone and is of a purely commercial nature, but it has numerous consequences. Admittedly, the international comparison of size and type of relationships between the press—which wants to educate and objectively inform the public about politics and other subject matters—and the business community, whose needs for publicity are reflected in advertising, is extremely different, if one uses France as an example. Why? With what general consequences? These are questions, although frequently addressed, that we will have to raise again because only a partial consensus of opinions exists.

But let us continue: a current characteristic, in particular, is the growth of capital needs for press enterprises. The question is (and this question has not yet been decided because the best-informed experts disagree about it), To what extent does the increasing need for capital mean an increasing monopoly of already existing enterprises? This could perhaps vary depending on the circumstances.

Regardless of the effect of increasing capital needs, the strength of the monopoly position of already existing newspapers differs, depending on whether the press relies regularly on subscriptions or single sales. Abroad, the individual has the choice each day of buying a different paper than he bought the day before, which (so it seems at first glance) perhaps facilitated the founding of new newspapers. Perhaps this phenomenon should be examined and combined with the effect of increasing capital needs to answer the question, Does increasing investment also mean increasing power to mold public opinion according to one's own judgment? Or vice versa—as it has been stated but without clear proof—does it mean an increasing sensitivity of individual enterprises to fluctuations in public opinion? It has been said that the obvious opinion change of certain French papers—one usually recalls the *Figaro* at the time of the Dreyfus affair—can simply be explained by the fact that the large, fixed capital investment of the modern newspaper enterprise becomes increasingly sensitive to, and therefore dependent on, the public at times of public dissatisfaction, which results in cancellations that it finds economically unfeasible—taking into account the prevalent single-copy sales in France that accommodate the ease of change. This would mean, therefore, that an increasing dependence on current opinions is a consequence of a growing need for capital. Is this true? That is the question we must raise. It has been supported by press experts (I am not such an expert) while others have denied it.

Furthermore, are we facing a move toward newspaper trusts as a result of increasing capital investments among newspapers perhaps, as is often the case with increasing capital needs? What are the possibilities of such a trend? Gentlemen, this has been denied most vigorously by renowned press experts, theoreticians as well as practitioners. Of course, their major spokesman, Lord Northcliffe, could know more than he is saying, perhaps, since he is one of the most important press magnates. [Lord Northcliffe (1865–1922) was founder of England's first mass-circulation newspaper, the *Daily Mail*, in 1896; he owned several other newspapers with his brother, Lord Rothermere.] What would be the consequences for the character of newspapers if this would happen? That newspapers of large, already existing companies often display characteristics different from other papers is obvious. Enough—I only used these examples to show how much the business side of press enterprises must be taken into account. We must ask ourselves, What is the meaning of capitalism and its development within press enterprises for the sociological position of the press in general and its role in the process of forming public opinion?

Another problem: the "institutional" character of the modern press in Germany is expressed by the anonymity of what appears in newspapers. An infinite amount has been uttered "for" and "against" the anonymity of the press. We do not take sides but ask, How is it that this phenomenon can be found in Germany, for instance, while different conditions prevail abroad, for example, in France, while England is more closely related to us? Actually, there is only one French newspaper, the *Temps*, that operates strictly on the basis of anonymity. In England, on the other hand, newspapers like the *Times* have most rigorously adhered to anonymity for quite different reasons, perhaps. It could be (as it seems to be the case with the *Times*) that personalities who supply the newspaper with information are frequently too important to release information under their own names. In other cases, anonymity may be used for exactly the opposite reason. It depends: how does this question look in light of conflicts of interest that exist undeniably between the interests of an individual journalist to become well-known and the interests of a newspaper not to become too dependent on cooperating with this individual journalist? Again, there are differences, depending on commercial interests and on whether single sales dominate or not. And above all, the political nature of society plays a role. For instance, depending on whether a nation (and Germany is an example) tends to be impressed more by the institutional powers of a newspaper that acts like a "superindividual" than by the opinion of an individual—or whether it is free from this type of metaphysics?—these are questions that lead into the domain of part-time journalism, which looks different in Germany than in England and in France, for instance, where the part-time journalist is a common phenomenon.

This invites questions such as, Who writes for the newspaper from outside the field and what? And who doesn't and what isn't written? And why not? More general questions include, How does the press obtain the material that it offers to the public? And what does it really have to offer at all? Is the steady increase in the importance of purely factual accounts a general phenomenon? This is certainly the case in England, America, and Germany, but not entirely so in France—the Frenchman wants primarily an opinion sheet. But why? The American, for instance, wants nothing but facts from his newspaper. Whatever opinions about these facts are published in the press, he disregards as not worth reading; as a democrat he is convinced that, in principle, his interpretation is as good as the editorial writer's, perhaps even better. But the Frenchman, too, wants to be a democrat. Where does the difference come in? In any event, in both cases the social function of the press is an entirely different one.

The presence of the news service—which despite these differences not only burdens the budget of the press increasingly in all countries of the world, but is also coming to the fore more prominently—raises the next question: What ultimately are the sources of news, and the next problem: What is the position of large news agencies and their international relations among themselves? Important studies about these phenomena must be conducted, and the beginnings of some are already available. The statements about the condition of this area of study have been partly contradictory, and the question remains whether objectively it would be possible to secure more material than can currently be obtained.

However, as long as the content of the newspaper consists neither of news nor boilerplate material (as is well known, there is a mass production of press contents, from sports and puzzle corner to the novel, a variety of items, by large, independent enterprises), I say, as far as neither syndicated materials nor straight news fills the pages of the press, there still remains the production of what is being offered today as journalistic accomplishment in the press, which is fundamentally important to evaluating the individual newspaper, at least in Germany as opposed to other countries.

We cannot be satisfied with examining the product at hand, but we must respect its producer and ask about the fate and status of journalism as a profession. The situation of the German journalist, for instance, is quite complex compared with that of journalists abroad. In England, under certain circumstances, journalists and publishers have entered the House of Lords. Men who were known for no other accomplishments than having created for their party an excellent paper that undercut (in this case did surpass) everything else. Journalists became ministers in France, and in large numbers. In Germany, however, this would be a great exception. And, even disregarding this obvious superficiality, we must ask, How have the conditions of professional journalists changed in individual countries in the recent past?

What is the origin and education, and what are the professional demands made, of the modern journalist? And what is the professional destiny of the German as compared with the foreign journalist? And finally, what are his chances in life—possibly outside his profession—here and abroad? The general situation of journalists is, apart from other aspects, rather variable, depending on parties, type of newspaper, and so on, as everyone knows. The socialist press, for instance, is a special phenomenon that must be treated separately, as must be the position of socialist editors; and even more so the Catholic press and its editors.

Finally, what are the effects of this product, which represents the complete newspaper, as it is to be examined by us in this way? There is an enormous amount of literature, which is highly valuable in parts but also contains extreme contradictions, even though experts have contributed to it. Gentlemen, as we know, there has been an attempt to examine the effects of the press on the human mind, raising a question about the consequences of the fact that modern man—before he leaves for his daily work—has become used to absorbing a journalistic hotch-potch that forces him on a hurried trip through all areas of cultural life, from politics to the theater, and many other subjects. That this makes a difference is obvious. It is quite possible and easy to make some general remarks about how this development joins certain other influences on modern man. But the problem cannot be moved easily beyond the most elementary stages.

We must start with the question, What is the effect of newspapers on the kind of reading habits of modern man? In regard to this issue, all kinds of theories have been constructed. There was also the argument that the book is being replaced by the newspaper. It is possible, although German book production quantitatively "blossoms" in unbelievable ways as in no other country in the world; nowhere are there as many books thrown onto the market as here. The sales figures for the same books, however, show an inverse ratio. Russia (and this happened before the introduction of press freedom) recorded printings of 20,000 and 30,000 copies for such unlikely books like *Neue Sittenlehre*. [Weber refers here to Anton Menger's *Neue Sittenlehre* (1905), in which the author describes the role of the press and public opinion as social powers.] There exist widely read magazines that unfailingly experimented with a "final" philosophical foundation of their individuality. This would be impossible in Germany, and it would be impossible in Russia under the influence of at least relative press freedom; the beginnings are already visible. The press is involved in making what are without a doubt tremendous shifts in reading habits and immense changes in the character and manner in which modern man absorbs the external world. The enormous weight of constant transformation and the acknowledgment of widespread changes of public opinion among the universal and inexhaustible possibilities of points of views and interests rest on the uniqueness of modern man. But how?

This we must examine. I cannot go into details and consequently I close with the following remarks. We must examine the press first to this end: what does it contribute to the making of modern man? Second, how are the objective, supra-individual cultural values influenced, what shifts occur, what is destroyed and newly created of the beliefs and hopes of the masses, the *Lebensgefühle* (as they say today), what is destroyed forever and newly created of the potential point of view? These are the last questions we must raise, and you see immediately, honored members of the audience, the road to the answers is extremely long.

You will ask now, Where is the material to begin such studies? This material consists of newspapers themselves, and we will start now, to be specific, quite narrowly with scissors and compasses to measure quantitative changes of newspaper content during the last generation, especially in the advertising section, feuilleton, between feuilleton and editorial, between editorial and news, and between what is generally carried as news and what is not presented at all. Because conditions have changed significantly, the first steps of such investigations, which try to substantiate these practices, have been made, but only the beginnings. From quantitative analyses we will proceed to qualitative ones. We will have to pursue the type of stylistic approach of the newspaper, the way in which the same problems are discussed in newspapers and outside of them, the apparent repression of emotion in the newspaper, which at the same time has formed the basis for its own existence, and similar topics. And finally we could approach the point where we may hope to slowly close in on the wide-ranging question; it is our goal to answer it.

References

Aron, Raymond. 1967. *Main Currents in Sociological Thought*. Vol. 2. Garden City, N.Y.: Doubleday.

Baumgarten, Edward, ed. 1964. *Max Weber: Werk und Person*. Tübingen: J. C. B. Mohr, Paul Siebeck.

Bendix, Reinhard. 1962. *Max Weber: An Intellectual Portrait*. New York: Doubleday Anchor.

Bendix, Reinhard, and Guenther Roth. 1971. *Scholarship and Partisanship: Essays on Max Weber*. Berkeley: University of California Press.

Burckhardt, Jakob. 1898. *Griechische Kulturgeschichte*. Berlin: W. Spemann.

Dronberger, Ilse. 1971. *The Political Thought of Max Weber: In Quest of Statesmanship*. New York: Appleton-Century-Crofts.

Freund, Julien. 1968. *The Sociology of Max Weber*. New York: Random House.

Gerth, H. H., and C. Wright Mills. 1946. *From Max Weber: Essays in Sociology*. New York: Oxford University Press.

Groth, Otto. 1915. *Die Politische Presse Württembergs*. Stuttgart: Scheufele.
———. 1960. *Die Unerkannte Kulturmacht: Grundlegung der Zeitungswissenschaft*. Vol. 5. Berlin: Walter de Gruyter.
Hardt, Hanno. 1974. "The Development of Mass Communication as a Field of Study in Germany: An Introduction." Unpublished paper, School of Journalism, University of Iowa, February.
Heuss, Theodor. 1958. "Max Weber in seiner Gegenwart." In Johannes Winckelmann, ed., *Max Weber: Gesammelte Politische Schriften*. Tübingen: J. C. B. Mohr, Paul Siebeck.
Honingsheim, Paul. 1968. *On Max Weber*. New York: Free Press.
Jaehrisch, Ursula. 1971. "Max Weber's Contribution to the Sociology of Culture." In Otto Stammer, ed., *Max Weber and Sociology Today*. New York: Harper & Row.
Kirchner, Joachim. 1962. *Das Deutsche Zeitschriftenwesen: Seine Geschichte und seine Probleme*. Wiesbaden: Otto Harrassowitz.
Koszyk, Kurt. 1966. *Deutsche Presse im 19. Jahrhundert*. Berlin: Colloquium Verlag.
Lachmann, Ludwig M. 1971. *The Legacy of Max Weber*. Berkeley, Calif.: Glendessary.
Lazarsfeld, Paul, and Anthony R. Oberschall. 1965. "Max Weber and Empirical Research." *American Sociological Review* 30, no. 2: 185–99.
Löbl, Emil. 1903. *Kultur und Presse*. Leipzig: Duncker & Humblodt.
MacRae, Donald G. 1974. *Max Weber*. New York: Viking.
Menger, Anton. 1905. *Neue Sittenlehre*. Jena: Gustav Fischer.
Mitzman, Arthur. 1970. *The Iron Cage: An Historical Interpretation of Max Weber*. New York: Knopf.
Mommsen, Wolfgang J. 1974. *Max Weber und die Deutsche Politik, 1890–1920*. Tübingen: J. C. B. Mohr, Paul Siebeck.
Oberschall, Anthony. 1965. *Empirical Social Research in Germany, 1848–1914*. The Hague: Mouton.
Parsons, Talcott. 1965. "Max Weber, 1864–1964." *American Sociological Review* 30, no. 2: 171–75.
Paupit, Kurt. 1973. "Frankfurter Zeitung (1856–1943)." In Heinz-Dietrich Fischer, ed., *Deutsche Zeitschriften des 17. bis 20. Jahrhunderts*, 241–56. Pullach: Verlag Dokumentation.
Runciman, Walter G. 1972. *A Critique of Max Weber's Philosophy of Social Science*. Cambridge: Cambridge University Press.
Stammer, Otto, ed. 1965. *Max Weber and Sociology Today*. New York: Harper Torchbooks.
Taubert, Rolf. 1973. "*Die Hilfe* (1894–1943)." In Heinz-Dietrich Fischer, ed., *Deutsche Zeitschriften des 17. bis 20. Jahrhunderts*, 255–64. Pullach: Verlag Dokumentation.
Weber, Karl. 1937. "Zur Soziologie der Zeitung." *Festgabe Fritz Fleiner zum siebzigsten Geburtstag*. Zürich: Polygraphischer Verlag.
Weber, Marianne. 1926. *Max Weber: Ein Lebensbild*. Tübingen: J. C. B. Mohr, Paul Siebeck.
Weber, Max. 1924. *Gesammelte Aufsätze zur Soziologie und Sozialpolitik*. Tübingen: J. C. B. Mohr, Paul Siebeck.
———. 1966. "Politik als Beruf." In Johannes Winckelmann, ed., *Max Weber: Staatssoziologie*. Berlin: Duncker & Humblodt. Originally presented in 1918 as a lecture in Munich; originally published in *Gesammelte Politische Schriften* (Munich: Duncker & Humblodt, 1921), 396–450. An English-language version appears in Gerth and Mills 1946, 77–128.
Winckelmann, Johannes. 1958. *Max Weber: Gesammelte Politische Schriften*. Tübingen: J. C. B. Mohr, Paul Siebeck.

CHAPTER 8: THE "AMERICAN SCIENCE" OF SOCIETY

Notes

1. Albion Small (1924, 326) recalls a number of individuals who had spent some time at German universities, "during the seventies, on the whole the most stimulating decade in German social science." They include William G. Sumner (in the previous decade), social sciences, Marburg and Göttingen; Herbert B. Adams, history, Johns Hopkins, Heidelberg, 1876; John W. Burgess, political sciences, Columbia, Leipzig, Berlin, 1871–1873; Richard T. Ely, economics, Johns Hopkins, Wisconsin, Halle, Heidelberg, Geneva, and Berlin, 1877–1880; Henry W. Farnam, political economy, Yale, Strassburg, 1878; Frank J. Goodenow, political sciences, Columbia, Paris, and Berlin, 1879–1882; Arthur T. Hadley, economics, Yale, Berlin, 1878–1879; George E. Howard, sociology, Leland Stanford, Nebraska, Munich, and Paris, 1878–1880; Edmund J. James, political and social sciences, University of Pennsylvania, Halle, 1878–1879; Simon N. Patten, economics, University of Pennsylvania, Halle, 1878; E. R. A. Seligman, economics, Columbia, Berlin, Heidelberg, Geneva; William M. Sloane, history, Princeton and Columbia, Leipzig, 1877; Albion W. Small, sociology, Chicago, Berlin, and Leipzig, 1879–1881; Frank W. Taussig, economics, Harvard, Berlin, 1879; William H. Tillinghast, history, assistant librarian, Harvard, Berlin, 1878–1880.

2. Among those who write on the press are social critics and sociologists who produced a rich literature of early media criticism. Victor S. Yarros (1899–1900) articulates the press conflict between the duty to inform the people and the desire to make money, which inevitably results in slanted news coverage. Sixteen years later, he advocates the founding of privately endowed newspapers to improve the service of the press. "We have plenty of syndicated trash, syndicated falsehood, syndicated malice, syndicated vulgarity and sensationalism. Why should not decency and integrity, sobriety and common-sense use the resources of cooperation and beneficence"(1916–1917, 211)?

George Vincent, who collaborated with Albion Small, describes a journalism course he taught for three years at the University of Chicago. It covered practical and theoretical aspects of the field, including "The History and Organization of the American Press" (1905–1906).

Frances Fenton investigates the question of the effects of crime reporting on criminal activities in a two-part series asking, "Do people get the idea of, or the impulse to committing criminal and other anti-social acts from the reading of such acts or similar acts in the newspaper"(1910–1911)?

A year earlier, an "independent journalist" had published an article that questioned the possibility of an honest and sane press in the United States (1909–1910).

There were other outlets for critical essays dealing with the press as well, which afforded social scientists an opportunity to participate in the general discussion. Thus W. I. Thomas writes on "the psychology of the Yellow Journal" in *American Magazine* (1908) and Edward A. Ross reports on "The Suppression of Important News" in *Atlantic Monthly* (1910).

Other typical examples are contributions such as "Our Chromatic Journalism," by John A. Macy in *Bookman* (1906) and Samuel W. Pennypacker's "Sensational Journalism and the Remedy" in the *North American Review* (1909).

References

Anonymous. 1909–1910. "Is an Honest and Sane Newspaper Press Possible?" *American Journal of Sociology* 15: 321–34. Written by "an independent journalist."

Fenton, Frances. 1910–1911. "The Influence of Newspaper Presentations upon the Growth of Crime and Other Anti-Social Activities." *American Journal of Sociology* 16: 342–71, 538–64.
Filler, Louis. 1976. *The Muckrakers*. University Park: Pennsylvania State University Press.
Herbst, Jürgen. 1965. *The German Historical School in American Scholarship: A Study in the Transfer of Culture*. Ithaca: Cornell University Press.
Hinkle, Roscoe C., Jr., and Gisela J. Hinkle. 1954. *The Development of Modern Sociology: Its Nature and Growth in the United States: Studies in Sociology*. New York: Random House.
Luhan, Mabel Dodge. 1936. *Movers and Shakers*. New York: Harcourt, Brace.
Macy, John A. 1906. "Our Chromatic Journalism." *Bookman* 24 (October): 127–33.
McClure's Magazine. 1903. "Concerning Three Articles in This Number of McClure's and a Coincidence That May Set Us Thinking." January.
Pennypacker, Samuel W. 1909. "Sensational Journalism and the Remedy." *North American Review* 190 (November): 586–93.
Ross, Edward A. 1903–1904. "Moot Points in Sociology." Pts. 2–4. *American Journal of Sociology* 9: 105–23, 188–207, 349–72.
———. 1904–1905. "Moot Points in Sociology." Pt. 6. *American Journal of Sociology* 10: 189–207.
———. 1910. "The Suppression of Important News." *Atlantic Monthly*, March, 303–11.
———. 1912. "The Suppression of Important News." In *Changing America: Studies in Contemporary Society*. New York: Century.
———. 1916–1917. "The Organization of Thought." *American Journal of Sociology* 22: 306–23.
———. 1917–1918. "Social Decadence." *American Journal of Sociology* 23: 620–32.
———. 1918. *Social Psychology*. New York: Macmillan.
———. 1928. "What the Films Are Doing to Young America." In *World Drift*. New York: Century.
———. 1938. *Principles of Sociology*. New York: Appleton-Century.
———. 1940. *New-Age Sociology*. New York: Appleton-Century.
Small, Albion. 1896–1897. "Review of *Bau und Leben des Sozialen Körpers*." *American Journal of Sociology* 2: 310–15.
———. 1899–1900. "The Scope of Sociology." Pts. 2–3. *American Journal of Sociology* 5: 617–47, 778–813.
———. 1900–1901. "The Scope of Sociology." Pts. 6–7. *American Journal of Sociology*. 6: 324–80, 487–531.
———. 1904–1905. "The Scope of Sociology." Pt. 9. *American Journal of Sociology* 10: 26–46.
———. 1905. *General Sociology*. Chicago: University of Chicago Press.
———. 1912–1913. "General Sociology." *American Journal of Sociology* 18: 200–214.
———. 1912–1913. "The Present Outlook of Social Science." *American Journal of Sociology* 18: 433–69.
———. 1914–1915. "The Bonds of Nationality." *American Journal of Sociology* 20: 640.
———. 1915–1916. "Fifty Years of Sociology in the United States." *American Journal of Sociology* 21: 773.
———. 1923–1924. "Some Contributions to the History of Sociology." Pts. 10, 12, 15. *American Journal of Sociology* 29: 305–24, 455–79, 707–25.
———. 1924. *Origins of Sociology*. Chicago: University of Chicago Press.

———. 1924–1925. "Some Contributions to the History of Sociology." Pts. 17–19, 23. *American Journal of Sociology* 30: 177–94, 302–10, 310–36, 479–88.
Small, Albion, and George E. Vincent. 1894. *An Introduction to the Study of Society*. New York: American Book.
Sumner, William Graham. 1906. *Folkways: A Study of the Sociological Importance of Usages, Manners, Customs, Mores, and Morals*. Boston: Ginn.
———. 1911."The Absurd Attempt to Make the World Over." In *War and Other Essays*, edited by Albert G. Keller. New Haven: Yale University Press.
———. 1914. *The Challenge of Facts and Other Essays*. Edited by Albert G. Keller. New Haven: Yale University Press.
———. [1901] 1932–1933. "Bequests of the Nineteenth Century to the Twentieth." *Yale Review* 22: 732—54.
———. 1934. *Essays of William Graham Sumner*, edited by Albert G. Keller and Maurice R. Davie, 1: 233–34. New Haven: Yale University Press. Contains parts of "Bequests of the Nineteenth Century to the Twentieth" on the newspaper press, which did not appear in the Yale review essay.
———. [1883] 1974. *What Social Classes Owe to Each Other*. Caldwell, Idaho: Caxton.
Sumner, William Graham, Albert Galloway, and Maurice R. Davie. *The Science of Society*. Vol. 4. New Haven: Yale University Press.
Sumner, William Graham, and Albert G. Keller. 1934. *The Science of Society*. Vol. 1. New Haven: Yale University Press.
Thomas, W. I. 1908. "The Psychology of the Yellow Journal." *American Magazine*, March, 491–96.
Vincent, George. 1905–1906. "A Laboratory Experiment in Journalism." *American Journal of Sociology* 11: 297–311.
Yarros, Victor S. 1899–1900. "The Press and Public Opinion." *American Journal of Sociology* 5: 372–82.
———. 1916–1917. "A Neglected Opportunity and Duty in Journalism." *American Journal of Sociology* 22: 203–11.

CHAPTER 9: COMMUNICATION AND SOCIAL THOUGHT

References

Carey, James W. 1974. "The Problem of Journalism History." *Journalism History* 1:1, 3–5, 27.
———. 1997. "Afterword: The Culture in Question." In Eve Stryker Munson and Catherine A. Warren, eds., *James Carey: A Critical Reader*, 308–39. Minneapolis: University of Minnesota Press.
Hardt, Hanno. 1992. *Critical Communication Studies: Communication, History, and Theory in America*. London: Routledge.
Mauther, Fritz. 1901–1903. *Beiträge zu einer Kritik der Sprache*. 3 vols. Stuttgart: Cotta.
———. 1910. *Wörterbuch der Philosophie: Neue Beiträge zu einer Kritik der Sprache*. Munich: Müller.
Peters, John Durham. 1999. *Speaking into the Air: A History of the Idea of Communication*. Chicago: University of Chicago Press.

Index

About the Author

Hanno Hardt is John F. Murray Professor of Journalism and Mass Communication and professor of communication studies at the University of Iowa and professor of communication at the University of Ljubljana, Slovenia. He is the author of numerous scholarly articles and books, including *Ferdinand Tönnies on Public Opinion: Selections and Analyses* (with Slavko Splichal, 2000).